GULF COAST
KITCHENS

bright flavors from
key west to the yucatán

GULF COAST KITCHENS

* * *

CONSTANCE SNOW
PHOTOGRAPHS BY TINA RUPP

clarkson potter/publishers
new york

Portions of this book originally appeared in a different form in the
Times Picayune.

Published by Clarkson Potter/Publishers, New York, New York.
Member of the Crown Publishing Group, a division of Random House, Inc.
www.randomhouse.com

CLARKSON N. POTTER is a trademark and POTTER and colophon are
registered trademarks of Random House, Inc.

Printed in the United States of America

Designer: Jan Derevjanik
Food stylist: Paul Grimes
Assistant food stylist: Abigail Crisp
Prop stylist: Roy Finamore

Library of Congress Cataloging-in-Publication Data
Snow, Constance.
Gulf coast kitchens : bright flavors from Key West to the Yucatán /
Constance Snow; photographs by Tina Rupp.—1st ed.
Includes bibliographical references and index.
1. Cookery—Mexico, Gulf of.   I. Title.
TX714 .S598   2003
641.59'16364—dc21   2002009037

ISBN 0-609-61011-2

10 9 8 7 6 5 4 3 2 1

First Edition

For Ken

acknowledgments

* ❋ *

First thanks go to Dale Curry, food editor of the New Orleans *Times-Picayune*, for giving me a great job and years of fun times, reliable friendship, and Doug's barbecue. I'm also indebted (in a nonbinding sense) to Millie Ball for laughing at my morose humor and recommending me to a world of other editors who pay more than she does, and to Keith Marshall for his inspiring turn of phrase.

I can't believe my good luck in making it over the transom to literary agent Liv Blumer, who changed my life before I knew what hit me. Now she's even got me thinking all kinds of heretical un-Louisiana thoughts, like "change is good" and "I love New York."

Above and beyond his duties as editor, Roy Finamore designed and orchestrated the photographs, shopped for props, and opened his own home and kitchen to us for four days of shooting. Once I got past the initial panic, it was a joy to watch the pictures come together under Roy's direction and the cool vision of photographer Tina Rupp. And it was a relief to surrender responsibility for the appearance of the food to stylist Paul Grimes, master of space, time, and tweezers. Paul's associate, Abigail Crisp, was a fun and energetic presence who helped make everything look "crisp like uniform." I'll never forget the weird glamour of it all.

It was another thrill when messengers delivered the first mock-ups of the jacket and inside pages by designer Jan Derevjanik. I'm also grateful to production editor Camille Smith, copy editor Carole Berglie for her sharp eyes and light touch, editorial assistant Lance Troxel for explaining how my computer works, and to all of the other people at Clarkson Potter who helped get this book into your hands.

As usual, Priscilla Vayda was the first person I called with any questions about cooking, etiquette, or generalized anxiety. Among other good deeds, Kathy Clark and Dan Rich pushed me to draft the proposal for *Gulf Coast Kitchens*, then helped me find an agent. Thanks also to Ed Sherrill, first cause of all things; Carolyn Kolb, a walking encyclopedia of southern culture; Leigh Harris for testing recipes, general commiseration, and twisted e-mails; Steve Lasky for years of unsolicited advice and solicited photo equipment; Victor Andrews for juicy cuisine and haute gossip; Bonnie Warren for steadfast encouragement; Jackson Mahaney and other editors at *Endless Vacation* magazine for Gulf Coast assignments that helped finance my research; Sam and Kathy Boyd for always being ready to celebrate; and the majestic Zella Funck and Martin Laborde just for being so damn strange.

All of the chefs and restaurateurs listed in the appendix contributed recipes and/or regional lore, particularly JoAnn Clevenger, owner of Upperline Restaurant in New Orleans and one of the greatest creative forces in the city. I owe her for everything from costuming advice to putting out a bounty on a redfish (when I couldn't find one through normal channels for a photo shoot), and for years of enthusiastic support.

Many home cooks shared their recipes for this book, and I was often inspired by the readers who corresponded with me through my food columns in the *Times-Picayune*. I also depended upon some fearless tasters, especially my husband's colleagues at McDonogh 39 Elementary School and the staff at Bed and Breakfast, Inc. (next door to my house in New Orleans), who were always happy to try anything, even the disasters. And special thanks to their manager, Susan Smith, for chopping down a banana leaf and FedExing it to me in New York, among other odd services.

I was fortunate to grow up with devoted parents in a big family that loves to laugh and appreciates good food. I have learned from all of them, especially my sister, Kathleen Masson Hill, who taught me how to read, cook, and maintain a sense of irony (still working on that grace-under-pressure thing).

And finally I'd like to thank all of the little people who made this possible, the hundreds of public school students that my husband, Kenneth Snow, has educated during twenty years of subsidizing my freelance career. As always, Ken has been a full partner in this book, collaborating on the outlines, research trips, grocery shopping, recipe testing, writing, and rewriting. He turns everything into a wild ride. Can't wait to see what happens to us next.

contents

* ✳ *

introduction

If you're looking for tea cakes and mint juleps,
you've come too far south.

* * *

Pinpoint the major settlements around the Gulf of Mexico, America's third coast, and you've got a road map to good times and great food. Start light in the Floribbean cafés of Key West, then it's on to Tampa Bay for the Cuban nightlife of Ybor City and the Greek tavernas of Tarpon Springs. Old South fish fries and porch suppers fill lazy days from the Florida Panhandle through Alabama and Mississippi. A few miles and a world away, Louisiana is famous for its Creole/Cajun cuisine and pagan work ethic.

Tex-Mex goes uptown in the cosmopolitan restaurants of Houston, while it covers the waterfront in freewheeling cantinas and crab shacks from Galveston to South Padre Island. Go even deeper and you'll taste its sophisticated tropical roots in the Mexican coastal states of Tamaulipas, Veracruz, Tabasco, Campeche, and Yucatán.

It's a long strange trip, more than 3,000 miles, so think of this book as a friendly introduction, an invitation to make a few connections and discover just how much these different peoples have in common. One of the greatest pleasures of cooking (and eating) your way around the Gulf Coast is discovering the world of foods that can be created with the same simple ingredients.

The Gulf of Mexico, like other great seas, is fringed by a colorful jumble of cultures that share a common history. Ancient native civilizations, French and Spanish colonials, African slaves—all contributed to the exotic regional character. The warm waters and sunny climate also attracted huge communities of later immigrants who stirred their own traditions into the melting pot, adding the rich flavors of Sicily, Greece, Cuba, Latin America, India, and Vietnam, among many others.

Long before it had a name, this authentic "fusion cuisine" evolved naturally, over centuries, in Gulf Coast kitchens where African *jambes* and Spanish paellas morphed into jambalayas. You'll taste the earthy seasonings and ancient grains of the American Southwest, but also the lavish produce and cultural diversity that propelled California style into a national trend.

People around the Gulf grow up on fresh fish, tomato sauces, olive oil, crusty rustic breads, rice, pasta, greens, and polenta (*a.k.a.* grits). In recent years, Asian and Caribbean influences have inspired crisp stir-fries and tropical salads. Meanwhile, beans and grains have been at the center of the menu since the Mayan pyramids were still on the drawing board. Here's the fact: many of the great regional foods are naturally healthy and simple to prepare.

That said, independent and fun-loving Coasters are not afraid of splurging. When you spend life in the path of the next hurricane, there's always good reason to seize the day.

GET COOKING!

Don't be fooled by the casual entertaining of the Gulf Coast. That lighthearted attitude masks a serious devotion to good food, properly prepared.

My original recipes, and others from home cooks, stick to traditional methods and reasonable shortcuts. (Food processors and packaged tortillas are reasonable; nondairy whipped topping and bottled lemon juice are not.) The recipes from restaurant chefs incorporate fresh regional ingredients and simple techniques (no precarious towers drizzled with truffle oil). The emphasis is on homestyle foods that are naturally light and easy. When appropriate, I've included tips for advance preparation.

In my life on the Coast, I have encountered a lot of exotic ingredients, but I've tried to include only those that are available in well-stocked supermarkets. You might need to make an occasional side trip to a Latin or Asian grocery, or contact the mail-order sources on pages 384–85. Otherwise, I've recommended substitutes wherever possible. Most of these Gulf Coast staples will be familiar to adventurous cooks. When in doubt, consult this glossary.

STRANGE GROCERIES

ACHIOTE * Rock-hard and brick-red, the little seeds are used to flavor and color Latin sauces, marinades, and rice dishes. They put the yellow in Cuban-style yellow rice and Yucatecan barbecues. Also known as *annato*, they're commonly used to tint margarines and cheeses, as well. You'll find achiote (or annato) in many supermarkets and all Latin groceries, where you can also buy spicy achiote paste.

AJI AMARILLO CHILES * Grown in South America and the Caribbean, these medium-hot chiles range in color from yellow to bright orange. They're available in some Latin markets. Serranos or jalapeños are easier to find and make a good substitute.

ANAHEIM CHILES * The so-called long greens are mild chiles produced in New Mexico and California. When they ripen to red, they're strung into the pendulous *ristras* that hang from the eaves of adobe houses like fish on a line (the inspiration for those strings of twinkling chile lights). Broad-shouldered poblano chiles are a good substitute, but they tend to be hotter. Again, check Latin markets.

ANCHO CHILES * The name means "broad," and the dried poblano chiles are both wide and widely used in Mexican cooking. Sweeter and milder than the equally popular chipotle powder, ground ancho chiles are a fine addition to dry rubs, moles, and stews. Both are available by mail order (Sources, page 384).

ANDOUILLE * A Cajun specialty, the lean and spicy smoked sausage is stuffed with chunks of ham. The authentic version is definitely worth seeking out (Sources, page 384); otherwise, substitute smoked beef sausage or kielbasa.

BITTER ORANGE * A tart Seville orange, like those used to make marmalades and liqueurs, its juice is a common ingredient in Cuban and Yucatecan cooking. You might find the fresh fruit in Latin groceries, but the bottled juice is more prevalent. A better substitute is two parts fresh orange juice to one part fresh lemon juice.

CAJUN SEASONING * A Cajun or Creole seasoning blend generally contains cayenne pepper, paprika, garlic and/or onion powder, and salt. I've included it here because recipes from home cooks often call for this ubiquitous flavoring. You could easily substitute your own mixture of salt, freshly ground chiles, and spices. Otherwise, be sure to choose one that doesn't contain MSG. Tony Chachere's, Zatarain's, and Konriko are three popular regional brands. They're available in many supermarkets and from the Sources on page 384.

CANE SYRUP * Thinner than molasses, with a slightly milder flavor, cane syrup is another product of the process from sugarcane stalk to granulated sugar. A traditional sweetener in Louisiana and the Caribbean, cane syrup is used like honey or maple syrup. The most popular brand is Steen's (Sources, page 384). Otherwise, molasses is a good substitute.

CANE VINEGAR * Rich and slightly sweet, made from sugarcane, this rustic product has become very trendy in Creole/Cajun cuisine. Again, Steen's is the best-known bottler (Sources, page 384). For a substitute, try balsamic vinegar.

CAYENNE * Long before other chiles became a familiar ingredient in the United States, cooks north of the border spiced their food with cayenne. Many of them called it "red pepper," which is actually more accurate, as the supermarket ground spice is made from a variety of hot red chiles, not all of them cayenne.

CHAYOTE * Ancient Mexicans depended on this "vegetable pear," with a pale green color and delicate flavor reminiscent of cucumber or zucchini. It is also known as a *mirliton* in Louisiana, or *christophene* or *cho-cho* in the Caribbean. It is available seasonally (fall and winter) in some supermarkets and many Latin groceries.

CHIPOTLE CHILES * Though usually made with jalapeños, *chipotle* is an ancient Mexican term for any smoked chiles, from the Aztec words for "hot pepper" (*chil*) and "smoked" (*poctli*). Ground into chipotle powder, smoked chiles are great for an instant infusion of slightly sweet heat and deep red color. Canned *chipotle chiles en adobo*, packed in a thick tomato-based sauce, can be puréed in a food processor to make an earthy paste that will add punch to salsas, soups, and gravies. Whole and ground chipotles are among the most common dried chiles, generally available in the produce or import sections at supermarkets, always at Latin groceries, and from the Sources on page 384. You'll find the canned *chipotle chiles en adobo* at many supermarkets and all Latin groceries.

CHORIZO * Sold fresh or smoked, in casings or as loose ground meat, the Latin pork sausage is highly seasoned with ground chiles, cumin, garlic, and oregano. It is usually available at groceries in Cuban and Mexican neighborhoods.

CILANTRO * The green leaves of the coriander plant look like flat-leaf parsley (hence the nickname, "Chinese parsley"). Definitely an acquired taste, at first cilantro seems sharp and soapy; but it soon becomes addictive, especially when combined with hot chiles and other pungent spices for Mexican, Asian, and Floribbean dishes.

CRAB BOIL * A mixture of dried pickling spices and peppers, "crab boil" is actually used to season the pot for any sort of boiled seafood, including shrimp and crawfish. It is available in cheesecloth bags, as well as in liquid and powdered forms. Look for it in the spice or seafood departments of most supermarkets. The most common brands are Zatarain's and Rex (Sources, page 384).

CREOLE MUSTARD * A cross between a coarse whole-grain mustard and a creamy brown mustard; the most popular brand is Zatarain's (Sources, page 384). Substitute any grainy brown mustard.

EPAZOTE * Mexicans add this pungent herb to their beans as a flavoring agent, but also because it helps to control gas. It's found in Latin markets, sometimes fresh, but usually dried.

FILÉ * A contribution by the Choctaw tribe to the melting pot of Creole/Cajun cuisine, the powdered sassafras leaves (Sources, page 384) are used to season and thicken gumbos.

FISH SAUCE * A salty coffee-colored condiment, *nuoc mam* is thinner than soy sauce and is an essential ingredient in Vietnamese and other Southeast Asian foods. Made from fermented fish, it has a pungent flavor that blends surprisingly well with the usual additions of garlic, lime juice, hot red chiles, and sugar. Flavor and quality can vary quite a bit. I prefer Squid, a popular brand bottled in Thailand, which is available in many supermarkets and most Asian groceries. Look for the big squid on the label and the fluorescent green cap.

HARDTACK BISCUITS * Thick and floury crackers were originally dried to harden and preserve them for long sea voyages. They're an essential ingredient for the famous gaspachee salad of Pensacola, where they're produced by the Premier Baking Company and available by mail order (Sources, page 385). Otherwise, substitute Pilot Biscuits.

JALAPEÑO CHILES * One of the most popular chiles was born in (and named for) the Mexican city of Jalapa, capital of the coastal state of Veracruz. Since then, they've reached icon status in Texas, where they star in everything from ballpark nachos to homemade jams. Smoked and dried, they're known as chipotles. Keep a jar of pickled jalapeños in the refrigerator to pinch-hit in recipes when you don't have any fresh chiles on hand.

JAMAICAN CURRY POWDER * Caribbean curries are seasoned with a sweet-hot blend of turmeric, coriander, cumin, fenugreek, black pepper, ginger, mustard, fennel seed, allspice, and pepper. Badia is one brand of Jamaican curry powder that is widely available (Sources, page 385). If you can't find it at your supermarket, try a Latin grocery.

JAPONE CHILES * Popular in Asian stir-fries and named for "Japan," the red-hot devils originated in the Mexican coastal state of Veracruz.

JICAMA * Also known as *Mexican potato*, the bulbous Latin tuber adds snap to stir-fries with its texture similar to water chestnuts. In Mexico it is often served raw, a refreshing snack sliced and sprinkled with chile powder, also a crunchy addition to salsas and salads. You'll find it in many supermarkets and most Latin groceries.

LEMONGRASS * Also known as *citronella*, it looks like a stiff woody scallion and lends a unique lemony flavor to Vietnamese and Caribbean foods. Lemongrass is becoming more common in supermarkets; otherwise, you can pick it up at an Asian grocery.

PEPITAS * This is the name for pumpkin seeds in Mexico, where they're toasted and seasoned with chile powder for snacks, tossed into salads and stews, or ground into thickeners for sauces.

PIÑONS * It's the Mexican name for pine nuts, known to Italians as *pinoli*. Found inside certain varieties of pine cones, they're used for pestos, salads, desserts, even piñon brittle. Because of their high fat content, they tend to become rancid quickly and are best stored in the freezer.

PLANTAIN * The fat "cooking banana" is common in Latin, Caribbean, and African cookery. It is used to make chips and starchy purées when unripe (green or yellow). When the skin ripens to a brownish black, the sweet flesh is cut into slices and fried, a common accompaniment to Cuban pork dishes or black beans and rice.

POBLANO CHILES * The broad-shouldered poblanos are stout enough to hold a variety of savory fillings for *chiles rellenos* (stuffed chiles). Mild and dark green when fresh, the dried red pods are known as anchos.

RICE PAPER * It looks like a round sheet of translucent plastic, but when dipped into hot broth or water, the sheet becomes extremely pliable, a bit sticky, and pleasantly chewy. It is used as a wrapper for Vietnamese spring rolls, also for enclosing salads or meats, much as you might employ a tortilla to roll your own soft tacos or fajitas. Rice papers of various sizes are available in many supermarkets and most Asian groceries.

SERRANO CHILES * The name means "from the mountains." These lively peppers resemble pointy jalapeños, though they tend to be hotter. Green or red, they make salsas extra tingly.

SPINY LOBSTER * The clawless crustacean, also known as a *Florida lobster* or *rock lobster*, is actually more closely related to the crawfish. It is native to the waters around southern Florida and Mexico.

YUCA * Also known as *cassava* or *manioc*, the starchy tuber looks like a gnarly root covered with tree bark, but the flesh is white and crisp. Like potatoes in the United States, it is eaten boiled, mashed, or fried—a common staple in Mexico, Africa, the Caribbean, and South America. Yuca is also the source for tapioca starch, as well as the namesake for the Mexican coastal state of Yucatán.

part 1

QUICK BITES and FRESH STARTS

What's your pleasure? A picnic under moss-draped live oaks or a backyard fiesta? Sherry and tapas on the patio or jasmine tea and spring rolls in the garden? A sunset toast on the beach or a fishing-camp poker game? These lively flavors and colors are sure to energize casual celebrations or light meals. Some are rich enough for a real splurge, others are cool and refreshing. But all are high in adventure and low in fuss, so the cook can enjoy the party, too.

finger food

✳creole meets floribbean✳

Get out your iron skillet for some piquant snacks that will add tropical sizzle to any party. The Cubans of South Florida meet Louisiana's Creoles over a hot stove, where everybody throws in dashes of Africa, Spain, France, and the New World. Pour yourself a cold beer and light the fire.

CRISPY BANANA SHRIMP
with mango mojo

SERVES 6–8

A crunchy coating of pulverized banana chips enlivens Gulf shrimp dusted with a warm blend of spices common in Floribbean curries and Jamaican-style jerks. You could use the same seasonings and methods to cook strips of firm-fleshed fish, such as red snapper, grouper, or catfish.

4 cups	banana chips
1 cup	all-purpose flour
2	eggs
1 teaspoon	salt
1 teaspoon	ground allspice
½ teaspoon	grated nutmeg
½ teaspoon	cayenne pepper
¼ teaspoon	ground cinnamon
2 pounds	large head-on shrimp, peeled and deveined (tails left on)
	Peanut oil for frying
	Mango Mojo for serving (page 22)

1. Line a baking sheet with waxed paper. Pulse the banana chips in a food processor to make a slightly coarse powder, about the consistency of coffee grounds; transfer to a 1-gallon plastic bag. Place the flour in another 1-gallon plastic bag. Crack the eggs into a small bowl and beat them well with a whisk.

2. Mix the salt, allspice, nutmeg, cayenne, and cinnamon in a small bowl; stir to blend thoroughly. Sprinkle generously over the shrimp, tossing to coat them evenly.

3. Working in three or four batches, shake the shrimp in the flour bag to coat; holding them by their tails, dip the floured shrimp quickly into the beaten eggs and shake off excess moisture; then transfer the shrimp to the bag of pulverized bananas, shaking gently until they're thoroughly coated. Continue until all of the shrimp are coated, arranging them well apart in a single layer on the baking sheet. Cover them with a second sheet of waxed paper and refrigerate for 30 minutes to 1 hour. (This helps to set the coating, so it adheres well; plus the chilled shrimp won't overcook before the crust browns.)

(recipe continues→)

4. Pour oil to a depth of 2 to 3 inches in a deep iron skillet, or fill an electric deep fryer according to the manufacturer's directions; heat to 350° F. (As always when frying seafood, it's essential to maintain the correct temperature, so use a dependable thermometer.) Working in three or four batches, drop in the shrimp one at a time, without crowding. Cook just until browned, about 1 minute. Allow the oil to return to 350° F for each batch. Drain well on paper towels and serve immediately with a bowl of Mango Mojo for dipping.

mango mojo
MAKES ABOUT 2 CUPS

Traditional Cuban mojo (pronounced mo-ho, regardless of what you may have heard from Austin Powers and assorted blues singers) is a garlicky olive oil with a squeeze of lemon, often served with boiled or sautéed yuca. Here, ginger-infused mango purée replaces most of the oil for a tangy sweet-hot dip that tastes of the tropics.

2 tablespoons	olive oil
1 tablespoon	minced fresh ginger
1 tablespoon	minced fresh garlic
½ teaspoon	red pepper flakes, plus more for garnish
2 cups	finely chopped ripe mango (from 2 or 3 mangoes)
¼ cup	water
¼ cup	rice wine vinegar
1 tablespoon	sugar

1. Warm the olive oil in a small saucepan over medium heat; add the ginger, garlic, and red pepper flakes and cook until the garlic is tender, but not at all browned. Stir in the mango, water, vinegar, and sugar; bring to a boil; reduce the heat to low, cover, and simmer for 30 minutes.

2. Cool the mixture slightly, then purée in a food processor or blender. Strain through a fine sieve; discard any remaining fibers or other solids. Add a bit more water, if needed, for a consistency similar to ketchup. Refrigerate for at least 24 hours. Taste and adjust salt, if needed.

Plan ahead: Mango Mojo must be refrigerated for at least 24 hours and it gets better with age. It may be stored in a tightly covered jar in the refrigerator for up to 2 weeks.

3. Serve in a small deep bowl for dipping. Garnish with additional red pepper flakes.

SEAFOOD FRITTERS

MAKES ABOUT 2 DOZEN

In the Florida Keys, these savory little puffs would be studded with minced conch
(see page 24) for the ubiquitous conch fritters. In Louisiana, the same basic
recipe would produce seafood beignets, made with an equal amount of chopped
cooked shrimp, crawfish, or crabmeat in place of the conch.
The lightest fritters rise as they cook. If you want to double the recipe, mix only one
batch at a time. It's alright to stir together the dry ingredients in advance, but once the
buttermilk and seafood are added the batter should be used up within 15 minutes at most.

	Peanut oil for frying
1 cup	all-purpose flour
2 teaspoons	sugar
1 teaspoon	baking powder
¼ teaspoon	baking soda
½ teaspoon	ground ginger
⅛ teaspoon	white pepper, or to taste
1	egg
½ cup	buttermilk
½ pound (about 1 cup)	finely minced conch, chopped cooked shrimp or crawfish tails, or flaked crabmeat
⅓ cup	finely minced onion
¼ cup	finely minced red bell pepper
2 tablespoons	minced fresh flat-leaf parsley
1	seeded and minced fresh jalapeño or serrano chile (optional)
	Salt

1. Pour the oil to a depth of 3 inches in a deep iron skillet, or fill an electric deep fryer according to the manufacturer's directions; heat to 350° F. (Use a thermometer to maintain the correct temperature.)

2. While the oil heats, sift the flour, sugar, baking powder, baking soda, ginger, and white pepper into a large mixing bowl. Make a well in the center. Whisk the egg and buttermilk until smooth in a separate bowl. Stir together the chopped seafood, onion, bell pepper, parsley, and chile (if using) in another bowl.

(recipe continues→)

3. When the oil reaches a steady 350° F, and not a minute sooner, stir the egg and buttermilk into the dry ingredients, just until moistened; then quickly fold in the seasoned seafood. Add salt to taste. Drop the batter into the hot oil by rounded teaspoons, without crowding. Fry until the fritters float and are golden brown on all sides, 2 to 3 minutes. (They should turn over by themselves as they cook, but it's okay to give them a nudge.) Allow the oil to return to 350° F for each batch. Drain on paper towels.

Note: The traditional dip for Florida's conch fritters is a simple combination of 1 cup mayonnaise with ¼ cup each of brown mustard and freshly squeezed lime juice. Chill for at least 1 hour to allow the flavors to blend. The fritters are also good with Mango Mojo (page 22).

∗ ∗ ∗ conched out ∗ ∗ ∗

Most Americans are more familiar with the giant pink shells sold at roadside souvenir stands than the creatures that live inside. However, these meaty mollusks have been a favorite in South Florida for generations and have recently begun turning up in fresh seafood markets around the country. And there's no need to feel out of the loop if you can only find conch flown in from the Bahamas or Costa Rica. Truth is, harvesting has been outlawed in Florida waters for years, so you'll be cooking with the same imports they use in Key West.

How do you spot the good stuff? Fresh conch has flecks of white, pink, and gray that are bright in color, not dull like fresh fish. The whiter, the better—you don't want it when it gets real gray—and it should be firm to the touch. Most of the commercial product is already cleaned, but you should trim off any bits of dark membrane that might remain.

Finally, be prepared for a fight. Conch has a lot of elasticity and it can be tough. For Fritters (page 23) it's best to pound the meat with a mallet to flatten and tenderize it before you mince it by hand (tedious), grind it with a meat grinder (easier), or chop it in a food processor (easiest).

∗   ∗   ∗   ∗   ∗   ∗

BLACK-EYED PEA FRITTERS,
african-style

MAKES ABOUT 3 DOZEN

Nearly everywhere that Africans left their culinary mark in the New World, you'll find
some version of these crisp snacks, called akara in Louisiana, bollitos or bollos in Cuba
and Florida, accra in the Caribbean. And if you didn't know that the airy little fritters
were made with ground black-eyed peas, you'd never guess. The secret is skinning the
beans, a bit of optional effort that yields fluffy white interiors with a more delicate flavor.
Try them with the preceding Mango Mojo, or with one of the salsas on pages 85–87 and 90–91.

1 cup	dried black-eyed peas
⅓ cup	chopped onion
4	garlic cloves, coarsely chopped
1–2	fresh hot chile peppers, such as serranos, seeded and chopped
2 teaspoons	salt
¼ teaspoon	ground white pepper, or to taste
2	eggs
	Peanut oil for frying

1. Cover the peas by 2 inches with cold water and soak for 24 hours in the refrigerator; drain, then cover again with fresh water. Briskly rub the peas between your hands; the skins will float to the surface and the inner white peas will settle to the bottom. Discard the skins, then drain the peas.

2. Place the peas in the work bowl of a food processor with the onion, garlic, chile pepper, salt, and white pepper. Grind to a paste, scraping the sides often, 3 to 4 minutes. Add the eggs; process for 2 minutes longer. Scrape the batter into a large bowl and set aside for 30 minutes.

3. Pour the oil to a depth of 3 inches in a deep iron skillet, or fill an electric deep fryer according to the manufacturer's directions; heat to 360° F. (Use a thermometer to maintain the correct temperature.) Meanwhile, beat the batter vigorously with a whisk for at least 1 minute to aerate the mixture. Gently drop the batter by rounded tablespoons into the hot oil, without crowding, and fry the *akara* in batches until golden brown, about 2 minutes. Drain on paper towels. Allow the oil to return to 360° F and whisk the batter well every time you spoon out a new batch.

Plan ahead: Prepare through step 2 and refrigerate the batter for up to 2 days. Whisk vigorously before frying.

SWEET POTATO CHIPS

SERVES 6

Earthy orange crisps are great on their own, or mix them with a basket of tortilla chips to serve with black bean dip or salsa. They'll also brighten simple meals of soup or salad.

3   medium sweet potatoes
Peanut or canola oil for frying
Salt

1. Scrub the sweet potatoes and slice them crosswise as thin as possible (a mandoline helps). Cover with water and refrigerate overnight. Drain and dry thoroughly on paper towels.

2. Pour the oil to a depth of 3 inches in a deep iron skillet, or fill an electric deep fryer according to the manufacturer's directions; heat to 365° F. (Use a thermometer to maintain correct temperature.) Working in batches, fry the sweet potatoes for 5 to 8 minutes, until crisp and very lightly browned. Allow the oil to return to 365° F for each batch. Drain the chips on paper towels and season them to taste with salt. Serve hot or at room temperature. They're best freshly made.

Note: For baked sweet potato chips, heat the oven to 375° F. Toss the sliced potatoes with 2 tablespoons of peanut or olive oil, coating them thoroughly on both sides. Season to taste with salt. Spread in a single layer on baking sheets lightly coated with oil. Bake until crisp and very lightly browned, 35 to 45 minutes.

CUBAN-STYLE PLANTAIN CHIPS
* mariquitas *

SERVES 6

Though they look like jumbo bananas, green plantains have little of the sweet flavor that will eventually develop as they ripen to black, so the starchy flesh actually makes better chips, without the sugars that could cause scorching. If you can't find green plantains at your supermarket, try a Latin grocery.

3   green plantains
    Peanut or canola oil for frying
    Salt

1. Slit the tough skin of each plantain with a sharp knife, then use the blade to gently pull the peel away in strips, leaving the flesh whole (like a banana). Cut the flesh into paper-thin slices.

2. Pour the oil to a depth of 3 inches in a deep iron skillet, or fill an electric deep fryer according to the manufacturer's directions; heat to 350°F. (Use a thermometer to maintain the correct temperature.) Fry the plantain chips in batches until crisp, but not at all browned, about 1 minute. Allow the oil to return to 350°F for each batch. Drain the chips on paper towels and season to taste with salt. Serve hot or at room temperature. They're best freshly made.

north and south of the border

The Mexican Gulf Coast, isolated from the rest of the country by high mountain ranges, actually has stronger culinary ties to the Caribbean and southern Louisiana. Besides our common history of French and Spanish occupation, we have depended upon many of the same seafoods, spices, citrus fruits, and tropical tubers. In fact, Yucatán gets its name from yuca, just one of the dietary staples that native Maya share with their neighbors in Cuba.

Creole recipes from the preceding section (Crispy Banana Shrimp, Black-Eyed Pea Fritters, Sweet Potato Chips) would seem right at home on tables in Mérida or Veracruz. You might also see similar versions of the Isleño Omelet or Marinated Crab Fingers that are detailed in the next section on tapas and antipasti. All were stirred up in the same melting pot of Mediterranean, African, and Native American influences.

VERACRUZ-STYLE SAUCES
for fresh seafood

In the Mexican state of Veracruz, oysters on the half-shell might be presented alone or as part of the region's famous vuelve a la vida *(return-to-life cocktail), a bountiful platter of cooked crabs, shrimp, mussels, and other prizes from the day's catch. Either way, forget the ketchup and set out this pair of piquant sauces.*

✳ garlic-lime aïoli ✳

MAKES ABOUT 1 CUP

3	egg yolks
2 tablespoons	strained fresh lime juice
2	garlic cloves, minced
¾ teaspoon	salt, or to taste
⅛ teaspoon	cayenne pepper
1 cup	extra-virgin olive oil

Place the egg yolks, lime juice, garlic, salt, and cayenne pepper in a blender; purée until smooth, about 5 seconds. With the machine still running, slowly pour in the olive oil until the aïoli emulsifies. Serve immediately or refrigerate for up to 2 days.

✳ sauce for oysters ✳
salsa para ostiones

MAKES ABOUT 1 CUP

¼ cup	olive oil
¼ cup	chopped scallions, white and green parts
2	garlic cloves, minced
1 cup	finely chopped, peeled, and seeded fresh tomatoes
⅓ cup	minced fresh parsley
	Salt and freshly ground black pepper

Warm the olive oil in a small skillet over medium heat; add the scallions and garlic and cook until tender, but not browned. Add the tomatoes and stir until soft, 1 to 2 minutes. Remove from the heat; cool to room temperature. Stir in the parsley; season highly with salt and black pepper. Set aside for 30 minutes to allow the flavors to blend. Serve within 2 hours.

* * * oyster shucking 101 * * *

Whether you like your oysters with beer or Champagne, learn to handle them with care and to spot the signs of quality. If they're already shucked (typically sold in containers from 8 ounces to a gallon), they should be plump and creamy-colored. Don't buy any that look shriveled or discolored. The liquid should be clear, not cloudy, with no shell particles or grit. And it should make up no more than 10 percent of the volume.

Live oysters (those still in the shell) might be sold by the dozen or by the sack. They should have a fresh marine scent, rather than a strong fishy odor. Look for shells that are clean, unbroken, and moist. Beware of those that are gaping, muddy, or dried out. They should be tightly closed, or they should clamp shut when you tap them. Discard any that do not.

Now that you've chosen well, buy a sack of live oysters and learn how to wrest them from their shells. It's a valuable skill for parties, also the freshest beginning for luxurious appetizers like those on pages 69–71. With a little practice and a lot of caution, you can become a competent shucker. Read these instructions and follow them carefully, or the combination of slippery bivalves and sharp tools could lead to a nasty gash.

1. First, line up the right equipment. You can buy a proper oyster knife and protective rubber mitt at such culinary shops as Williams-Sonoma or at restaurant supply houses. At the very least, wear the toughest work gloves you can find. Some people pry the shells apart with a heavy screwdriver or old-fashioned can opener (the one with the triangular tip that we used before pop-tops). Never resort to kitchen knives, which are too flexible for this work and very likely to cause accidents.

2. Scrub the shells with a stiff wire brush under cold running water to remove grit and debris. Then put on your mitt or gloves.

3. Work over a bowl to collect the juices, *a.k.a.* liquor. Cradle an oyster in the palm of one gloved hand. Gently insert the blade of an oyster knife into the gap between the shells at the hinge end. Firmly twist the handle until the hinge pops and separates. (Be sure to move the blade away from your hand. This will prevent injury if the knife slips out of the gap.)

4. Now you'll be able to see the adductor muscle, which connects the shells near the hinge end. Gently slide the knife blade between the two shells to sever this muscle, being careful not to damage the meat. Remove and discard the shallow top shell. (The oysters won't slide off the deeper bottom shell, which is best for serving.) Finally, slip the blade under the oyster to cut the adductor muscle where it joins the oyster to the floor of the bottom shell.

5. Before arranging them on beds of ice (to serve raw) or rock salt (for baking), use the knife to flick off any bits of shell that could be clinging to the meat. Also scrape away any mud or debris that might have collected near the hinge.

There is a much simpler way to open oysters that are intended for cooking, though it won't work for those you plan to consume raw. Purists can just avert their eyes because I'm about to use the "M" word.

Microwave the scrubbed oysters in a single layer, tightly covered, in a shallow dish. Ovens vary, but approximate times on high setting are 2 minutes for a half-dozen or 4 minutes for a dozen. When they come out, you should be able to twist the shells apart.

✳ ✳ ✳ vibrio warning ✳ ✳ ✳

Residents of the Gulf Coast are famous for their devil-may-care attitude toward diet, but we need to be aware that consuming raw shellfish is dangerous for people with certain health conditions. The greatest threat is for those with liver disease, diabetes, or an immune system that has been compromised by HIV, chemotherapy, kidney failure, or medications taken after an organ transplant to prevent rejection. Heavy drinkers are also at risk, as are those who take antacids (because stomach acids combat bacteria).

Though pollution may sometimes lead to viral infections, the main culprit is a bacterium known as *Vibrio vulnificus*, which grows naturally in brackish marsh water. Cooking kills the microorganism.

✳　✳　✳　✳　✳　✳

BITE-SIZE TURNOVERS
⁕ *empanaditas* ⁕
MAKES 24 (3-INCH) EMPANADITAS OR 12 (5-INCH) EMPANADAS

*Known to Texas and Louisiana cooks as "hand pies," empanadas are Mexican-style
turnovers, while empanaditas are "little turnovers," the finger-food version.
The traditional Spanish pastries were brought to these shores by early colonists,
who also introduced the wheat flour that was necessary to make the dough.
In addition to using the fillings that follow, you could stuff empanaditas with the deviled crab
or jaibas rellenas mixtures on pages 188 and 190; crumbled Queso Blanco (page 267); or apples, roasted
sweet potatoes, and pine nuts. Just keep any filling on the dry side and chill it well before stuffing
the dough to prevent leaks and soggy crusts. You'll need about 2 cups for this amount of dough.*

2 cups	unbleached all-purpose flour
½ teaspoon	salt
8 tablespoons	chilled unsalted butter
½ cup	ice water
1	egg white
1	recipe filling (recipes follow, on pages 33 and 34, but see the headnote as well)

1. Place the flour and salt in the bowl of a food processor and process for 30 seconds to blend well. Cut the chilled butter into 16 pieces and add to the bowl; pulse several times until the mixture resembles coarse meal with bits of butter the size of small peas. With the machine running, add the ice water in a steady stream. Stop the machine as soon as the dough comes together in a shaggy mass. (If you don't have a food processor, sift the dry ingredients into a bowl, then cut in the butter quickly with a pastry cutter or two knives. Make a well in the center, pour the ice water into the well, and stir briskly with a fork just until the dough comes together, being careful not to overblend.)

2. Turn the dough out onto a floured board. Gather it into a ball and use your hand to flatten it into a disk. Whisk the egg white in a small bowl until frothy.

3. Roll the dough to a thickness of ⅛ inch. Use a cookie cutter or glass to cut 24 (3-inch) circles of dough. Place a rounded teaspoon of the chilled filling in the center of each circle. Lightly moisten

Plan ahead: Prepare through step 3 and refrigerate overnight or freeze for up to 1 month. (Freeze in a single layer on a cookie sheet, then store in zipper bags. Do not thaw; bake the frozen empanaditas for 30 to 35 minutes at 375° F.)

QUICK BITES AND FRESH STARTS
32

the edges of the dough with a fingertip dipped in the beaten egg white; fold the dough over the filling; press the edges firmly with the tines of a fork to seal. Prick the tops with the fork to allow the steam to escape.

4. Heat the oven to 375° F. Place the *empanaditas* on lightly greased baking sheets. Bake for 20 to 25 minutes, until the crust is browned. Serve warm.

caramelized onion and wild mushroom filling

MAKES ABOUT 2 CUPS

3 tablespoons	unsalted butter
1	large red onion, quartered and thinly sliced
2	garlic cloves, minced
½ teaspoon	sugar
1 teaspoon	balsamic vinegar
½ pound	fresh wild mushrooms, chopped
1 tablespoon	chopped fresh rosemary
¼ cup	Crema (page 267) or sour cream
	Salt and freshly ground black pepper

Warm the butter in a large skillet over medium-low heat; cook the onion and garlic slowly until the onion is tender and translucent, about 10 minutes. Sprinkle with the sugar and vinegar and continue cooking until browned and syrupy, about 5 minutes longer. Stir in the mushrooms and rosemary; raise the heat to medium-high and toss until the mushrooms are cooked and any liquid has evaporated, 2 to 3 minutes. Stir in the Crema or sour cream; chill the mixture thoroughly. After chilling, taste it and season highly with salt and pepper. (The dough will absorb a lot of the flavor.)

spicy orange chicken filling

1	boneless, skinless chicken breast half
	Salt and freshly ground black pepper
2 tablespoons	olive oil
½ cup	finely chopped red onion
2	garlic cloves, minced
½ teaspoon	ground cumin
¼ teaspoon	ground cinnamon
⅛ teaspoon	ground cloves
Pinch	of allspice
2 tablespoons	golden raisins
3 tablespoons	frozen orange juice concentrate, thawed
1 teaspoon	chipotle paste (see page 37)
2 tablespoons	slivered almonds, lightly toasted and coarsely chopped

1. Season the chicken breast with salt and pepper. Warm the olive oil in a large nonstick skillet over medium heat; cook the chicken breast; remove it from the pan and set it aside to cool slightly. Add the onion, garlic, cumin, cinnamon, cloves, and allspice to the hot pan; cook until the onion is tender and lightly browned.

2. Finely chop the chicken and add it to the pan, stirring to absorb the spices, then add the raisins, orange juice concentrate, and chipotle paste. Stir until combined. Add the chopped almonds and chill thoroughly. After chilling, taste it and season highly with salt and pepper. (The dough will absorb a lot of the flavor.)

TEXAS CHAYOTE PICKLES

MAKES 5 PINTS

Perhaps because of the German influence, Texans are big on pickling. This simple recipe adds spark to the vegetable pears known as chayotes in Texas and Mexico, mirlitons in Louisiana, and christophenes in Cuba and the Caribbean. They were a primary food source for ancient Aztecs and Maya, and they still grow like mad once the vines get started, so regional cooks use them in everything from slaws to coffee cakes.

8	medium chayotes
4	medium yellow onions
1 tablespoon plus 1 teaspoon	coarse salt
2½ cups	cider vinegar
2½ cups	sugar
4 teaspoons	mustard seed
2 teaspoons	ground turmeric
1 teaspoon	red pepper flakes (optional)
10	whole cloves
5	whole allspice
5	small, dried red chiles, such as *japones*

1. Peel the chayotes; cut in half lengthwise and remove the center seed; cut the flesh crosswise into slices about ¼ inch thick. Peel the onions; cut them in half lengthwise, then slice them into thin half-moons. Toss the onion and chayote slices with 1 tablespoon of the salt in a large bowl; let stand for 2 hours. Drain well.

2. Place the drained chayotes and onions in a large nonreactive saucepan with the remaining teaspoon of salt, the vinegar, sugar, mustard seed, turmeric, and red pepper flakes (if using); bring just to a boil.

3. Pack the pickles into hot sterilized pint jars, leaving ½ inch of headspace. Push 2 cloves, 1 allspice, and 1 chile into each jar, being sure the spices are submerged in the liquid. Seal and process in a boiling water bath for 10 minutes. Store in a cool dark place for at least 2 weeks before serving.

LULU'S L.A. CAVIAR

SERVES 12–16

Singer Jimmy Buffet is more closely identified with the Florida Keys, but he actually grew up in laid-back L.A. (Lower Alabama), where his sister Lucy Buffet still lives. She owns and operates Lulu's Sunset Grill in Point Clear, and this is one of her signature appetizers. Marinated black-eyed peas are popular all along the Gulf Coast and known variously as Texas caviar, Cajun caviar, even redneck caviar. This recipe makes enough for a big party, particularly appropriate on New Year's Day, when all good Southerners eat black-eyed peas to ensure luck in the coming year.

6	(15-ounce) cans black-eyed peas, rinsed and drained
½ cup	chopped red onion
⅓ cup	chopped green bell pepper
⅓ cup	chopped red bell pepper
⅓ cup	chopped yellow bell pepper
1 cup	quartered cherry tomatoes
½ cup	chopped parsley
½ cup	balsamic vinegar
½ cup	olive oil
¼ cup	sugar
	Salt and pepper

Combine all of the ingredients and season to taste with salt and pepper. Marinate for 24 hours. Serve with tortilla chips or saltines.

* * *instead of the usual chips * * *

For a light and simple refresher, re-create the ubiquitous Mexican street snack—cool slices of jicama and melon sprinkled with lime juice, salt, and ground ancho chiles. Serve them as they would appear on a vendor's cart, mixed bouquets of five or six slender spears standing upright in parchment cones or clear plastic cups.

* * * * * *

HONEY-CHIPOTLE PECANS

MAKES 2 CUPS

Not your usual beer nuts, these get a flash of smoky fire from ground chipotle chiles (the dried red version of jalapeños). The toasty sweet-hot pecans are also great in place of croutons for soups and salads.

2 tablespoons	honey
1½ teaspoons	chipotle powder
½ teaspoon	ground cinnamon
2 cups	pecan halves
2 tablespoons	sugar
½ teaspoon	salt

1. Heat the oven to 325° F. Warm the honey with the chipotle powder and cinnamon in a non-stick skillet; add the pecans, stirring to coat evenly. Spread the pecans in a single layer on a rimmed baking sheet lined with waxed paper. Bake for 10 minutes. Cool slightly.

2. Stir the sugar and salt together in a mixing bowl. Add the warm pecans and toss to coat evenly. Spread the pecans out on a fresh sheet of waxed paper to dry completely. Store airtight for up to 1 week.

✳ ✳ ✳ ¡arriba! speedy chipotle paste ✳ ✳ ✳

When jalapeños are slowly dried over smoke, they shrivel into leathery brick-red chipotle chiles, which are often ground and marketed as chipotle powder. It's tasty and convenient, but you can make a simple chipotle paste that will add a much stronger punch of mysterious and earthy flavor to many dishes. Look for *chipotles en adobo,* which are packed in a thick tomato sauce seasoned with spices and vinegar. The little 7-ounce cans, once limited to Latin groceries, are now appearing in many supermarkets. (Goya and Embasa are two common brands.) Just empty the contents into a food processor or blender, purée until smooth, and you've got instant *wow* power. Add a spoonful to Tex-Mex sauces, salsas, chili, marinades, or grilling rubs. A little goes a long way, but you can store the leftover paste in the refrigerator for up to 2 weeks or freeze it for up to 6 months. And use a glass jar—this stuff stains.

✳ ✳ ✳ ✳ ✳ ✳

third coast antipasti and tapas

Italians, who began immigrating to the Gulf South in great numbers during the late nineteenth and early twentieth centuries, settled near the ports of Galveston, New Orleans, Mobile, Pensacola, and Tampa Bay. Many of the lively foodways they brought to the Gulf Coast soon spread into the general community, especially the delightful custom of antipasto, still known in some regions of Cajun country as an "Italian hand salad." Though *antipasto* actually means "before the meal," a platter of the colorful hors d'oeuvre can make a light summer lunch or dinner, as well as a substantial cocktail buffet. In their traditional role, two or three antipasti tease the eye and the palate for bigger dishes to come.

The same is true of kindred snacks from Spain, where they're known as tapas. Translated literally, tapas are "lids," originally slices of bread placed over wineglasses to keep out flies (a bit of trivia you may or may not choose to share with your guests).

ISLEÑO OMELET

*Known in Italy as a frittata, and in Spain as a tortilla or torta, this recipe comes from a
source who is reliable on both counts. Louise Bonomo Perez is an Italian American who
married into a family of Isleños (Gulf Coast descendants of Spain's Canary Islanders).
You may modify her basic directions, as you might with any omelet, using whatever
ingredients you have on hand. Similar versions are served in Mexican and Cuban homes.
Perez also contributed the following recipe for Isleño-Style Marinated Shrimp.
Cut this rustic flat omelet into small diamonds for tapas or an appetizer tray.
Or slice it into wedges for brunch or a simple supper.*

3–4 tablespoons	olive oil
6	red-skinned potatoes, cut in half and thinly sliced
1	medium onion, chopped
1	bell pepper, chopped
½ pound	cooked shrimp, peeled and coarsely chopped
5	eggs
	Salt and pepper

1. Warm the olive oil in a nonstick skillet over low heat. Cook the potatoes with the onion and bell pepper, covered, stirring occasionally. When the potatoes are soft, stir in the cooked shrimp.

2. Beat the eggs in a large bowl; add the shrimp and potato mixture, plus salt and pepper to taste. Heat more olive oil in the skillet, if necessary, then pour in the egg mixture. Cook over low heat so the omelet won't brown.

3. When the underside is cooked and the surface appears dry, place a large plate over the skillet and invert the omelet onto the plate, then gently slide it back into the pan to cook the other side.

4. Serve warm or at room temperature.

ISLEÑO-STYLE MARINATED SHRIMP

SERVES 4–6

*Louise Bonomo Perez's recipe for Isleño-Style Marinated Shrimp is similar to
Spanish, Mexican, and Cuban versions served all along the Gulf Coast.
She said she sometimes adds cleaned bodies (the interior, meat-filled white shell,
with the outer red shell and innards discarded) of Basic Boiled Crabs (page 187)
to the marinade, along with the shrimp.*

2 pounds	shrimp
	Salt and black pepper
1 teaspoon	liquid crab boil (see Note)
4	garlic cloves
1	medium red onion
2	celery ribs (preferably tender hearts), chopped
½ cup	olive oil
¼ cup	balsamic vinegar
	Crackers

1. Peel and devein the shrimp. Cover them with water seasoned to taste with salt and pepper. Add the liquid crab boil and garlic. Bring to a boil, then cook until the shrimp just turn pink, about 5 minutes (depending upon the size of the shrimp).

2. Drain the shrimp and place them in a deep bowl with the cooked garlic. Cut the onion in half and cut each half into thin half-moons. Add to the bowl with the celery. Whisk together the olive oil and balsamic vinegar, then pour over the shrimp and stir to combine. Adjust salt and pepper to taste. Cover and refrigerate for several hours, preferably overnight, stirring occasionally. Serve with crackers.

Note: Liquid crab boil is an unsalted flavoring for boiled seafood, most commonly sold under the brand name Zatarain's. It is available in many supermarkets or from Sources on page 384. You could substitute 1 to 2 teaspoons of Old Bay Seasoning, but decrease salt accordingly.

✶ ✶ ✶ the couple ✶ ✶ ✶
that fishes together

The Isleños, descendants of Spain's Canary Islanders, have fished the Gulf from coastal communities in Louisiana and Texas since the 1700s. Louise Bonomo Perez has always lived on or around water, even though she never learned to swim. Raised in an Italian-American family, she was introduced to Isleño life as a seventeen-year-old bride, when she first began accompanying husband Irvin on his boat out of Poydras, Louisiana.

"We used to get up at 3 A.M. to go out shrimping," Perez said. "We'd pick a bayou to trawl and put the nets down right at daylight; then I'd nap until it was time to pick up the trawl. I used to be so anxious to pull it in. I loved to watch the shrimp fall down onto the tail of the deck. We'd put them into the cleaning pen and I would clean all the shrimp and ice 'em up while he navigated.

"It was exciting to see the sun go up, and sometimes go down, too," she said. "The breeze from the boat, I used to love it. I'd tell my husband, 'I think I could get rich and I'd still love to go shrimping.'"

When health problems put an end to the demanding life of commercial fishing, Louise and Irvin Perez continued in their second career as unofficial ambassadors of Isleño culture. His woodcarvings are in the collection at the Smithsonian Institution and he has performed the traditional songs of his people at Carnegie Hall, among other venues. She has demonstrated Canary Islander cooking at the Smithsonian, the 1984 World's Fair, and the New Orleans Jazz and Heritage Festival.

✶ ✶ ✶ ✶ ✶ ✶

MARINATED CRAB FINGERS

SERVES 8

A platter of cracked crab claws, blanketed in a beautiful green sauce of chopped fresh herbs, is one of the most popular appetizers at Ralph & Kacoo's, a chain of Gulf-area restaurants based in Destin, Florida. They agreed to share this recipe, which has much in common with the zesty seafood marinades of coastal Mexico and Cuba.

1½–2 pounds	cooked crab claws
1 cup	olive oil
½ cup	red wine vinegar
¼ cup	lemon juice
1 teaspoon	dried tarragon leaves
10	garlic cloves, minced
1 cup	chopped scallions, white and green parts
1 cup	chopped parsley
1 cup	chopped celery
¾ teaspoon	salt
¾ teaspoon	sugar
¾ teaspoon	black pepper

Crack the crab claws and remove half of the shell. Set aside. Mix all of the remaining ingredients and refrigerate. When ready to serve, place the crab claws on a serving platter and pour the marinade over them.

SICILIAN-STYLE FRIED VEGETABLES
★ frittura ★
SERVES 6–8

An initial dusting in flour, followed by a dip in thin batter and herbed bread crumbs,
yields surprisingly light and nongreasy fried vegetables. Serve them as hors d'oeuvre or
with pasta and sauce for a meatless main course.

1 cup	all-purpose flour
1 teaspoon	salt
½ teaspoon	black pepper, or to taste
1 cup	Italian seasoned bread crumbs
1	egg, lightly beaten
½ cup	milk
1 pound	peeled eggplant wedges, fresh whole mushrooms, sliced zucchini, small cauliflower florets, slices of fennel bulb, or a mixture of these
	Vegetable oil for deep frying
	Warm pasta sauce for dipping

1. Shake the flour with the salt and pepper in a 1-gallon plastic bag to mix. Place the bread crumbs in a second plastic bag. Whisk the egg and milk together in a wide bowl.

2. Working in three or four batches, shake the prepared vegetables in the flour bag to coat; dip the floured vegetables quickly in the egg batter and shake off excess; then transfer the vegetables to the bread crumb bag and shake gently until the pieces are thoroughly coated with a layer of crumbs. Continue until all of the vegetables are breaded.

3. Heat the vegetable oil in an iron skillet or deep fryer to 375° F. Fry the vegetables in batches, without crowding, until they are well browned and tender, 2 to 3 minutes depending upon the vegetable and its size. Serve with a bowl of warm pasta sauce for dipping.

ARTICHOKE and CRABMEAT BALLS

MAKES ABOUT 4 DOZEN

Though more common at office Christmas parties or Italian wedding receptions, good old artichoke balls are a simple and breezy snack, perfect for antipasto trays. I've enhanced the traditional mix with crabmeat, which is purely optional but delicious.

2	(14-ounce) cans artichoke hearts, drained and finely chopped
2	large garlic cloves, minced
½ cup	grated Parmesan cheese
½ cup	Italian seasoned bread crumbs, plus more for coating
3 tablespoons	olive oil, plus more if needed
	Salt and pepper
½ pound	cooked crabmeat (optional)

1. Heat the oven to 350° F. Stir together the chopped artichokes, garlic, Parmesan, bread crumbs, and olive oil. Add salt, if needed, and pepper to taste. Pick over the crabmeat to remove any bits of shell; carefully stir it into the artichoke mixture, being careful not to break up the lumps of crabmeat. Mold the mixture into small balls about the size of cherry tomatoes. (If they aren't holding together properly, add more oil to the mixture.)

2. Just before baking, roll the artichoke balls in the bread crumbs to coat. Bake for 15 minutes on jelly-roll pans. Serve warm.

Plan ahead: Complete through step 1 and refrigerate overnight, or freeze for up to 2 months. Without the crabmeat, the unbaked artichoke balls may be refrigerated for up to 1 week. Either way, you can take out a handful at a time and bake them in a toaster oven for smaller parties.

✶ ✶ ✶unraveling the mysteries✶ ✶ ✶
of the artichoke

You'd never know it from their handsome crop, but Al and Lucy Capdebosq were told by a county agent that artichokes couldn't thrive in South Louisiana. Lucy knew otherwise. She was born into the Liuzza family, Sicilian-American truck farmers who have worked the same land for three generations, cultivating everything from arugula to zucchini, including artichokes.

"My grandmother told me she used to purchase homegrown artichokes," says Richard McCarthy, director of the Crescent City Farmers Market, which convenes every Saturday morning in the Warehouse District of New Orleans. "Moreover, just imagine how short memories are. This used to be an artichoke region. I've been told that the Warehouse District was first developed as an artichoke plantation in the eighteenth century."

Simmered into soups, marinated in salads, or chopped atop Muffulettas (page 360), artichokes are still at the heart of many Sicilian Creole dishes. And for hors d'oeuvre, a big basket of whole steamed artichokes, with an assortment of dipping sauces, is a striking alternative to the usual chips or crudités. Try herb-infused olive oil, melted butter, Creole Remoulade Sauce (page 94), Cioppino Sauce (page 62), vinaigrette, red bell pepper coulis, or yogurt seasoned with puréed roasted garlic.

Those big thistles might look intimidating, but they're easily tamed. To prepare a whole artichoke for cooking, use a stainless steel knife to lob off the top, cutting straight across about 2 inches down. Immediately rub the cut edge with a lemon wedge or it will turn dark and ugly. Trim off the stem to make a flat bottom, so the globe will stand upright on a plate without wobbling. Pull off the small dark leaves around the base, then use kitchen shears to clip the thorny points from all of the other leaves.

Stand the artichokes in a large nonreactive pot, surrounded by an inch of water acidulated with the juice of 1 lemon. Cover the pot and bring it to a boil, then reduce the heat to low. Begin checking after 20 minutes. The artichokes are done when you can easily pull out a leaf and pierce the bottoms with the tip of a knife. Drain them upside down.

✶ ✶ ✶ ✶ ✶ ✶

bright flavors from vietnam

Craig Claiborne called it "the Nouvelle Cuisine of the Orient" and Vietnamese restaurants have prospered for decades in Paris, where they far outnumber Chinese. Likewise, a history of Gallic occupation left many marks on the small Asian country, including a love of French bread, pâtés, white potatoes, and asparagus (known in their language as "Western bamboo").

This French connection helped ease the transition for Vietnamese immigrants to the Gulf Coast, where they found plenty of other familiar flavors in the regional seafood, hot peppers, sweet potatoes, rice, tropical fruits, chayotes, and sugarcane. Like the Sicilians and Greeks who came before them, they gravitated to the major ports, especially New Orleans and Houston, settling on the outskirts of the cities and in nearby fishing communities.

LEMONGRASS BEEF SKEWERS

SERVES 8

The Vietnamese love charcoal-grilled foods, and their garlicky lemongrass marinades share many flavors with the peppery citrus rubs of Texas, Louisiana, and Florida. Serve these meaty skewers as appetizers, or arranged over steamed rice for a main course. They're also a fine addition to Vietnamese Rice Noodles (page 152). Don't want beef? Substitute chicken. For an artful—and tasty—touch, skewer the meat on spears of lemongrass.

1 pound	lean beef (top or bottom round) or boneless, skinless chicken breasts
3 stalks	fresh lemongrass
2	shallots, peeled and quartered
3	garlic cloves, halved lengthwise
1	small red chile, halved lengthwise and seeded
1 tablespoon	brown sugar
1 tablespoon	bottled fish sauce (Sources, page 385)
1 tablespoon	toasted sesame oil
2 tablespoons	sesame seeds, toasted golden brown
	Nuoc Cham (page 49)
	Peanut Sauce (page 49)

1. Cut the beef or chicken diagonally against the grain into thin slices; place in a glass or stainless steel bowl. Pull away the outer leaves of the lemongrass and trim off the tough tops of the stalks, leaving about 4 inches of the tender lower stalks; finely chop and add to the bowl with the meat slices.

2. Place the shallots, garlic, chile, and brown sugar in the work bowl of a food processor; pulse several times to make a rough paste, scraping down the sides as needed. Add the fish sauce and sesame oil; process very briefly to blend; pour over the meat slices. Stir well to combine all ingredients; marinate for 1 hour. Meanwhile, soak bamboo skewers in water to cover for 1 hour (so they won't catch fire on the grill).

3. Thread the beef or chicken onto the soaked bamboo skewers. Place on a hot charcoal grill (or stovetop grill pan); cook for 2 minutes on each side. Arrange on a platter and sprinkle with the toasted sesame seeds. Serve with the dipping sauces.

Plan ahead: Prepare through step 2 and refrigerate for up to 24 hours.

LITTLE SHRIMP CAKES
on sugarcane skewers

Like the Gulf Coast, Vietnam was once colonized by European sugar planters, whose crops inspired this traditional dish. The moist and fibrous inner core of a sugarcane stalk is cut into skewers, which release traces of sweet juice as your teeth scrape off the little "meatballs" of shrimp paste. This recipe is from Thu Cao, who also contributed the Vietnamese Spring Rolls (see page 50).

2 pounds	head-on shrimp, peeled and deveined
2 tablespoons	vegetable oil
1 teaspoon	salt
1 teaspoon	sugar
1 teaspoon	finely minced garlic
½ teaspoon	black pepper
1	egg white
	Peeled fresh or packaged sugarcane (Sources, page 384), cut into 36 matchstick-size skewers
	Nuoc Cham (page 49)
	Peanut Sauce (page 49)

1. Rinse the shrimp well; drain in a colander; dry individually with paper towels. Place the dry shrimp in a bowl with the oil, salt, sugar, garlic, pepper, and egg white; toss to coat well. Marinate in the refrigerator for 1 hour.

2. Place the shrimp mixture in the work bowl of a food processor and grind to a paste. Wet your hands and divide the shrimp paste into 35 to 40 portions. Form each into a compact ball, about the size of a small cherry tomato, around the base of a sugarcane matchstick. Flatten the bottoms slightly so the sugarcane matchsticks stand straight up.

3. Steam the shrimp cakes for 10 minutes, then brown the bottoms on a charcoal grill or nonstick pan. Serve immediately with the dipping sauces.

Note: These shrimp cakes are also one of the traditional toppings for the Vietnamese Rice Noodles (page 152).

Plan ahead: Prepare through step 2 and refrigerate for several hours.

VIETNAMESE DIPPING SAUCES

Like American ketchup or Tabasco sauce, pungent and spicy nuoc cham *is always on Vietnamese tables. The basic ingredients are universal, though some recipes call for lemon or vinegar instead of lime, and most contain less water (you can decrease the amount as you grow accustomed to the taste). Taken straight it will seem far too strong, but a quick dip really wakes up the flavor of food. Peanut sauce is similar to the peanut dip for Indonesian satays and is so easy to re-create if you start with bottled hoisin sauce.*

✳ nuoc cham ✳

MAKES ABOUT ½ CUP

2	garlic cloves
2 tablespoons	sugar
⅓ cup	water
3 tablespoons	bottled fish sauce (Sources, page 385)
1 tablespoon	fresh lime juice
3	hot red chiles, seeded (for less heat) and thinly sliced
1 tablespoon	coarsely shredded carrot

Put the garlic through a press, then use a fork to mash it with the sugar and make a paste. Add the water, fish sauce, and lime juice; stir until the sugar is dissolved. Pour into a small serving bowl and stir in the sliced chiles. Set aside for at least 30 minutes to allow the flavors to blend. Just before serving, sprinkle the shredded carrot over the surface.

✳ peanut sauce ✳

MAKES ABOUT ½ CUP

3 tablespoons	bottled hoisin sauce
3 tablespoons	Nuoc Cham (see above)
3 tablespoons	ground roasted peanuts
1 tablespoon	coarsely shredded carrot
1 tablespoon	chopped roasted peanuts
Several drops	Tuong Ot Toi Sriracha Hot Chili Sauce (Sources, page 385) or Tabasco sauce

Mix the hoisin sauce, Nuoc Cham, and ground peanuts. Spoon the shredded carrot over the surface, then sprinkle with the chopped peanuts and hot chile sauce.

VIETNAMESE SPRING ROLLS

MAKES 8 ROLLS

*These translucent beauties were among the first Vietnamese foods to be adopted
by other Coasters, who are always happy for a new way to bite into some of their favorite
ingredients. Spring rolls look like see-thru eggrolls, but they are a refreshing alternative to
the deep-fried Chinese appetizer. More like a cool and crisp salad that you hold in your
hand, they are beautifully layered packages of shrimp, roasted pork, noodles, and assorted
herbs, usually served with a piquant peanut sauce for dipping.*

*Assembly is easy once you get the hang of it. After a quick dip in steaming broth
or water (use tongs), the stiff rice papers become extremely pliable and rather sticky,
so they adhere well as you roll. Though many recipes recommend working on a kitchen
towel to take up extra moisture, a wooden cutting board is much better, absorbing
the slight dampness without getting tangled up in the process.*

*My early attempts produced a lumpy mess, but I've since learned a few
secrets from an expert. Thu Cao, co-owner of Pho Tau Bay Restaurants in Gretna
and Metairie, Louisiana, showed me the following method that is best for beginners.
Her trick of "cross bracing" the main sheet with a second half-sheet makes all the difference,
for a tight finish with no unsightly bulges or splits.*

12	rice papers, 8½ inches in diameter (sold at Asian markets)
2 ounces	dried rice vermicelli, cooked according to package directions
1 cup	fresh bean sprouts
½ cup	fresh mint leaves
½ cup	fresh cilantro leaves
8	cooked medium shrimp, peeled, deveined, and halved lengthwise
4	lettuce leaves (Boston, red leaf, or another soft variety), torn in half lengthwise
8 ounces	cooked pork loin or tenderloin, cut very thinly into 24 2-by-1-inch slices (barbecued pork loin is available at many Asian markets)
	Nuoc Cham (page 49)
	Peanut Sauce (page 49)

1. Break four of the rice papers in half, for a total of eight full circles and eight half-circles. Fill a large bowl with steaming hot water for dipping.

2. Make the spring rolls one at a time. For each, dip one whole rice paper in the hot water, gently shake off any excess moisture, and place on a work surface. Dip a half-paper, gently shake off excess moisture, then center the half-circle lengthwise over the full circle to brace the middle of the roll.

3. Center a good pinch of vermicelli (10–15 strands) 1 inch from the bottom of the rice paper circle, leaving a border of 1 inch on either side. Lay an equal amount of bean sprouts on the rice paper right above the vermicelli, then a few leaves of fresh mint and cilantro above the sprouts. Finally, top the lineup with two shrimp halves, pink sides down. Altogether, the tiered ingredients should extend halfway up the rice paper circle.

4. Back at the bottom, just over the sprouts and noodles, place a small piece of lettuce torn from the softest edge of the leaf. Cover the lettuce with three very thin slices of pork tenderloin, laid side by side in a single layer.

5. Now you're ready to roll. Working from the bottom up, make two very tight turns to enclose the stacked pork loin, lettuce, vermicelli, and bean sprouts. Fold in both sides of the rice paper, then continue rolling to the top edge to form a firm cylinder that looks like a translucent egg roll.

6. Place seam side down on a serving plate. Cover with a slightly damp towel until all of the rolls are made. Serve with the dipping sauces.

Plan ahead: Spring Rolls may be assembled and refrigerated up to 3 hours before serving, a good idea if this is your first attempt. Just be sure to cover them airtight with plastic wrap.

little plates, big flavors

FLASH IN THE PAN

Little Crabcakes with Papaya Salsa • 55

Stir-Fried Shrimp on Sliced Mango • 57

Black Beans and Scallops • 58

Alabama Butterbean Cakes • 59

* ✳ *

SEAFOOD COCKTAILS

Drunken Shrimp (*Camarones Borrachos*) • 61

Gulf Shrimp "Martinis" with Cioppino Sauce • 62

Fire and Ice Shrimp Cocktail • 64

Crabmeat and Crema • 66

Bill Bayley's West Indies Salad • 67

* ✳ *

ON THE HALF-SHELL

Oysters in Champagne Sabayon with Wilted Spinach • 69

Oysters in Roasted Garlic Sauce • 70

Oysters Mexicali • 71

✳flash in the pan✳

Serve one of these colorful sautés as an appetizer or light lunch, two or more to replace a larger main course. All are flavorful examples of the cross-cultural cooking of the Gulf Coast, where every kitchen makes good use of the regional seafoods, citrus, spices, rice, beans, and tropical fruits—sometimes all at once.

LITTLE CRABCAKES
with papaya salsa

MAKES 1 DOZEN CAKES, SERVES 4–6

The next time you're in an Asian market, look for the Japanese-style bread crumbs called panko. They're processed and flaked for an extra-light and crackly coating that won't go soggy when fried foods cool, great for keeping party hors d'oeuvre crisp— although that won't be a problem with these airy crabcakes. They always disappear as fast as they come out of the pan.

1 pound	lump crabmeat, carefully picked over to remove any bits of shell or cartilage
2 tablespoons	all-purpose flour
1 teaspoon	baking powder
1 teaspoon	sugar
½ teaspoon	salt, or more to taste
½ teaspoon	dried oregano, preferably Mexican, crumbled
¼ teaspoon	ground white pepper
3	scallions, white and green parts, thinly sliced
2	garlic cloves, minced
2 tablespoons	minced fresh cilantro
1	pickled jalapeño chile, seeded and minced (see Note)
2 teaspoons	fresh lime juice
1	egg
2 tablespoons	vegetable oil, plus more for frying
2	egg whites, lightly beaten
	Dry bread crumbs, preferably Japanese panko (see headnote)
	Papaya Salsa for serving (page 56)

1. Place the crabmeat in a large bowl; gently flake with a fork, leaving a few larger lumps. Whisk together the flour, baking powder, sugar, salt, oregano, and white pepper; stir into the crabmeat along with the scallions, garlic, cilantro, jalapeño, lime juice, and egg. Refrigerate for at least 2 hours.

(recipe continues→)

2. Divide the crabmeat mixture into 12 portions and use your hands to mold each portion into a ball. (It will be very loose and sticky, and rather difficult to work with, but that's what makes these crabcakes cook up so light and moist.) Arrange the balls on a pan or platter covered with waxed paper, gently flattening and compacting them into small round cakes. Refrigerate for at least 2 hours.

3. Just before serving, warm 2 tablespoons of oil in a large nonstick skillet over medium-high heat. Dip each cake in the egg whites and lightly coat it with bread crumbs. Working in two or three batches (replenishing oil if necessary), fry the cakes in hot oil for 2 minutes on each side, turning once. Drain on paper towels. Serve immediately, two or three crabcakes per plate, arranged around a small mound of the Papaya Salsa (recipe follows).

Note: Pickled jalapeños are sold in jars at most supermarkets, usually stocked with the other pickles or with Latin imports.

Plan ahead: Prepare through step 2 and refrigerate for up to 8 hours.

papaya salsa

MAKES ABOUT 2 CUPS

2 cups	finely diced ripe papaya
1 tablespoon	fresh lime juice
2 tablespoons	minced scallion, green and white parts
1–2	fresh serrano or jalapeño chiles, seeded and minced
1 tablespoon	minced fresh cilantro
½ teaspoon	finely grated fresh ginger
½ teaspoon	salt
⅛ teaspoon	white pepper

Stir together all of the ingredients and set aside for 30 minutes to allow the flavors to blend. For best flavor and texture, serve within 3 hours.

STIR-FRIED SHRIMP
on sliced mango

SERVES 4

This Asian-inspired tropical salad is especially refreshing as a light meal or appetizer, enlivened by crisp greens and piquant spices that really hit the spot on a humid summer night. If you prefer, skip the fruit and lettuce and serve the garlicky shrimp over steamed rice or noodles.

2	mangoes, peeled and sliced
4 cups	(loosely packed) mixed salad greens
2 tablespoons	roasted peanut oil, preferred, or cooking oil
2 teaspoons	finely minced garlic
2 teaspoons	finely minced fresh ginger
1–3	fresh red chiles, seeded and cut into thin rings
1 pound	jumbo shrimp, peeled and deveined
	Salt and freshly ground black pepper
	Fresh cilantro leaves for garnish

1. Arrange the mango slices atop a small bed of mixed greens on each of four salad plates. Set aside.

2. Heat a wok or heavy skillet over high heat, then add the oil. When the oil is very hot (just beginning to smoke), add the garlic, ginger, chiles, and shrimp. Stir-fry until the shrimp are cooked, 2 to 4 minutes. Season with salt and pepper, then divide among the salads, arranging the shrimp over the mango slices. Garnish with fresh cilantro. Serve immediately.

Plan ahead: Wash the greens, chop the seasonings, and peel the shrimp several hours ahead; refrigerate.

BLACK BEANS and SCALLOPS

SERVES 4

Here's a quick sauté from Eddie Cass, who escaped the cold winters and big-city pace of his native Boston to open Chef Eddie's Magnolia Grill in Apalachicola, Florida. (Don't know where that is? Residents will tell you it's halfway between Sopchoppy and Wewahitchka.) He created this Latin-inspired appetizer to showcase the local Calico Bay scallops. Have everything ready and keep a close watch on the scallops, as they can go from perfect to overcooked in a matter of seconds.

¼ cup	unsalted butter
⅓ cup	chopped yellow onion
2	garlic cloves, minced
½	shallot, finely chopped
1	plum tomato, diced
1 pound	bay scallops
1½ cups	cooked and drained black beans (see Note)
2 cups	steamed basmati rice
4 tablespoons	sour cream for garnish
	Chopped fresh tomato, red or yellow bell pepper, and scallions for garnish

1. Warm the butter in a sauté pan over high heat; add the onion, garlic, and shallot; toss until the onion is crisp-tender and lightly browned around the edges, about 1 minute. Add the tomato and the scallops, tossing just until the scallops are heated through, but still barely translucent. Add the black beans, stirring just until heated.

2. Serve immediately over basmati rice. Garnish with a dollop of sour cream and chopped fresh tomato, bell pepper, and scallions.

Note: Cook the beans in water to cover by 3 inches, seasoned with 1 chopped onion, 1 garlic clove, ½ teaspoon dried thyme, a bay leaf, salt, and black pepper.

Plan ahead: Cook black beans up to 3 days in advance. If you must use canned, be sure to rinse them first.

ALABAMA BUTTERBEAN CAKES

MAKES 8 CAKES, SERVES 4

*The restaurant Justine's is set in the original Bank of Mobile, an 1852 beauty in the
downtown historic district. One of Chef Matt Shipp's signature dishes, humble
butterbeans are dressed in high style for these tasty cakes.*

BUTTERBEAN CAKES

3 cups	cooked and drained butterbeans
2 tablespoons	fresh lemon juice
4 dashes	Tabasco sauce
2 teaspoons	minced garlic
2 teaspoons	minced red onion
4 ounces	feta cheese, crumbled
1	red bell pepper, minced
1	large leek, white part only, thinly sliced
1	green or yellow bell pepper, minced
½ cup	plain dry bread crumbs
	Salt and pepper
	Olive oil or vegetable oil for browning

SAUTÉED VEGETABLE TOPPING

2 tablespoons	unsalted butter
1	red bell pepper, seeded and thinly sliced
1	green bell pepper, seeded and thinly sliced
1	yellow bell pepper, seeded and thinly sliced
1	large leek, white part only, thinly sliced
1 cup	sliced shiitake mushrooms
	Salt and freshly ground black pepper

1. For the butterbean cakes: Combine all of the ingredients except the oil. Divide into eight portions, each about ½ cup; use your hands to form the mixture into compact cakes about ¾ inch thick.

2. Heat the oven to 400° F. Warm the oil in a large skillet over medium heat; brown the cakes, about 2 minutes per side. Transfer to an oiled pan and bake for 8 to 10 minutes.

3. For the sautéed vegetable topping: While cakes are baking, warm the butter in a large skillet over medium heat. Sauté the vegetables until tender and lightly browned. Season to taste with salt and pepper. Arrange two cakes each on four warmed plates; top with sautéed vegetables.

seafood cocktails

Coast dwellers like their shrimp and crabs in great heaps, still warm and peppery, dumped straight from the boiling pot onto newspaper-lined tables. However, if you're planning one of those strange dinner parties where people don't eat with their hands, try one of these fresh ideas.

DRUNKEN SHRIMP
camarones borrachos

SERVES 6

Serve these tequila-spiked cocktails with an icy beer chaser. A cousin of Isleño-Style Marinated Shrimp, Camarones Borrachos are popular all along the Texas and northern Mexico Gulf Coast. Presentation in salt-rimmed margarita glasses elevates this beach-house poker snack to party food. Make the shrimp a day in advance, so they'll have plenty of time to soak up the piquant marinade.

1 recipe	Isleño-Style Marinated Shrimp (page 40), the cooking water replaced by 3 (12-ounce) beers
2 tablespoons	chopped cilantro or flat-leaf parsley
1–2	jalapeño chiles, seeded and chopped
1	lime
	Coarse salt
2	Florida avocados or 3 Hass avocados
	Salt and pepper
	Tomato and Tequila Salsa (page 91)

1. Prepare the Isleño-Style Marinated Shrimp, cooking them in beer instead of water, then add the cilantro and chopped jalapeño to the oil-and-vinegar marinade. Refrigerate for several hours or overnight.

2. When ready to serve, cut the lime into eight wedges; set aside six wedges for garnish. Rub one lime wedge over the rims of six margarita glasses and roll each in coarse salt. Set them aside for a few minutes to dry, so the salt will really stick.

3. Peel and pit the avocados; mash them coarsely, leaving some big chunks; sprinkle with lime juice from a second wedge and season highly with salt and pepper. Divide the mashed avocado among the margarita glasses, being careful not to disturb the salt-coated rims. Top with the drained marinated shrimp, then 2 heaping tablespoons of the salsa. Garnish with a lime wedge.

GULF SHRIMP "MARTINIS"
with cioppino sauce

SERVES 8

This recipe was inspired by a similar dish that used to be served at the historic Hotel Galvez, grande dame of the Gulf beaches on Galveston Island, Texas. The Mediterranean-accented appetizer is a spicy reminder of the many Italian immigrants who landed and settled in the Galveston area, once known as the "Ellis Island of the South."

The usual ketchup-based cocktail sauce is replaced by a fragrant and chunky tomato brew, which is based on the Italian seafood soup known as cioppino. Though it may taste rather spicy when hot off the stove, remember that chilling will dull the flavors slightly, and that much of the seasoning will be absorbed by the shrimp and leek toppings in the final dish.

CIOPPINO SAUCE

¼ cup	olive oil
½ cup	very finely chopped red onion
½ cup	very finely chopped celery
1 tablespoon	minced garlic
2	large fresh tomatoes, peeled, seeded, and finely chopped
1 cup	shrimp stock (see page 159)
⅓ cup	dry white wine
2 teaspoons	chopped flat-leaf parsley
2 teaspoons	chopped fresh oregano
¼ teaspoon	sea salt, or to taste
½ teaspoon	red pepper flakes, or to taste

ASSEMBLY

½ cup	finely julienned leeks
¼ cup	minced flat-leaf parsley
¼ cup	balsamic vinegar
24	jumbo cooked shrimp, peeled, deveined, and chilled
8	Kalamata olives
8	rosemary sprigs

1. For the sauce: Warm the oil over medium heat in a small heavy saucepan. Cook the onion, celery, and garlic until the onion is translucent and golden, but not browned, about 5 minutes. Stir in all of the remaining sauce ingredients and simmer slowly for 1 hour. Chill thoroughly.

2. To assemble: Toss the leeks and parsley with the balsamic vinegar until combined. Scoop about 2 tablespoons of the chilled Cioppino Sauce into eight stemmed martini glasses. In each glass, arrange three chilled shrimp atop the sauce, then top the shrimp with the leek mixture. Garnish each glass with an olive skewered on a rosemary sprig.

Plan ahead: Refrigerate the completed Cioppino Sauce for up to 3 days.

* * * weighing your options * * *

Having trouble gauging the amount of shellfish you need for a recipe? Here's the scoop:

* One pound of shrimp with heads and shells is roughly equivalent to ½ pound of cleaned meat. One pound of headless shrimp with shells yields slightly more than ½ pound of cleaned meat. (The weight is typically 40 percent heads, 10 percent shells, 50 percent meat.)

* Six medium crabs yield 1 pound (2 cups) of crabmeat.

* One pint of shucked oysters will contain 1½ to 2 dozen, depending upon their size.

* Six pounds of cooked whole crawfish yield 1 pound of tailmeat.

* A 1-pound lobster will yield 2 cups of cooked meat.

* * * * * *

FIRE and ICE SHRIMP COCKTAIL

SERVES 4

During the late nineteenth and early twentieth centuries, several Japanese colonies sprang up in the Rio Grande Valley around Brownsville and Harlingen, where the new immigrants earned their livings as truck farmers or nurserymen. Others helped develop the Texas rice industry, directing research and working the coastal fields near Houston. Today their children and grandchildren are primarily urban dwellers, and many of their foodways have crossed over into the mainstream, most notably the ubiquitous sushi bars. However, the cultures cross both ways, producing such culinary spectacles as the Banzai Chili Team, who stir their pots at regional cookoffs with samurai swords.

"Sleet" is a traditional Japanese salad, so called because the shredded daikon (white Japanese radish) with its simple coating of lemon juice and salt takes on an iridescent sheen similar to frozen rain. Of course, sleet is about as common on the Gulf Coast as a Japanese appetite, and the original is a bit spare for Western tastes. However, it makes a cool base for a thoroughly modern shrimp cocktail, topped by wasabi-spiked avocado.

1⅓ cups	shredded daikon (Japanese radish) or seeded cucumber
1 tablespoon	fresh lemon juice
	Salt
1	ripe avocado
¼ teaspoon	wasabi paste, or more to taste (Sources, page 385)
24	large boiled shrimp, peeled and deveined
	Black and white sesame seeds
	Pickled ginger, cut lengthwise into thin shreds (Sources, page 385)
	Thin slices of lemon for garnish
	Sesame rice crackers

1. Toss the shredded daikon with the lemon juice and salt. (If using cucumber, roll the shreds in a paper towel and squeeze out the excess moisture before tossing with the lemon juice and salt.)

2. Mash the avocado, adding salt and wasabi paste to taste.

3. For each serving, arrange six shrimp atop ⅓ cup of the shredded daikon. Spoon a small mound of wasabi-flavored mashed avocado alongside. Sprinkle with the sesame seeds and pickled ginger. Garnish with a thin slice of lemon. Serve with sesame rice crackers.

✳ ✳ ✳ treasures of the gulf ✳ ✳ ✳

In general, finfish and shellfish should have a fresh briny scent. Always store them in the coldest part of your refrigerator, preferably on a bed of crushed ice. Buy from a market you trust on the day you intend to cook. Whole finfish should have shiny scales and bright eyes that are not sunken. Fillets and shellfish should appear as follows.

Amberjack: The sweet, firm flesh should be translucent and unblemished. Any dark, oily flesh should be cut away before storing or cooking fillets.

Blackfin tuna: The mild, red flesh has a firm and meaty texture. It should be translucent and moist and bounce back when pressed with a finger.

Blue crabs: Look for hard shells and some movement. Live crabs that have been refrigerated may be sluggish, but they shouldn't be motionless.

Drum: Sweet and mild, with a soft and flaky texture, it's a fine substitute for the pricier redfish. The flesh should be translucent and cohesive, not falling into flakes.

Grouper: The mild, white flesh is sweet and flaky. It should be translucent and cohesive, not falling into flakes.

Mahimahi: Yes, it's a type of dolphin, hence the exotic alias. The dark meat turns white when cooked, with firm large flakes and a mildly sweet flavor.

Redfish: Look for the characteristic black spot on the tail to identify authentic redfish, which may be difficult to find due to overfishing in recent years. Drum or red snapper are economical substitutes.

Shark: Similar to swordfish, it has a mild flavor and a firm, lean texture with no bones (as shark is a cartilaginous fish). It's usually cut into steaks or cubes for brochettes.

Shrimp: Look for translucent shells with a grayish-green, pinkish-tan, or light pink tint and a minimum of black spots or edges. Don't buy any that smell fishy or have a red tinge around the heads.

Swordfish: Raw flesh of different varieties might be gray, orange, white, or pink, but it's always white and sweet when cooked, with a lean and firm texture. It is also relatively boneless, other than the central backbone, which is easy to avoid when cut into steaks.

Tilefish: The sweet, firm flesh has a flavor similar to grouper. Golden tilefish is most prized, although the less colorful blueline tilefish tastes nearly the same.

Yellowtail snapper: This Florida delicacy is meltingly tender and sweet, quite different from the strong and oily fish labeled as Pacific or California yellowtail. If you can find it, cook it right away, as it deteriorates rapidly.

✳ ✳ ✳ ✳ ✳ ✳

CRABMEAT and CREMA

SERVES 4–6

Like the living creature, jumbo lump crabmeat is not to be trifled with.
One of nature's most perfect foods, the sweet and delicate white flesh should
never be masked by complicated seasonings or heavy sauces. Mexican Crema
(a soured cream), lightly spiced with scallions and minced
jalapeño, makes a smooth and unobtrusive dressing.

1 pound	jumbo lump crabmeat, picked over to remove any bits of shell or cartilage
⅓ cup	Crema (page 267) or crème fraîche
2	scallions, white and green parts, thinly sliced
1–2	pickled or fresh jalapeños, seeded and minced (see Note)
	Salt and freshly ground black pepper
1	avocado, peeled, pitted, and sliced
1	mango, peeled and sliced
2	limes

1. Combine the crabmeat, crema, scallions, and jalapeños, stirring very gently to avoid breaking up the crabmeat. Season to taste with salt and pepper. Refrigerate for at least 1 hour to allow the flavors to blend.

2. On each plate, alternate slices of avocado and mango. Cut one lime into wedges and reserve; squeeze the other lime over the avocado and mango slices. Divide the dressed crabmeat mixture evenly among the plates. Garnish each with a wedge of lime.

Note: Pickled jalapeños are milder and less likely to overpower the flavor of the crabmeat. Use fresh if you'd like a little more bite.

Plan ahead: Prepare through step 1 and refrigerate for up to 8 hours.

BILL BAYLEY'S WEST INDIES SALAD

SERVES 4–6

Now served in Gulf Coast restaurants from South Florida to the tip of Texas, this simple luxury originated at Bayley's Restaurant in Mobile, Alabama. It was created by Bill Bayley, who founded the landmark steakhouse in 1947. The mild vinaigrette lets the flavor of the crab shine through, but it's still an assertive blend that is better suited to the less expensive claw meat.

1	medium onion, finely chopped
1 pound	fresh lump crabmeat or claw meat, carefully picked over to remove any bits of shell
	Salt and pepper
½ cup	salad oil (Bayley's uses Wesson, but some cooks substitute olive oil)
½ cup	apple cider vinegar
½ cup	ice water

Spread half of the chopped onion over the bottom of a large bowl. Spread the crabmeat over that, followed by a final layer of onion. Season to taste with salt and pepper. Pour the oil over the top, followed by the vinegar, then the ice water. Do not stir. Cover and place in the refrigerator to marinate for 2 to 12 hours. When ready to serve, fluff carefully (being careful not to break up the crabmeat), but do not stir.

on the half-shell

Oysters cradled in their own shells, served atop glittering
beds of rock salt, have been a Gulf Coast specialty since the
turn of the last century, when Antoine's Restaurant in New
Orleans created a money-green topping that was "rich
enough for a Rockefeller." The original formula for oysters
Rockefeller remains a secret, but there's no need to resort to
counterfeit when we have so many luxurious alternatives.

OYSTERS IN CHAMPAGNE SABAYON
with wilted spinach

SERVES 6

This dazzler from the Mississippi Gulf Coast took second prize at the 22nd Annual National Oyster Cookoff in Maryland. It was created by Mike Christensen, a native of Chicago and graduate of the Culinary Institute of America, who has worked in the Biloxi-Gulfport area since 1990. When I caught up with him, he was chef at Murano's Restaurant in Grand Casino Gulfport.

24	oysters in the shell
6 cups	rock salt
1½ cups	Champagne
4	shallots, minced
Pinch	of saffron threads
6	egg yolks
¾ cup	clarified butter
3 tablespoons	olive oil
¼ cup	minced garlic
1 pound	spinach, washed and dried

1. Open the oysters over a bowl to catch the liquor (see page 30); discard the top shells. Scrub the bottom shells and arrange on rock salt, 1 cup per plate, topped with 4 shells.

2. Pour the oyster liquor into a small pot; add the Champagne, shallots, and saffron. Cook over medium heat until reduced to ¼ cup; strain out and discard the shallots.

3. Place the egg yolks in a bowl set over simmering water; whisk until thick. Slowly add most of the Champagne reduction (reserving about 1 tablespoon), whisking constantly. Slowly pour in the clarified butter, whisking until thick.

4. Warm the olive oil in a sauté pan; add the garlic and spinach, along with the reserved tablespoon of Champagne reduction; stir until the spinach is wilted.

5. Place a bit of the wilted spinach on the bottom of each oyster shell, then place an oyster on the spinach and top with the Champagne sabayon.

OYSTERS
in roasted garlic sauce
SERVES 4

Legendary bed-hopper Giacomo Casanova called oysters "a spur to the spirit and to love."
Ancient Romans chomped down whole bulbs of garlic for strength, courage, and
endurance. And this double shot of aphrodisiacs is sure to get some hearts pumping.
The recipe is from the Upperline Restaurant in New Orleans.

3	whole heads of garlic
1 tablespoon	olive oil
½ teaspoon	dried thyme
1 teaspoon	kosher salt
1	egg
1 teaspoon	fresh lemon juice
½ teaspoon	onion powder
1 teaspoon	Dijon mustard
1	garlic clove, peeled and minced
⅛ teaspoon	salt
¾ cup	pure olive oil
4 cups	rock salt
24	cleaned oyster shells
24	fresh Louisiana medium-plump oysters
	Lemon wedges

1. To make the sauce: Heat the oven to 350° F. Cut the tops off the whole garlic so that the cloves are exposed. Pour the tablespoon of olive oil into a small shallow baking dish; add the thyme and kosher salt. Coat the garlic with the oil mixture, then place it cut side down on the baking dish. Bake for 30 minutes; cool the garlic.

2. Squeeze the cooked garlic from the pods into a food processor bowl. Add the egg, lemon juice, onion powder, mustard, minced garlic, and salt. With the machine running, slowly add the oil.

3. To complete the dish: Heat the oven to 400° F. Divide the rock salt among four pie pans and arrange six oyster shells on each pan. Place an oyster on each shell and top with a tablespoon of the Roasted Garlic Sauce. Bake the oysters for 10 minutes, then brown them under a hot broiler for 2 minutes. Serve immediately with lemon wedges.

OYSTERS MEXICALI

SERVES 4

Simple and beach-y, here's a showy appetizer that doesn't require hours of preparation.
It's adapted from a similar dish at The Sea Ranch Restaurant on South Padre Island,
a Gulf resort that serves the border cities of Brownsville, Texas, and Matamoros, Mexico.

4 cups	rock salt
24	oysters in the shell
2 tablespoons	olive oil
¼ cup	finely chopped yellow onion
2	garlic cloves, minced
1 cup	peeled, seeded, and finely chopped fresh tomato
1	jalapeño, seeded and minced
2 tablespoons	minced fresh flat-leaf parsley
2 tablespoons	minced cilantro
	Salt and freshly ground black pepper
	Shredded Monterey Jack cheese
24	thin slices of jalapeño
4	lime wedges

1. Heat the oven to 400° F. Divide the rock salt among four ovenproof dishes or pie plates. Open the oysters; discard the top shells. Scrub the bottom shells and arrange on the beds of rock salt, six shells per dish. Place an oyster on each shell.

2. Warm the olive oil in a small skillet over medium heat; cook the onion and garlic until tender, but not browned. Add the tomato and minced jalapeño; stir until the tomato is just soft and most of the moisture is absorbed, 1 to 2 minutes. Remove from the heat. Stir in the parsley and cilantro; season highly with salt and black pepper.

3. Spoon about 1 tablespoon of the sauce over each oyster; top with a pinch of shredded cheese and a slice of jalapeño. Bake for 10 minutes, then broil until the cheese is lightly browned, about 2 minutes. Garnish with lime wedges.

salads and salsas

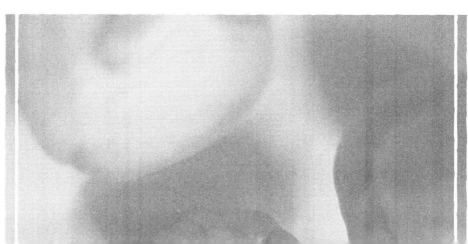

SALADS WITH SPICE

Chicory with Queso Fresco and Honey-Chipotle Pecans · 75

Vietnamese Cabbage and Chicken Salad · 76

Pensacola Gaspachee Salad · 77

Jamie Shannon's Watermelon and Summer
Vegetable Salad · 78

Mexican Fruit Salad with Cinnamon Syrup · 79

* ✳ *

TWO COOL TUBERS

Shrimp Boil Potato Salad · 81

Louis Pappas's Famous Greek Salad · 82

* ✳ *

SPONTANEOUS SALSAS

Citrus-Avocado Salsa · 85

Honeydew and Ginger Salsa · 86

Grilled Vegetable Salsa · 87

Summer Garden Salsa · 90

Tomato and Tequila Salsa · 91

* ✳ *

SOUTHERN-FRIED SALADS

Fried Okra Salad · 93

Fried Green Tomatoes with Shrimp Remoulade · 94

Spinach and Fried Oyster Salad · 96

salads with spice

People here joke that the Gulf Coast has two seasons, summer and February, but even February can be kind of muggy. The good news: it's always salad weather. Around the time we see the last of the homegrown tomatoes, the earliest crops of citrus and pecans are hitting the stands. Whatever the date, there's something fresh and colorful to toss in with the lettuce, from January's Ruby Red grapefruit to July's watermelons.

CHICORY WITH QUESO FRESCO
and honey-chipotle pecans

SERVES 4

Chicory is not just for Creole coffee. A cousin of endive, the curly bitter leaves are best mixed with a milder soft lettuce, such as Boston or Bibb, for a salad that stands up to a garlicky orange vinaigrette spiced with chipotle chiles. The Mexican cheese known as queso fresco, now available in many supermarkets, has a crumbly texture and salty tang similar to feta (which is a good substitute). It balances the bite of the sweet-hot nuts. If you like, add some julienned ham or smoked turkey.

ORANGE VINAIGRETTE

1	garlic clove, minced
¼ teaspoon	salt
¼ teaspoon	chipotle powder
¼ teaspoon	ground cumin
1 tablespoon	fresh lime juice
¼ cup	frozen orange juice concentrate, thawed
2 tablespoons	olive oil

SALAD

1	small heart of chicory (curly endive), torn into pieces
1	small head of Boston or Bibb lettuce, or another mild variety
1	avocado, peeled and thinly sliced
2	seedless oranges, peeled and sectioned
4 ounces	crumbled queso fresco or feta cheese
½ cup	Honey-Chipotle Pecans (page 37), very coarsely chopped
	Salt and freshly ground black pepper

1. For the vinaigrette: Use a fork to mash the garlic clove with the salt, chipotle powder, and cumin. Stir in the lime juice, whisking until the salt is completely dissolved and the mixture is well blended. Whisk in the thawed orange juice concentrate. Drizzle in the oil, whisking to blend. Set aside for at least 30 minutes to allow the flavors to blend.

2. To finish: Toss all salad ingredients together, adding the Orange Vinaigrette to taste, then season with salt and pepper. Serve immediately.

VIETNAMESE CABBAGE
and chicken salad

SERVES 4

This stuff is addictive, a quick and easy meal in one bowl, sparked by the bright flavors of fresh herbs, lime juice, and roasted peanuts. Like other Vietnamese imports, it tastes both familiar and slightly exotic to Gulf Coasters, who have long appreciated the refreshing qualities of similar sweet-and-sour slaws. I like napa cabbage for its tender leaves and milder taste, but it's okay to substitute regular green cabbage. The recipe is one of my favorites, a frequent dinner at my house. It's adapted from a similar version by cookbook author Nicole Routhier.

LIME DRESSING

2	fresh green or red jalapeño peppers, seeded and minced
3	garlic cloves, minced
2 tablespoons	sugar
¼ cup	fresh lime juice
3 tablespoons	fish sauce (Sources, page 385)
3 tablespoons	roasted peanut oil, preferred, or vegetable oil
½	small red onion, sliced into paper-thin half-moons

SALAD

3 cups	shredded napa cabbage
2 cups	shredded cooked chicken
1 cup	coarsely shredded carrots
½ cup	shredded fresh basil leaves
⅓ cup	shredded fresh mint leaves, preferably spearmint
⅓ cup	chopped roasted peanuts
	Fresh cilantro leaves for garnish

1. For the dressing: Combine all of the ingredients and set aside for at least 30 minutes to allow the flavors to blend.

2. To complete the salad: Stir together the cabbage, chicken, carrots, basil, and mint in a large bowl. Add the Lime Dressing and toss well to blend. Sprinkle with the peanuts and cilantro leaves.

PENSACOLA GASPACHEE SALAD

SERVES 8

A taste for the famous cold soup of Andalusia traveled with Spanish settlers to the Florida Gulf Coast, where the dish evolved from gazpacho soup to "gaspachee salad." (These things happen down South.) Today the refreshing Panhandle specialty is most strongly identified with Pensacola, one of the only places where you can still obtain the required hardtack biscuits. The recipe was contributed by Marianne Beckman of Pensacola, who credits her grandmother, Margaret Gonzales Sheppard. She dresses her version with a vinaigrette, though some cooks use mayonnaise.

2	(2½-ounce) hardtack biscuits (Sources, page 385)
3	ripe tomatoes
1–2	cucumbers, peeled
1	sweet onion
1	large green bell pepper
	Salt and black pepper
½ teaspoon	dry mustard
¼ cup	vinegar
½ cup	olive oil

1. Soak the hardtack in water for about 2 hours, or until soft. Squeeze the water out of the hardtack until it's as dry as possible. Fluff the hardtack and pull it apart. Place it in a bowl.

2. Dice the tomatoes, cucumbers, onion, and green pepper. Toss in a colander; place the colander over a bowl so the vegetables can drain for about 30 minutes. Add the drained vegetables to the hardtack. Season to taste with salt and pepper. Refrigerate until well chilled, for at least 2 hours and up to 1 day.

3. Just before serving, whisk together ½ teaspoon salt, ½ teaspoon black pepper, the dry mustard, and vinegar until the mixture is well combined and the dry ingredients have dissolved. Whisk in the olive oil until smooth.

4. Toss the salad with the dressing. Serve cold.

JAMIE SHANNON'S WATERMELON
and summer vegetable salad

SERVES 10

Early one Saturday morning, the late Jamie Shannon, then chef of Commander's Palace in New Orleans, roared up to the Crescent City Farmer's Market on his Harley-Davidson. As he searched for homegrown produce for a special Fourth of July menu, other shoppers tagged along, crowding up afterward to sample the results at his on-site cooking demonstration. Shannon said you should not be limited by his choices; use any summer vegetables that are at their peak in your own garden or green market. Whatever you toss in the big bowl, this salad will be the life of your party because it is topped with rum-spiked watermelon.

¼	large watermelon
1 cup	New Orleans Rum or another dark sugarcane rum, such as Mount Gay
¼ cup	fresh orange juice
¼ cup	cane vinegar (Sources, page 384)
	Kosher salt and cracked black peppercorns
1½ cups	good-quality olive oil
2 pounds	baby lettuces, such as red oak, arugula, mizuna
2	yellow squash
2	zucchini
2	baby cucumbers

1. Remove the watermelon flesh from the rind; remove the seeds and cut the flesh into 1-inch cubes. Place it in a bowl and douse it with rum. Set aside.

2. To make the vinaigrette, mix the orange juice and cane vinegar in a bowl with salt and pepper to taste. Slowly pour in the olive oil, while whisking vigorously, until it is fully incorporated.

3. Wash the lettuces in cold water and pat them dry. Cut the squashes and cucumbers in half lengthwise, then cut them into thin half-moons. Toss the greens and vegetables in a bowl, adding vinaigrette to taste. (Refrigerate any leftover vinaigrette for up to 3 days.) Adjust salt and pepper, if needed. Top with the marinated watermelon. Drizzle with a small amount of watermelon marinade, if desired.

MEXICAN FRUIT SALAD
with cinnamon syrup
SERVES 8

Mangoes or papayas poached in cinnamon syrup are a popular sweet throughout Mexico. Here the same spiced citrus syrup energizes a big bowl of fresh tropical fruit, a colorful salad that can stay on the table through dessert at cookouts, potlucks, or children's parties.

CINNAMON SYRUP

1 cup	water
½ cup	sugar
¼ cup	lime juice
	Zest of 1 lime, removed in wide strips
2	(3-inch) cinnamon sticks
4	whole cloves
1	whole allspice

SALAD

10–12 cups	chunked ripe fruit (mango, papaya, honeydew melon, watermelon, seedless red or green grapes)
	Crema (page 267) or sour cream (optional)
	Ground cinnamon (optional)

1. For the syrup: Bring the water and sugar to a boil in a saucepan over medium-high heat, stirring until the sugar dissolves. Add the lime juice, lime zest, cinnamon sticks, cloves, and allspice; reduce the heat and simmer for 20 minutes, then raise the heat and boil until the syrup is reduced to ½ cup, about 5 minutes. Strain and discard the solids. Cool the syrup to room temperature.

2. To complete the salad: Toss the syrup with the fruit; refrigerate until well chilled. If you like, top each serving with a drizzle of crema or sour cream that has been lightly seasoned with ground cinnamon.

Plan ahead: Cinnamon Syrup may be prepared a day or two in advance and refrigerated. The assembled salad should be served the day it is made.

two cool tubers

Potato salad turns up in some strange places around here. Some Louisianians serve it as a side dish with jambalaya, or with red beans and rice (for those occasions when two starches just aren't enough). Others have been known to scoop it right into a bowl of hot gumbo. In Texas and Mexico, potato salad could be spiked with fresh chiles or picante sauce, even julienned cactus paddles. Cubans might add a garlicky aïoli (see page 29) instead of mayonnaise, along with chunks of tuna, green peas, olives, and pimentos. Go play.

SHRIMP BOIL POTATO SALAD

*Use the leftovers from a backyard Shrimp Boil (page 352) to make a spicy
meal-size salad spiked with shrimp (and/or crabmeat or crawfish). Or skip the
optional fish and start from scratch, boiling potatoes in seasoned water for a jolt
of flavor enhanced by horseradish mayonnaise.*

2 pounds	small red-skinned potatoes, unpeeled
	Powdered or liquid crab boil (Sources, page 384)
1 cup	fresh corn kernels (see page 243)
½ cup	thinly sliced celery
¼ cup	thinly sliced scallions, white and green parts
2 cups	cooked and peeled shrimp, crabmeat, and/or crawfish tails (optional)
1 cup	mayonnaise, preferably homemade
½ teaspoon	celery seed
2 teaspoons	prepared horseradish, or to taste
	Salt and freshly ground black pepper
1 tablespoon	minced fresh flat-leaf parsley

Cook the potatoes in water seasoned with the crab boil according to the package directions.
Cool the unpeeled potatoes to room temperature, then quarter them. Place potatoes in a bowl
with the corn, celery, scallions, and boiled seafood (if using). Stir mayonnaise together with
celery seed and horseradish to taste, then toss with salad until well blended. Season to taste
with salt and black pepper. Refrigerate for at least 1 hour to allow flavors to blend. Just before
serving, stir in minced parsley.

LOUIS PAPPAS'S FAMOUS
greek salad

SERVES 4

One of the best-known regional novelties was created during World War I by army chef Louis M. Pappamichalopoulos (a name he changed to Louis Pappas, for obvious reasons). To satisfy the hungry troops of General Pershing's Wildcat Division, Pappas began adding scoops of potato salad to his massive Greek salad. It soon became his trademark, and it is still the house specialty at Louis Pappas' Riverside Cafe in the historic Greek community of Tarpon Springs, Florida. Today the landmark restaurant (established in 1925) is operated by the third generation, Louis Lucas Pappas and wife Nancy, who agreed to share the original family recipe. This salad's meant to be a full meal for hungry people.

POTATO SALAD

6	boiled russet potatoes, peeled and diced
2	medium onions, finely chopped
¼ cup	finely chopped green bell pepper
½ cup	finely chopped scallions, white and green parts
½ cup	mayonnaise

GREEK SALAD

1	large head of iceberg lettuce
2	ripe tomatoes, cut into 6 wedges each
1	cucumber, peeled and cut lengthwise into 8 wedges
1	avocado, peeled and cut into wedges
12	arugula leaves or 12 sprigs watercress
5 ounces	feta cheese, sliced
1	green bell pepper, cut into 8 rings
1	cooked beet, cut into 4 slices
4	cooked and peeled shrimp
4	anchovy fillets
12	Kalamata olives
12	Salonika peppers
4	radishes, cut fancily
4	whole scallions
½ cup	white distilled vinegar
½ cup	extra-virgin olive oil
	Chopped fresh oregano

1. For the potato salad: Stir together all ingredients. Add salt to taste, if you care to.

2. For the Greek salad: Line a large plate with the outside leaves of the lettuce and mound the potato salad in the middle of the platter.

3. Shred the remaining lettuce leaves and scatter them over the top of the potato salad. Place the wedges of tomato, cucumber, and avocado around the outer edges, making a solid base for the salad. Arrange the arugula or watercress on top, along with the sliced feta and green pepper. On the very top, place sliced beets with a shrimp on each beet slice and an anchovy fillet on each shrimp. Olives, peppers, radishes, and scallions can be arranged as desired. Sprinkle entire salad with the vinegar, olive oil, and oregano.

✳ ✳ ✳ quickie picnics ✳ ✳ ✳ and cocktail snacks

Even on the laziest afternoon, you can throw together a respectable spread at a moment's notice from a well-stocked pantry. Keep a stash of savories, such as breadsticks, dried figs and apricots, smoked almonds, salted nuts, marinated mushrooms and artichoke hearts, roasted red peppers in brine, different varieties of olives, *giardinera* (Italian-style pickled vegetables), cocktail onions, whole baby corn, sun-dried tomatoes, pickled green beans, caponata (Italian eggplant relish), cherry peppers, good-quality tuna packed in olive oil, smoked oysters, sardines packed in tomato sauce, hard salami, pickled quail eggs, anchovies, or little jars of pesto.

Minimal effort will produce prosciutto-wrapped melon slices, pears with cubed Italian or Spanish cheese, grilled sausages, or bruschetta (grilled crusty bread brushed with oil and garlic). Wine is traditional with antipasti, sherry with tapas; but on a steamy night, you could opt for cold beer or a big pitcher of iced tea with lemon and mint.

✳   ✳   ✳   ✳   ✳   ✳

spontaneous salsas

Salsa has become as American as ketchup, outselling the old faithful for years now. The basic ingredients are usually lime juice, fresh chiles, minced red onion, and tomatoes. But cooks from Key West to the Yucatán add plenty of regional color with tropical fruits and offbeat seasonings. Follow their lead and experiment with an impromptu blend of your own: watermelon, cantaloupe, mangoes, peaches, nectarines, pineapple, grilled vegetables, corn kernels, and black beans are all good candidates. Instead of the usual cilantro, add a bit of grated fresh ginger, chopped mint, rosemary, or other herbs.

CITRUS-AVOCADO SALSA

MAKES ABOUT 3 CUPS

Gulf Coast citrus adds a sweet-tart flash to this avocado salsa that's good with sweet potato chips or fried plantains, also with grilled fish, poultry, or pork. You could even serve it as a side salad or roll it into warm tortillas with fajitas for a tropical wrap.

1–2	fresh jalapeños
3 tablespoons	minced red onion
2 tablespoons	fresh lime juice
1 tablespoon	minced fresh mint leaves
1 teaspoon	grated fresh ginger
2 teaspoons	sugar
2	oranges
1	grapefruit
2	ripe avocados
½ teaspoon	salt, or to taste
	Freshly ground black pepper

1. Mince the jalapeños, discarding the seeds if you prefer less heat. Mix with the onion, lime juice, mint, ginger, and sugar. Peel and section the oranges and grapefruit, then chop the peeled sections into small pieces. Stir them together with the lime juice dressing and set aside for at least 30 minutes to allow the flavors to blend.

2. Just before serving, peel, pit, and chop the avocados. Toss them with the citrus. Season to taste with salt and black pepper and serve immediately.

Plan ahead: Prepare through step 1 and refrigerate for up to 1 day. Once the avocado has been added, the salsa should be consumed within an hour or so.

HONEYDEW and GINGER SALSA

MAKES ABOUT 2¼ CUPS

*This beautiful, pale green salsa really wakes up the flavor of grilled fish or chicken.
Mango makes a pretty companion salsa; just use the same recipe and substitute it for the
honeydew, with cilantro in place of the mint.*

2 cups	finely chopped ripe honeydew melon
1 tablespoon	fresh lime juice
2 tablespoons	minced red onion
1–2	serrano or jalapeño chiles, seeded and minced
2 tablespoons	minced fresh mint leaves
½ teaspoon	grated fresh ginger
½ teaspoon	salt
Dash	of white pepper

Stir together all of the ingredients and set aside for 30 minutes to allow the flavors to blend.
For best flavor and texture, serve within 3 hours.

＊ ＊ ＊ kinda hot and always ready ＊ ＊ ＊

Pickled jalapeños are sold in jars at most supermarkets, usually stocked near the other pickles or with Latin imports. They're convenient to keep on hand as a substitute for fresh chiles, also a good choice for recipes like this one, since the pickling tames the hot flavor that would overpower more delicate ingredients. Sometimes the jars also contain a few slices of hot pickled carrot. If you'd like, chop one of those and add it to the mix for extra color.

＊ ＊ ＊ ＊ ＊ ＊

GRILLED VEGETABLE SALSA

MAKES ABOUT 8 CUPS

*Charred tomatoes and chili powder add smoky flavor to a salsa that should help to kick off
any cookout. Grill the vegetables over the hottest fire; hungry guests can dip their chips
while you wait for the coals to burn down enough for cooking fish or meats.*

4	large ripe tomatoes
3	ears freshly shucked corn on the cob
1	zucchini, cut lengthwise into 4 slices
1	yellow squash, cut lengthwise into 4 slices
	Olive oil
	Salt and freshly ground black pepper
	Chili powder
3–4	serrano or jalapeño chiles, seeded and minced
2 tablespoons	fresh lime juice
2 tablespoons	minced fresh cilantro or flat-leaf parsley

1. Rub the whole tomatoes, shucked corn, and slices of zucchini and yellow squash with olive oil.
Generously sprinkle the corn and squash with salt, pepper, and chili powder. Place on a charcoal or gas grill (or a stovetop grill pan) over high heat. Grill, turning to brown all sides, until
lightly charred and tender (10 to 12 minutes total for the tomatoes, 6 to 8 minutes for the corn,
4 to 6 minutes for the squash).

2. Halve the tomatoes across the equator; squeeze out and discard the seeds; discard the cores.
Transfer the tomatoes to a food processor or electric blender and process to a slightly chunky
purée. Return the tomato purée to the bowl. Cut the kernels from the grilled corn (see page
243) and dice the grilled squash. Stir into the tomato purée, along with the chiles, lime juice,
and cilantro or parsley. Season to taste with salt, freshly ground black pepper, and chili powder.

* * * hot, hotter, hottest! * * *
a guide to chiles

On the dusty shoulder of a well-traveled Texas highway is a roadside stand run by one of the great American entrepreneurs. He peddles chiles of every size and color, red-hot jams and relishes—the usual tourist stuff. He sits behind his cash register, cantankerous as hell, next to a big basket of candy (marked "Habanero Suckers 5¢") and a freezer filled with Popsicles. The Popsicles cost three dollars. He sells an average of one per sucker.

Tongue-torching habaneros, also known as Scotch bonnets, may be the hottest peppers on earth, measuring some 100,000 to 300,000 Scoville units on the official heat scale. (By comparison, jalapeños weigh in at a wimpy 2,500 to 5,000.) Among the mildest are sweet bell peppers in splashy colors from gold to deepest purple. Moving up the scale, "long greens" (Anaheim, California, or New Mexico) can be used interchangeably in recipes for a little bite. Warmer still, broad poblanos (*a.k.a.* pasillas) are easy to stuff for classic chiles rellenos. At the higher reaches, familiar green jalapeños are surpassed by hot yellow wax peppers and even hotter cayennes and serranos.

In Southwestern states, when long greens mature to red, they're strung into ristras, similar to garlic braids, then hung from the eaves of houses to dry in the sun. Spicier ancho (dried red poblano) and chipotle (smoke-dried red jalapeño) are two other regional favorites for earthy red sauces or chili powders. And japone (dried red serrano) is that little devil you accidentally bite into at Chinese restaurants.

These are just a few of the hundreds of peppers, or capsicums, that have spread around the globe since Columbus first carried specimens back to Europe. One of the earliest plants to be domesticated in the New World, chiles eventually made their way from Italian sauces to Sichuan stir-fries, from Spanish stews to Indian vindaloos. Today supermarket produce shelves are stacked with several fresh and dried varieties that remain a mystery to many cooks. But read on, because there are hot times ahead.

pick a pepper

Look for a stem that's curved and firm, not shriveled, to indicate a good meaty pod. Check for taut skin and good shape; bypass any that are wrinkled or deflated. Generally, the broader the shoulder, the milder the pepper. Sharp pointed tips (especially on serranos, cayennes, and habaneros) mean extra heat.

Flavor comes from the meat of the pod, which can contain more vitamin C than citrus fruit, as well as a significant amount of vitamin A. Capsaicin (the oily compound that makes peppers hot) is most concentrated in the ribs and seeds, which may be removed to temper the fire.

As the pepper matures, starches in the wall convert to sugars, for a paradoxical sweet-hot blend. Mature peppers usually change from green to red or orange, although ripe colors can range from chartreuse to purple, depending on the variety.

handle with care

Never touch your eyes or other sensitive areas, especially cuts and abrasions, after handling peppers. You may need to wear gloves for the hottest varieties, which can cause pain just from contact with unbroken skin.

Unbearably hot peppers can be toned down a little by soaking for at least 40 minutes in a mixture of 1 cup water, 1 tablespoon distilled vinegar, and 2 teaspoons of salt.

Before tasting, be prepared. If you bite off more than you can chew, heat-wise, experts say you can best extinguish the flame with tomato juice or a fresh lemon or lime. (Apparently the acid counteracts the alkalinity of the capsaicin.) Bread or rice are good, too. Milk helps, but water only makes it worse (by distributing the oily capsaicin to more areas of the mouth). True chileheads claim the only real cure is to eat another pepper.

Speaking of chileheads, you'll find recipes scattered throughout this book that could make one helluva dinner—fired with peppers from appetizer to dessert—a great treat for friends who love spicy food or a subtle torture for unwelcome guests.

Begin with mean margaritas, made by steeping four jalapeños (halved lengthwise) in your bottle of tequila for at least 3 days . . .

*　*　*　*　*　*

SUMMER GARDEN SALSA

MAKES ABOUT 8 CUPS

This crisp and colorful salsa is packed with earthy flavors that are native to the Gulf Coast (tomatoes, corn, beans, squashes, peppers, and avocado). To serve it as a vegetarian main course or side salad, just cut the tomato, squashes, and avocado into larger chunks.

2	garlic cloves
½ teaspoon	salt
2 tablespoons	fresh lime juice
¼ cup	olive oil
½ cup	bottled picante sauce (hot, medium, or mild)
½ teaspoon	ground cumin
1½ cups	cooked and drained black beans (rinsed, if canned)
2	ripe tomatoes, seeded and finely diced (about 2 cups)
1½ cups	fresh corn kernels (see page 243)
1	medium zucchini, finely diced (about 1 cup)
1	yellow crookneck squash, finely diced (about 1 cup)
1 cup	finely diced jicama
⅓ cup	finely diced red onion
⅓ cup	finely diced red bell pepper
1	small ripe avocado, peeled, seeded, and finely chopped
¼ cup	minced fresh cilantro (optional)
	Salt and freshly ground black pepper

1. Mash the garlic cloves with the salt in a large serving bowl to make a paste; add the lime juice, whisking until the salt is completely dissolved. Whisk in the olive oil, picante sauce, and cumin until smooth.

2. Add the beans and all of the vegetables, except for the avocado, to the bowl; toss gently until the vegetables are coated evenly with the dressing. Sprinkle with the cilantro (if using) and toss again. Chill for 3 to 4 hours, occasionally stirring gently.

Plan ahead: Prepare through step 2 and refrigerate for up to 1 day. Once the avocado has been added, the salsa should be consumed within an hour or so.

3. Just before serving, carefully stir in the chopped avocado. Taste and add salt and pepper, if needed. Serve chilled or at room temperature.

TOMATO and TEQUILA SALSA

MAKES ABOUT 3 CUPS

Make this tasty relish sans tequila for a basic tomato-based salsa. It's great with
Drunken Beans (page 139) or boiled seafood, as well as chips. Prepare the
salsa no more than 2 hours before serving.

2	large ripe tomatoes, seeded and finely chopped
2 tablespoons	minced red onion
1–2	fresh jalapeños, seeded and minced
2	tablespoons fresh lime juice
1	tablespoon minced fresh cilantro
¼ teaspoon	salt, or to taste
2 tablespoons	tequila, optional

Combine all of the ingredients in a nonreactive bowl; then set aside for 30 minutes at room temperature, so flavors can blend.

southern-fried salads

From the land that gave you deep-fried whole turkeys and fried sushi, here's yet another corruption of a former health food. Still, Southerners do know how to handle their iron skillets, and these "salads," while definitely not rabbit food, are based on a trio of golden oldies: fried green tomatoes, fried oysters, and fried okra. (Within the recipes that follow, you'll find traditional directions for making all three. Each is also tasty on its own, as an appetizer or a side dish, or as the centerpiece for an old-fashioned supper of garden vegetables.)

FRIED OKRA SALAD

"This recipe was given to me by a friend about ten years ago in the course of a conversation about okra, of all things," says Bebe Gauntt of Gulf Shores, Alabama. "The sign of a southern cook, I guess, is when you say to 'use a big bowl of okra, a couple of tomatoes, any kind of onions you have, good lean bacon . . .' and the other person knows exactly what is meant. Southern cooks will adjust the amounts of ingredients to suit their tastes." Gauntt says her salad must be served warm, while the fried okra is still crisp, and that it is especially good with fresh fish.

½ pound	bacon
1 cup	yellow cornmeal
1 cup	all-purpose flour
	Salt and black pepper
About 2 pounds	okra (a big bowlful), sliced ¼ to ½ inch thick
3	or more fresh ripe tomatoes, cored and chopped
½ cup	chopped onion, any kind, including scallions, white and green parts

1. Fry the bacon in a large heavy skillet over medium heat until crisp. Drain it on paper towels, then crumble it. Reserve the fat.

2. Stir the cornmeal and flour together; season the mixture well with salt and black pepper. Toss the sliced okra in the cornmeal mixture until well coated, then fry it in the hot bacon fat until crisp, turning once, about 1 minute per side. Drain on paper towels.

3. Toss the fried okra, tomatoes, onion, and crumbled bacon together. Season to taste with salt and pepper. Serve immediately, while the okra is still warm.

FRIED GREEN TOMATOES
with shrimp remoulade
SERVES ANY NUMBER

Unlike the creamy sauces of France, Creole remoulade is a spicy mustard-based
dressing that is usually mixed with chilled shrimp and served on a bed of shredded
lettuce. In fact, you could use the traditional sauce that follows to make that old
New Orleans classic, which has been a regional favorite for generations.
It inspired this cheeky upstart that arrives (sans lettuce) on a countrified raft of fried
green tomatoes. Now imitated all along the coast, the stylish appetizer originated at
Upperline Restaurant in New Orleans, says owner JoAnn Clevenger, who loves to tweak
convention with her uptown-downtown marriages of Southern comfort foods.
Her remoulade recipe yields about 4 cups of sauce, which is more than you'll probably
need, as each serving requires only ¼ cup. You could cut the ingredients by half for a
smaller batch, but it freezes well and also makes a good dressing for other salads.

CREOLE REMOULADE SAUCE

1 cup	virgin olive oil
1 cup	light salad oil
¾ cup	Creole mustard (or any spicy whole-grain mustard)
½ cup	finely chopped scallion, green parts only
½ cup	finely chopped celery
⅓ cup	prepared horseradish
¼ cup	ketchup
2 tablespoons	Tabasco sauce (or more to taste)
2 tablespoons	minced flat-leaf parsley
4 teaspoons	fresh lemon juice
4 teaspoons	Worcestershire sauce
4 teaspoons	sweet paprika
4 teaspoons	sugar
1 tablespoon	grated white onion
2½ teaspoons	minced garlic
1½ teaspoons	garlic powder

FRIED GREEN TOMATOES

Salad oil or very light olive oil

Green tomatoes (green all the way through), sliced ½ to ¾ inch thick

Egg wash (1 egg mixed with 1 cup milk)

Yellow cornmeal seasoned with salt and pepper

FOR EACH SERVING

3–4   medium boiled shrimp, peeled and chilled

1. For the sauce: Mix all of the ingredients and taste for salt. (Remoulade should be tangy and have a perky taste. Bland it is not!) Refrigerate the sauce until you're ready to use it. Covered and chilled, it will keep for up to 3 weeks.

2. For the tomatoes: Heat a thin layer of oil in a cast-iron skillet or heavy sauté pan over medium heat. Dip each tomato slice in the egg wash, then coat it with the seasoned cornmeal. Cook until it's golden brown on the bottom, then turn it and brown the other side, 1 to 2 minutes per side. (Watch your heat. If it's too high, the tomato slices will brown before they're thoroughly cooked.)

3. To serve: Place two hot slices of Fried Green Tomato on an individual serving plate. Top each serving with three or four chilled shrimp, then 2 tablespoons of the remoulade sauce.

Plan ahead: The shrimp may be boiled, peeled, and chilled a day in advance. The sauce may be refrigerated for up to 3 weeks, or frozen for up to 3 months. Fry the green tomatoes just before serving.

* * *what's that smell?* * *

"Here's a tip I learned from my grandmother," says my editor, Roy Finamore. "Put out a bowl of bleach (about a cup) when you're frying. Lord knows how it works, but it sucks up a lot of the smell."

Other cooks recommend boiling several cloves in a cup of water, or setting dishes of damp coffee grounds or baking soda near the stove. To remove fishy odors from your hands, rub them with a cut lemon, a slice of ginger, dry mustard, or toothpaste.

* * * * * *

SPINACH
and fried oyster salad
SERVES 4

Popeye was ahead of his time. Modern science has proved that spinach really does help us beat our enemies, from heart disease to cataracts. Best of all, it actually tastes good if you don't guzzle it straight from the can. Start by shaking up the usual spinach salad. Toss tender baby leaves with a Piquant Honey-Mustard Vinaigrette sparked by Tabasco sauce, then plop on some warm cornmeal-crusted oysters.

As always when frying seafood, temperature and timing are essential. Use a dependable thermometer and don't even take the oysters out of the refrigerator until the oil reaches the optimum 350° F. (The cold oysters will crisp on the outside and stay silky on the inside.)

PIQUANT HONEY-MUSTARD VINAIGRETTE

1 tablespoon	cane vinegar (Sources, page 384) or balsamic vinegar
1 tablespoon	Dijon mustard
2 teaspoons	honey
1 teaspoon	Tabasco sauce
¼ teaspoon	salt, or to taste
¼ cup	olive oil

SPINACH AND FRIED OYSTER SALAD

	Peanut or vegetable oil for deep frying
6 to 8 cups	fresh baby spinach leaves, washed and dried
	Salt
	Black pepper
2 dozen	shucked oysters
2 cups	yellow cornmeal
	Tabasco sauce

1. For the vinaigrette: Whisk together the vinegar, mustard, honey, Tabasco, and salt in a large bowl until the salt is dissolved. Slowly drizzle in the oil, whisking to make a smooth emulsion. Set aside for at least 30 minutes to allow the flavors to blend.

2. To finish the salad: Pour oil to a depth of 5 or 6 inches in a cast-iron frying pot, heavy saucepan, or electric deep fryer; heat to 350° F. While the oil heats, toss the spinach with the prepared

dressing. Taste and adjust the salt, if needed, and add a few grinds of black pepper. Divide the spinach salad among four serving plates.

3. When the oil reaches 350° F (and not before), remove the oysters from the refrigerator and drain off any liquid. (You'll need to fry the oysters in two or three batches, depending upon the size of your pot. Bread only as many as you intend to fry immediately, or the cornmeal will become soggy and fall off.) Roll oysters one at a time in the cornmeal to coat evenly; then place 8 to 12 in a fry basket and bang it sharply against the side of the sink to knock off excess corn-meal. Lower the basket into the hot oil and fry the oysters just until they float, 1 to 2 minutes. (Be very careful not to overcook them, or they'll be shriveled and tough.) Remove the oysters to a platter lined with paper towels to drain briefly, then quickly transfer six hot oysters onto the top of each salad. Shake a few drops of Tabasco onto each oyster. Serve immediately (and be sure to put the bottle of Tabasco on the table, so everyone can season his own salad to taste).

part 2

ONE BOWL

What's for supper? An iron-skillet jambalaya full of browned chicken and smoky andouille? Mexican fish soup scented with citrus and cilantro? Pasta sauce that simmers on a back burner for hours? Asian noodles layered with crisp vegetables and fragrant fresh herbs? A meal in a single dish is the ultimate comfort food, a tradition on the Gulf Coast since the Maya first stirred beans into their corn. It's a simple art seasoned by centuries of practice. Dig in.

gumbos, soups, and sopas

deconstructing bouillabaisse

A real stickler would inform you that bouillabaisse can only be prepared in and around Marseilles and that it must contain no shellfish, just seven different varieties of finfish found exclusively in Mediterranean waters. That's why we'd never invite him to dinner. Instead, round up some good company for a Third Coast brew that gives new life to the shrimp, crabs, and oysters we normally encounter in gumbo. And, in keeping with the go-to-hell theme, feel free to add or substitute any seafood that looks good in the market that day.

European roots also run deep in the Spanish *Sopa de Pescado* of the Mexican Gulf Coast. And the sweet-and-sour seafood soup is a favorite in the Vietnamese fishing communities of Louisiana and Texas. Even on the hottest nights, sluggish appetites will awaken to these bright flavors of sun and sea.

THIRD COAST BOUILLABAISSE

SERVES 6–8

A steaming pot of the freshest Gulf seafood makes a fun centerpiece for a party, especially when most of the work can be completed well in advance. Just add crusty French bread, a salad, and a carton of lemon sorbet. (And don't forget to phone your market early to reserve the bones and head from the fish fillets for a deeply flavored stock. Ask your fishmonger to remove the gills or snip them out with kitchen shears yourself.)

2 pounds	unpeeled jumbo shrimp, with heads
1 pound	firm fish fillets, cut into 2-inch pieces (plus bones and head—gills removed—for stock)
1	medium yellow onion, unpeeled and quartered
1	large garlic clove, unpeeled and halved
1	celery rib, with leaves
2 quarts	water
¼ cup	olive oil
2	medium yellow onions, coarsely chopped
1	large garlic clove, sliced
4 cups	seeded and coarsely chopped fresh tomatoes
3 sprigs	fresh thyme (or 1 teaspoon dried thyme leaves)
1	bay leaf
1 tablespoon	salt, or to taste
¼ teaspoon	thread saffron, crushed
⅛ teaspoon	cayenne pepper
1 dozen	cleaned small crabs (see page 189)
2 dozen	shucked oysters, with liquid
	Rouille (page 104)

1. Peel, devein, and refrigerate the shrimp; place the heads and shells in a stockpot with the fish bones and head. Add the unpeeled onion, garlic clove, and celery rib with leaves. Add the water, bring to a boil, then lower the heat and simmer for 1 hour. Strain out and discard the solids, then measure and reduce (if necessary) to make 6 cups of stock.

2. Warm the olive oil in a large pot over medium-low heat and cook the chopped onions until tender and golden, 3 to 5 minutes. Add the sliced garlic with the tomatoes, thyme, bay leaf, salt,

(recipe continues→)

saffron, and cayenne. Add the 6 cups of seafood stock and bring to a boil, then lower the heat and simmer for 30 minutes. Strain out and discard the solids.

3. Return the broth to the pot and bring to a boil. Add the cleaned crabs and cook for 10 minutes. Add the fish pieces and shrimp, return to a boil, then reduce the heat and simmer until the shrimp just begin to turn pink, 3 to 5 minutes. Add the oysters and cook for a minute or two longer, just until the edges curl. Serve immediately with the Rouille.

Plan ahead: Prepare through step 2 and refrigerate for up to 1 day.

ROUILLE

MAKES ABOUT 2 CUPS

Rouille is traditionally presented with Mediterranean-style fish soups, so guests can spice up their own bowls to taste. However, you could serve this garlicky seasoning paste with vegetable or bean soups, minestrone, gumbo, or any dish that needs a little attitude adjustment.

1	medium red-skinned potato
4	large garlic cloves, peeled and chopped
2	red bell peppers, roasted, peeled, and seeded (or bottled roasted peppers)
2	fresh jalapeños, seeded and chopped
½ cup	olive oil
	Salt and cayenne pepper

Steam or microwave the unpeeled potato until it's cooked, then peel it. Purée the garlic, roasted peppers, and jalapeños in a food processor or blender. Add the still-warm potato and process just until blended. Transfer to a bowl and whisk in the olive oil. Season highly with salt and cayenne pepper.

MEXICAN FISH SOUP
* sopa de pescado *

SERVES 4

Spain's orange-scented fish stew gets a New World spark from jalapeños and cilantro. The hearty classic featured here is common in the waterfront villages of Veracruz. Once you've got the fish cleaned, this is the easiest (and least expensive) of the soups in this section.

1	(3-pound) red snapper, or another firm-fleshed fish, filleted, bones reserved for stock
1	medium yellow onion, unpeeled and quartered
1	garlic clove, unpeeled and halved
1	celery rib, with leaves
½	small thin-skinned orange, scrubbed and sliced
1	bay leaf
6 cups	water
¼ cup	olive oil
1	medium yellow onion, chopped
2	garlic cloves, chopped
4	fresh tomatoes, peeled, seeded, and coarsely chopped
2–3	fresh jalapeños, seeded and finely chopped
¾ teaspoon	dried oregano, preferably Mexican
	Salt and freshly ground black pepper
1 tablespoon	minced fresh cilantro (optional)
	Lime wedges for garnish

1. Place the fish bones in a large saucepan. Add the unpeeled onion, unpeeled garlic clove, celery, orange, and bay leaf. Pour in the water and bring to a boil; lower the heat and simmer for 1 hour. Discard the solids; measure the stock and reduce (if necessary) to make 4 cups.

2. Warm the olive oil in a large pot over medium heat. Cook the chopped onion until it's tender and golden, about 3 minutes. Add the chopped garlic, tomatoes, jalapeños, and oregano. Cook briefly, until the garlic releases its fragrance, 2 to 3 minutes. Add the 4 cups of fish stock and bring to a boil; lower the heat and simmer for 30 minutes.

3. Add the fish pieces; simmer until fish just begins to turn opaque, 3 to 5 minutes. Season to taste with salt and pepper. Stir in the cilantro, if using. Serve immediately with lime wedges.

VIETNAMESE SWEET-and-SOUR
seafood soup
* *canh chua ca* *

SERVES 4–6

Many Vietnamese who settled on the Third Coast earn their living on the water, fishing
as they did in their homeland. One of their contributions to the regional melting pot is
this clear golden soup, stocked here with Gulf shrimp and red snapper, sometimes catfish.
It's a soul-satisfying bowl of flavors and textures, invigorated by tart pineapple, fresh
tomato wedges, crisp bean sprouts, lime juice, hot chiles, and a fragrant garnish of fresh
green herbs. If you prefer, substitute chicken broth for the seafood stock and 12 ounces of
boneless skinless chicken breasts (sliced crosswise) for the fish and shrimp.

1 pound	extra-large unpeeled shrimp, with heads
½ pound	firm fish fillets, cut into 2-inch pieces (reserve any bones for stock)
6 cups	water
1	celery rib, sliced
2	shallots, sliced
2	garlic cloves, chopped
2 tablespoons	peanut or vegetable oil
1	large ripe tomato, cored, seeded, and cut lengthwise into 8 wedges
1 cup	fresh pineapple chunks (or juice-packed canned chunks, drained)
2 tablespoons	sugar
3 tablespoons	fresh lime juice
3 tablespoons	Vietnamese or Thai fish sauce
1 teaspoon	salt
1 tablespoon	minced fresh red chile, or more to taste
½ cup	fresh bean sprouts
1	scallion, white and green parts, thinly sliced
	Shredded fresh basil and mint leaves

1. Peel, devein, and refrigerate the shrimp. For a quick stock, simmer the shrimp shells and heads, plus any fish bones, in the water (with the celery tops and the peelings from the shallots and garlic) for 30 minutes. Strain and reserve the stock, adding water if necessary to make 6 cups.

2. Warm the oil in a large saucepan over medium heat. Cook the sliced shallots and garlic until soft, but not brown. Add the tomato, pineapple chunks, sliced celery, and sugar; cook until the tomato wedges are barely soft. Add the reserved stock and bring to a boil over high heat. Stir in the lime juice, fish sauce, and salt. Reduce the heat to medium-low and simmer for 5 minutes. Stir in the shrimp and minced red chile; simmer until the shrimp are pink and cooked through, 2 to 3 minutes. Stir in the bean sprouts and scallion. Serve immediately, garnished with the shredded fresh basil and mint.

Plan ahead: Prepare through step 1 and refrigerate for up to 1 day.

✳ ✳ ✳ the other sunshine states ✳ ✳ ✳

Everybody knows about Florida citrus, but it's also big business on the Texas Gulf Coast, especially in the fertile Rio Grande Valley. Citrus fruits were introduced to both states, to Mexico, and to southern Louisiana by early Spanish missionaries.

✳ ✳ ✳ ✳ ✳ ✳

gumbo ya-ya

Louisiana's complex and earthy cuisine was cooked up in a French territory that was also controlled by the Spanish, served by African and Caribbean slaves, and settled by hordes of German, Italian, and Irish immigrants. If there's a signature dish it's gumbo, the dark and smoky stew that takes its name from the Bantu word for okra, though it's often thickened by oil-browned flour (roux) or ground sassafras leaves (filé) instead.

"Gumbo ya-ya" is an old slang expression that means "everybody talking at once." It's a fitting name for this section, which is devoted to the deliciously murky soup that is now part of nearly every Southern cook's repertoire, though no one can agree on exactly how it should be made. However, we are sure of one thing: gumbo is the perfect do-ahead meal because it always tastes better the second day.

AFRICAN-STYLE
smoked turkey and okra gumbo
✴ *nsouki-loppa* ✴

SERVES 6

Most cooks have experienced the oral history of their own families, trying to re-create favorite dishes under the direction of mothers or grandmothers who tell us to "add more flour until it feels right" or "take it out of the oven as soon as the top looks brown, but not too brown." In that spirit, we should have no trouble following this traditional African recipe from Fanta Tambajang, who moved to the Gulf Coast from Gambia. I have estimated her "four pitchers of water" to be around 4 quarts. As for the weight of the turkey, she recommends a "good-sized" one. And she offers no exact measurement for cayenne pepper either, as she always modifies food for guests who may request anything from extra mild to really really hot. ("When people boast like that," she says, "they don't know what they're asking for.")

"We use lots of garlic, like you do here, but lots of ginger, too," Tambajang says. "We don't make a roux. We thicken stews and sauces with okra or with ground nuts or melon seeds." Dried smoked fish is one African staple, a rarity in the United States, with a distinctive flavor that Tambajang finds hard to reproduce for this authentic gumbo that she remembers from her childhood. "Africans love a smoky flavor," she says. "Here we use smoked turkey and beef sausage, but it's not the same."

¼	whole smoked turkey
4 quarts	water
1 pound	beef smoked sausage, sliced
1 pound	okra, sliced
1	medium onion, chopped
1	ripe tomato, peeled and chopped
1 bunch	scallions, roasted until very dry, then ground
1	(½-inch) slice fresh ginger, ground
1	garlic clove, ground
	Salt and cayenne pepper to taste

Simmer the turkey in the 4 quarts of water until it's easy to remove the meat from the bones (about 1 hour). Tear the meat into small pieces and return it to the pot with the other ingredients. Boil for about 45 minutes. Serve over steamed rice.

CREOLE FILÉ GUMBO

SERVES 6

This rich elegant soup made with oysters and fowl, seasoned with aromatic vegetables and herbs, was contributed by New Orleans historian and writer Carolyn Kolb. It is her mother's Creole gumbo, thickened with filé (ground sassafras leaves), a contribution of the Native Americans of Louisiana.

"This is an old-fashioned recipe, in that ingredients are definite, but measurements are not," Kolb says. "It is also adaptable. You could use Louisiana-style smoked sausage, andouille sausage, cured ham, or other pork—just be sure that you don't use a 'hot' variety. Dried thyme and bay leaves are perfectly acceptable for herbs, and the amount of meat and vegetables can vary as to taste. The fowl might be chicken, leftover turkey, wild duck, or boneless chicken breasts. The chicken stock might be homemade or canned but, if possible, use a hen and simmer it in water flavored with onions, celery, parsley, thyme, and bay to make your stock; and be sure to de-fat and reduce it."

½ pound	smoked sausage, skinned and chopped
½ pound	andouille sausage, skinned and chopped
	Cooking oil (optional)
1	very large or 2 medium yellow onions, chopped
3	celery ribs, peeled and chopped
1	medium green bell pepper, chopped
½–1 teaspoon	dried thyme leaves
1	large dried bay leaf
1 pint	fresh raw oysters and their liquor
4–6 cups	good chicken stock
1 pound	cooked chicken, or other poultry meat, boned, skinned, and cut into 1-inch pieces
1 heaping tablespoon	filé powder (see Note)
	Kosher salt
	Cayenne pepper
	Chopped flat-leaf parsley
	Chopped scallions

1. Brown the sausages in a deep Dutch oven or skillet over medium heat until they begin to render fat. (If there is not any fat, add a tablespoon of oil.) Add the onion, celery, bell pepper, thyme, and bay leaf; cook slowly until the onion is clear.

2. Go through the oysters carefully and discard any shell fragments. In a separate saucepan, heat the oysters in their liquor just until the oysters' petticoats curl.

3. Add all but 1 cup of the stock to the sautéed vegetables; then add the oysters and their liquor. Now, add the chicken meat. Bring to a simmer but not to a boil, then let the gumbo cool on the stove awhile (until you can easily touch a spoonful of it).

4. Be sure the remaining cup of stock is cool. In a small bowl or cup, add the cool stock to the filé powder, stirring briskly. You should have a thick green paste.

5. Be sure the gumbo is not boiling, or anywhere near boiling. (Filé gets its name from the French word for "thread." When added to boiling liquid it forms unattractive threads, or becomes "ropey.") Stirring the gumbo very briskly, add the filé mixture. The gumbo should take on a greenish color. Warm it to serving temperature and remove the bay leaf. Season to taste with salt and a little cayenne pepper. Add the chopped parsley and scallions to the hot gumbo just before ladling it out into large soup bowls. Pass a big bowl of fluffy steamed white rice to add generously to each serving.

Note: Filé powder is available from the Sources on page 384. If using fresh home-ground filé, decrease the amount to 1½ teaspoons.

Plan ahead: Refrigerate completed gumbo for up to 3 days. Reheat slowly, being very careful not to let it come to a boil.

✳ ✳ ✳ the not-quite-holy trinity ✳ ✳ ✳

Cooking is practically a religion on the Third Coast and this is the crux of our belief: God has blessed us with a wondrous bounty that will taste even better if we doctor it up a little. That's why so many of our recipes begin by invoking the so-called Creole Trinity of onions, celery, and bell peppers. It's a sign of our Mediterranean roots, along with other kitchen essentials, like garlic, tomatoes, lemons, bay leaves, and thyme. Skinny bottles of hot sauce are regional icons. Our pepper comes in black, white, and red. And Emeril is right—pork fat does rule. Amen.

✳ ✳ ✳ ✳ ✳ ✳

COUNTRY DUCK GUMBO

"I grew up on a Louisiana bayou in a family of hunters," says my good friend Priscilla Fleming Vayda. "So we always had duck, either aging in a large outdoor icebox or neatly tucked away in a freezer. But the last time I craved this gumbo, I was living in Los Angeles. Undaunted, I went to the market and bought two free-range domestic ducks, and had the butcher quarter them. I saved one breast to grill later and proceeded with the following recipe." Vayda's gumbo is thickened with both roux and okra.

STOCK

3	large wild ducks, preferably mallards, or 2 free-range domestic ducks, around 4½ pounds each
	Salt and pepper
About ¼ cup	vegetable oil to brown the ducks
3 quarts	water
1	medium onion, quartered
4	celery ribs
4	carrots

GUMBO

⅓ cup	vegetable oil
⅓ cup	flour
1 cup	chopped onion
1 cup	chopped bell pepper, preferably a mix of red and yellow
½ cup	chopped celery
¼ cup	chopped scallions
2	garlic cloves, minced
1	bay leaf
¼ teaspoon	thyme
2 cups	sliced okra
1 pound	shrimp, peeled and deveined
	Salt and pepper
1 pint	small oysters, with liquor (about 2 dozen)
¼ cup	chopped parsley

1. For the stock: Clean and quarter the ducks; dry thoroughly with paper towels; season with salt and pepper. Brown the ducks in the ¼ cup of vegetable oil in a large heavy skillet over medium heat.

2. Remove the browned duck pieces to a large soup kettle; set the skillet aside to use in step 5. Add the water, onion, celery, and carrots to the soup kettle. Simmer, covered, for about 1 hour, until the ducks are tender.

3. Remove the ducks from the stock and pull the meat from the bones, discarding the bones and fat; set the meat aside. Strain the stock for the gumbo (you'll need about 3 quarts); discard the solids. Return the stock to the soup kettle, skim the fat, and hold at a simmer.

4. For the gumbo: Warm the ⅓ cup of oil in a clean heavy skillet over medium-high heat. Whisk the flour into the oil and cook, whisking, to make a very dark roux. The roux will take 3 or 4 minutes to reach this point, but browns quickly once it gets going, so be especially vigilant toward the end. Switch to a spoon and immediately stir in the onion, bell pepper, celery, scallions, and garlic; cook until the vegetables are limp. Spoon the roux and browned vegetables into the hot duck stock, stirring to blend. Add the duck pieces, bay leaf, and thyme; simmer.

5. Place the same skillet that you used to brown the ducks over medium heat, and use the same oil to brown the okra, stirring until it is no longer ropey. Add the okra to the soup kettle; set the skillet aside to use in step 6. Simmer the gumbo, covered, until all is tender and nice and thick, about 1½ hours. ("Gumbo should never be thin," Vayda insists.)

6. Just before serving, brown the shrimp in the same skillet that was used for the okra, then add them to the soup kettle; cook for 5 minutes. Skim any excess oil from the top of the gumbo and remove the bay leaf. Season to taste with salt and pepper. Add the oysters and their liquor; cook until the edges of the oysters just begin to curl. Remove the kettle from the heat and stir in the parsley. Serve the hot gumbo in soup bowls over fluffy steamed rice.

Plan ahead: "When I am preparing this gumbo for a dinner party," Vayda says, "I cook everything the day before, except the oysters. Then I reheat the gumbo and add the oysters while a pot of rice is cooking."

a chicken in every pot

The world's most popular protein, raised domestically for at least 4,000 years, is simmered into chicken soup by cooks from nearly every culture. Offered as relief for anything from a stuffy head to a broken heart, a steaming bowlful—whether it's stocked with noodles, tortillas, dumplings, or matzo balls—evokes mother love.

Like gumbo, chicken and dumplings is a ubiquitous Gulf Coast dish prepared in many different ways. The French Acadian fricot is similar to the version passed down in many Louisiana families. It tops browned meat and vegetables with biscuit-like "drop dumplings" (*a.k.a.* poutines). Head deeper south and such cozy brews are brightened by citrus and spice. Tex-Mex Tortilla Soup is crowned with chopped tomatoes and avocados, served with tortilla strips. Floribbean Chicken and Coconut Soup is quick and exotic, enlivened by fresh ginger and Jamaican curry powder.

FLORIBBEAN CHICKEN
and coconut soup

SERVES 4

*Definitely not your mother's chicken soup, unless she's a Bahama mama, this
tropical brew isn't meant to be soothing. It'll have you on your feet in no time—
all charged up by fresh ginger, garlic, and Floribbean spices—but the coconut milk
keeps everything smooth and sweet.*

2 tablespoons	unsalted butter
1 tablespoon	chopped fresh ginger
1 tablespoon	chopped garlic
¼ cup	chopped scallions, green and white parts
3 cups	chicken broth
1	(14-ounce) can unsweetened coconut milk
2½ teaspoons	Jamaican-style curry powder (such as Badia brand)
1½ teaspoons	sugar
½ pound	boneless, skinless chicken breast, cut crosswise into strips
1 tablespoon	fresh lime juice
1–2	fresh serrano chiles, seeded and minced
	Salt and white pepper
	Finely chopped scallions for garnish
	Lime wedges

1. Warm the butter in a large saucepan over medium heat; cook the ginger, garlic, and scallions until tender, but not browned. Stir in the chicken broth; bring to a boil, reduce the heat to a simmer, and cook for 20 minutes. Strain out and discard the solids.

2. Return the flavored broth to the pot with the coconut milk, curry powder, and sugar; bring to a simmer. Add the chicken and simmer until cooked through, about 5 minutes. Stir in the lime juice and chiles; cook for 1 to 2 minutes longer. Season with salt and pepper. Garnish each bowl with chopped scallions; serve with lime wedges.

ACADIAN CHICKEN and dumplings
* chicken fricot *
SERVES 6

Driven out of Canada by the English in 1755, French Acadians scattered down the Eastern seaboard all the way to the bayous of Louisiana. Their simple and hearty fricot is an ancestor of Cajun chicken and dumplings, but it could also be made with pork, rabbit, beef, seafood, game, or—vegetarians take note—no meat at all.

"Potato fricot was prepared when neither meat nor fish was available and was given the tongue-in-cheek name 'weasel fricot' (fricot à la belette)," according to Canadian folklorist Marielle Cormier-Boudreau. "If you ask Acadians about the origin of the name, they will smile and say, 'Parce que la belette a passé tout drouète' (Because the weasel went right on by)."

1	(5-pound) roasting hen, cut into serving pieces
	Salt and freshly ground black pepper
¼ pound	salt pork, diced (traditional), or 3 tablespoons olive oil
2 cups	diced onion
¼ cup	all-purpose flour
2 quarts	boiling water
5 cups	diced russet potatoes
4	carrots, thickly sliced

1. Season the chicken pieces with salt and pepper. Brown the salt pork (or warm the olive oil) in a large pot over medium heat; brown the chicken pieces in the rendered fat until lightly colored on all sides. Remove the meats and drain off all but 3 tablespoons of the fat. Sauté the onion until golden, then add the flour and stir for a minute or two, until smooth.

2. Return the meats to the pot with the boiling water and simmer until the chicken is tender. Add the potatoes and carrots; cook for 15 to 20 minutes longer. Season to taste with salt and pepper. The fricot may be served as is, or topped with the drop dumplings known as poutines (recipe follows).

Plan ahead: The fricot may be prepared a couple of days in advance. Reheat and add the dumplings, if using, just before serving.

Note: Vegetarians—use vegetable broth and leave out the meat for a "weasel fricot."

drop dumplings (poutines)

1 cup	flour
1 tablespoon	baking powder
½ teaspoon	salt
½ cup	cold water

Combine the flour with the baking powder and salt. Add the water and mix lightly, just until blended. Drop the dumplings by tablespoons onto the simmering fricot and steam, tightly covered, for 7 minutes.

✳ ✳ ✳ stock your soup pot right ✳ ✳ ✳

Since most of us only have access to supermarket stewing chickens (usually worn-out laying hens that cook up tough and dry), you should seek out the more tender birds labeled as roasters. Otherwise, substitute 7 to 8 pounds of fryers for a 5-pound hen.

✳ ✳ ✳ ✳ ✳

TEX-MEX TORTILLA SOUP

SERVES 6–8

Originally created as a thrifty use for leftover chicken carcasses and stale tortillas, this popular Tex-Mex soup is worth preparing from scratch. Browning fresh fowl with the seasoning vegetables creates an especially flavorful broth, much heartier than a pallid stock made from boiled bones. Topped with chunks of tomato and avocado, then a crackly mound of fried tortilla strips, it's truly a meal in one bowl.

FOR THE SOUP

1	(3-pound) fryer, cut into 8 pieces
	Salt and freshly ground black pepper
1 teaspoon	ground cumin
¼ cup	olive oil
2 cups	chopped onion
1 tablespoon	chopped garlic
2 cups	peeled, seeded, and diced tomatoes (or a 14½-ounce can of diced tomatoes, drained)
3	mild green chiles, such as Anaheim, roasted, peeled, seeded, and chopped (or 3 canned mild green chiles, drained, seeded, and chopped)
½ teaspoon	dried oregano, preferably Mexican
1	bay leaf
2 quarts	water
2 tablespoons	fresh lime juice

FOR THE TORTILLA STRIPS

	Peanut oil or canola oil for deep frying
12	tortillas, cut in half, then into ¼-inch strips

FOR SERVING

3	plum tomatoes, seeded and coarsely chunked
2	Hass avocados, peeled, seeded, and coarsely chunked
	Minced fresh cilantro leaves for garnish

1. For the soup: Wash and dry the chicken. Season highly with salt, black pepper, and ground cumin. Warm the oil in a heavy stockpot or Dutch oven over medium heat. Working in batches, without crowding, brown the chicken on all sides and remove to a platter. Strain off

and discard all but 2 tablespoons of the fat. Add the onion, tossing until it's browned at the edges and beginning to soften, 3 to 4 minutes. Add the garlic, tomatoes, chiles, oregano, and bay leaf; cook, stirring occasionally, until the garlic is fragrant and any excess moisture from the tomatoes has evaporated, 2 to 3 minutes.

2. Return the chicken pieces to the pan, along with the water. Bring just to a boil, then cover the pan, reduce the heat to low, and simmer for 20 minutes, or until the chicken is cooked.

3. Remove the chicken from the pot. When cool enough to handle, discard the skin and bones; use your fingers to pull the meat into rough shreds. Return the meat to the soup. Stir in the lime juice and remove the bay leaf.

4. For the tortilla strips: Heat the peanut or canola oil in a deep heavy skillet or electric fryer to a temperature of 375° F. Working in batches, without crowding, fry the tortilla strips until crisp and very lightly browned around the edges, less than 1 minute.

5. To serve: Place several tortilla strips in the bottom of each bowl. Ladle in the very hot soup. Top with a few chunks of tomato and avocado, a sprinkle of minced cilantro leaves, and more tortilla strips.

Plan ahead: Fried or baked tortilla strips may be stored airtight at room temperature for up to 2 days. Prepare soup through step 4 and refrigerate for up to 2 days.

from the earth

Throughout South Louisiana, a vegetarian gumbo made with fresh greens and herbs is traditionally served on Good Friday, when many Catholics still abstain from meat. This *Gumbo z'Herbes* ("grass soup") may include whatever the garden yields (spinach, turnip greens, collards, cabbage, kale, watercress, parsley, beet tops); but legend has it that you'll make a new friend for each different variety that you throw into the pot.

Though many people won't even think of sweet potatoes until next Thanksgiving, the New World's most nutritious vegetable is not just for pies and turkey dinners. It's an everyday staple on the Third Coast, a colorful addition to hearty soups and stews. The Spicy Sweet Potato Bisque that follows is seasoned with an earthy blend of roasted garlic, cumin, thyme, and sage.

Corn is another Gulf Coast product, and new supersweet varieties delay converting their sugar to starch for weeks, rather than minutes. Make the most of the harvest with Cuban-style corn soup that preserves the crunch and color of the main ingredient.

GUMBO OF GREENS AND HERBS
* gumbo z'herbes *

SERVES 6–8

This classic version of the vegetarian gumbo is from Priscilla Fleming Vayda, a food writer who grew up on Fleming Plantation in the tiny Louisiana fishing village of Lafitte. She directs carnivores to add a ham bone or ham hock to the sautéed seasonings before stirring in the stock.

3 pounds	mixed sturdy greens (such as spinach, turnip greens, collards, cabbage, kale, watercress, parsley, beet tops)
4 cups	water
2 tablespoons	cooking oil
2 tablespoons	all-purpose flour
1 cup	chopped onion
1 cup	chopped green bell pepper
½ cup	chopped celery
¼ cup	chopped scallions
2	garlic cloves, minced
1	bay leaf
1 sprig	fresh thyme
1 sprig	fresh marjoram
2 tablespoons	filé powder (Sources, page 384)
	Salt and pepper
	Hot steamed rice
6 tablespoons	chopped flat-leaf parsley

1. Cover the washed greens with 4 cups of water in a large pot and simmer for 30 minutes. Drain, and reserve the stock. Chop the greens.

2. Warm the oil in the same large pot over medium heat, then gradually add the flour, stirring all the while. Cook to a pale golden color. Add the onion, bell pepper, celery, and scallions. Cook until the vegetables are limp. Add the garlic and reserved cooked greens; simmer for several minutes. Pour in the reserved stock. Add the bay leaf, thyme, and marjoram. Simmer for 2 hours.

3. Just before serving, stir in the filé powder. (Do not let gumbo boil after adding filé; it will turn stringy.) Season to taste with salt and pepper. Serve over rice in soup bowls. Garnish with chopped parsley.

Plan ahead: Prepare the gumbo through step 2 and refrigerate for up to 2 days.

CREAM OF GARLIC SOUP

SERVES 8

*Like the sopa de ajo of Spain and Mexico, Chef Susan Spicer's Cream of Garlic Soup is
thickened by chunks of stale bread. But instead of the last-minute swirl of beaten eggs that
would enrich the Spanish version, she adds a simpler (and smoother) finish of half-and-
half. It's a fragrant introduction to Spicer's celebrated New World cuisine, and a signature
dish at her New Orleans restaurant, Bayona.*

2 pounds	onions, peeled and roughly chopped (about 4 cups)
2 cups	garlic cloves, peeled and chopped
2 tablespoons	olive oil
2 tablespoons	unsalted butter
6 cups	chicken broth, plus more if needed
1	bouquet garni (parsley stems, thyme sprigs, and a bay leaf, tied together)
2 cups	stale French bread, torn into ½-inch pieces
1 cup	half-and-half
	Salt and pepper

1. In a 1-gallon, heavy-bottomed pot, sauté the onions and garlic in the oil and butter. Stir frequently over low to medium heat until they turn a deep golden brown, about 30 minutes. Add 6 cups of the chicken broth and the bouquet garni; bring to a boil. Stir in the bread cubes and simmer for 10 minutes, until the bread is soft.

2. Remove the bouquet garni and purée the soup in a blender, working in small batches, so the hot soup doesn't overflow the container. Strain back into the pot through a medium strainer. Heat and whisk in more chicken broth if too thick. Add the half-and-half. Season to taste with salt and pepper.

SPICY SWEET POTATO BISQUE

SERVES 8–12

The puréed potatoes create a silken texture without any cream, but you could
swirl in a bit to enrich this savory soup for special occasions. Vegetarians will
find the nutty flavor of soy milk enhances the smokiness of the roasted vegetables,
as does the final sprinkle of toasted pecans.

6	medium sweet potatoes, about 3 pounds
1	large onion, unpeeled
8	garlic cloves, unpeeled
¼ cup	olive oil
2	celery ribs, chopped
1	large onion, peeled and chopped
2 teaspoons	ground cumin
½ teaspoon	dried rubbed sage
½ teaspoon	dried thyme leaves
½ teaspoon	white pepper
6 cups	chicken or vegetable stock, plus more if needed
	Salt
	Cream, milk, or soy milk (optional)
	Honey-Chipotle Pecans (page 37) for garnish

1. Heat the oven to 400° F. Place the sweet potatoes and the unpeeled onion in a lightly greased roasting pan and bake for 30 minutes. Add the unpeeled garlic cloves and continue baking until the potatoes are soft, about 30 minutes longer.

2. Warm the olive oil in a stockpot over medium heat; cook the celery and chopped onion until browned. Add the cumin, sage, thyme, and white pepper; stir for 1 to 2 minutes longer.

3. When the roasted vegetables are cool enough to handle, peel and place in a food processor; add the sautéed vegetables and spices; purée until smooth, adding a bit of stock, if necessary, to facilitate blending. Return the purée to the pot with the remaining stock and bring to a boil; reduce the heat and simmer very gently for several minutes to allow the flavors to blend. Season to taste with salt. Thin to the desired consistency with additional stock, cream, milk, soy milk, or water. Serve garnished with Honey-Chipotle Pecans.

CUBAN CORN SOUP
guiesso de maiz

SERVES 6

Common in the Florida Keys and Tampa Bay area, Cuban Guiesso de Maiz is almost identical to the traditional corn soups of Alabama and Mississippi, except for a final garnish of spicy chorizo sausage. Some Cuban cooks also top each bowl with chopped hard-cooked egg. A satisfying mix of textures and bright flavors, it's a colorful summer supper.

3 tablespoons	olive oil
1	medium onion, chopped
1	green bell pepper, chopped
1	celery rib, chopped
1	carrot, chopped
½ pound	smoked ham, diced
1	bay leaf
1 teaspoon	chopped fresh thyme, or ¼ teaspoon dried leaves
2	garlic cloves, sliced
1	(14½-ounce) can stewed tomatoes
3 cups	chicken broth
6–8	small red-skinned potatoes, quartered
1½ cups	fresh kernels from 3 large ears corn (see page 243)
	Salt and freshly ground black pepper to taste
2 tablespoons	minced flat-leaf parsley
3 links	chorizo sausage (Sources, page 384), cooked and sliced for garnish

1. Warm the oil over medium heat in a large saucepan and cook the onion, bell pepper, celery, carrot, and ham until the onion is golden and the ham is lightly browned. Add the bay leaf, thyme, and garlic and continue cooking for 1 to 2 minutes, until the garlic is fragrant. Add the tomatoes and chicken broth; bring to a boil, then reduce the heat and simmer for 15 minutes. Add the potatoes and continue cooking until tender, about 20 minutes.

2. Stir in the corn and simmer until tender, but still crisp, about 5 minutes. Adjust the salt and pepper to taste. Garnish each bowl with parsley and a few slices of chorizo sausage.

ROASTED POBLANO SOUP

SERVES 4–6

*Out near Beeville, Texas, potter and yoga instructor Debra Hanus makes
custom "ranchware" emblazoned with the client's brand (Sources, page 385).
One of the highlights of my research was a drive through cattle country to her rural
home studio, where the grounds are patrolled by a menagerie that includes a king
snake, a couple of buffalo, and a camel.*

*When I asked for a recipe, Hanus told me that this one is her favorite, a never-fail
starter for parties. Roasted fresh chiles are blended with cream cheese and sour cream (or
yogurt) for a pale green beauty that may be served hot or chilled. Poblanos do pack a spark,
but it's a relatively mild one. Use 1 for a slight kick, or up to 3 for rowdy tastes. Hanus
sometimes adds corn or chunks of chicken.*

1	large onion, chopped
2 tablespoons	unsalted butter
3 cups	chicken stock
1	(8-ounce) package cream cheese, chunked
1–3	poblanos, roasted, peeled, seeded, and chopped
1 cup	sour cream or plain yogurt
	Crumbled Queso Blanco (page 267) for garnish
	Lime wedges for garnish

Cook the onion in the butter in a medium saucepan over medium heat until soft and golden, but not browned. Add the chicken stock and cream cheese; stir until the stock is hot and the cheese is melted. Cool slightly, then purée with the poblanos in a food processor or blender. Return to the pot; add the sour cream or yogurt and heat through, but do not boil. Serve hot or chilled, each bowl garnished with crumbled queso blanco and a lime wedge.

cool and refreshing

Author Peter S. Feibleman remembers his first summer in Seville, when American refrigerators held places of honor in Andalusian living rooms and blenders were enshrined on red velvet in glass cases that were locked at night.

"The maid in the house where I lived prayed for a blender," he wrote, "and the cook went to church and promised the Virgin of the Macarena five candles if she could provide her with one by October."

Like their cousins in sunny Spain, residents of America's Gulf Coast have good reason to value a cool summer meal. They have developed a fine variety of chilled soups, including many spinoffs of gazpacho (the Andalusian specialty that was pounded by mortar and pestle before the advent of the electric savior).

Creamy avocado soup has been on the menu at bridge luncheons and grand Florida hotels since the 1890s. Here it is rejuvenated by lime juice and ginger, then topped with a luxurious mound of lump crabmeat.

Mango and Yogurt Soup is a sweet and flowery beginning to a romantic dinner for two. As quick to assemble as a smoothie, it also makes an unusual breakfast in bed.

CRAWFISH GAZPACHO

SERVES 4–6

This loose interpretation of the Spanish soup is from Palace Cafe in New Orleans. It was one of several courses (including three desserts) that President Bill Clinton tucked into during a surprise lunchtime visit in 1996. You could substitute cooked shrimp, scallops, crabmeat, or clams for the crawfish (or just delete it for a vegetarian meal).

6	cucumbers, peeled, seeded, and finely diced
6	ripe tomatoes, peeled, seeded, and finely diced
2	red onions, finely diced
1	green bell pepper, finely diced
1½ cups	fresh tomato purée
¼ cup	hot sauce, such as Tabasco sauce
¼ cup	Worcestershire sauce
¼ cup	minced fresh basil leaves
2 tablespoons	kosher salt
2 tablespoons	cracked black pepper
1 tablespoon	minced garlic
1 tablespoon	minced cilantro
1 pound	cooked Louisiana crawfish tails, peeled and deveined

Combine all of the ingredients and refrigerate for 1 hour. Serve in chilled bowls.

* * * something fishy? * * *

If you peel freshly boiled crawfish or obtain the tails from a reliable source, the yellow fat adds richness and flavor to any dish. However, fat from previously frozen meat can have an unpleasant fishy taste. If that's the case, rinse the fat from the tails and toss them with a few tablespoons of wine, or lemon or lime juice, to refresh the flavor.

* * * * * *

CHILLED AVOCADO
and crabmeat soup

SERVES 4

Older recipes call for cream, but avocado alone provides a smooth purée with a lovely pale-green hue. If crabmeat is too pricey, garnish bowls with boiled shrimp or one of the fresh salsas on pages 85–87 and 90–91. For Mexican sopa de aguacate, replace the ginger with a seeded and minced jalapeño, then garnish the soup with thin, crisply fried tortilla strips or slices of avocado.

2	Florida avocados (or 3 Hass avocados), peeled and seeded
¼ cup	fresh lime juice
2 tablespoons	dry sherry
1 teaspoon	finely grated ginger
½ teaspoon	Tabasco sauce
¼ teaspoon	white pepper
3 cups	cool chicken stock or broth, plus more if needed
	Salt
½ pound	lump crabmeat, picked over to remove any bits of shell

1. Purée the avocados with the lime juice in a food processor. Add all of the remaining ingredients except the salt and crabmeat; process until smooth. Season to taste with salt. Transfer to a bowl and place plastic wrap directly on the surface of the soup to seal. Refrigerate for 4 to 6 hours.

2. Taste and adjust the seasonings. Serve in chilled bowls, topped with lump crabmeat.

MANGO and YOGURT SOUP

SERVES 2

Mangoes and oranges are the very essence of the Gulf Coast, enhanced here by a wisp of orange flower water, recalling the fragrance of groves in full bloom. If you really want to get lavish, float an edible blossom in each bowl.

2	mangoes, peeled, pitted, and sliced
1 cup	plain yogurt
½ cup	fresh orange juice
½ teaspoon	orange flower water (see Note; optional)
	Ground allspice

Purée the mangoes in a blender or food processor. Add the yogurt, orange juice, and orange flower water (if using); process until smooth. Strain the soup and chill for a few hours or overnight. Serve in chilled bowls, lightly sprinkled with ground allspice.

Note: Look for orange flower water in liquor stores or Middle Eastern markets, or order from one of the suppliers on page 384.

rice and beans

FORTIFIED RICE

Havana-Style Paella (*Paella Habana*) * 133

Mexican-Style Paella (*Arroz a la Tumbada*) * 134

Jambalaya * 136

* ✳ *

GOOD FOR YOUR HEART

Drunken Beans (*Frijoles Borrachos*) * 139

Cuban Black Beans and Rice (*Moros y Cristianos*) * 140

Red Beans and Rice * 142

Mayan Chili * 144

fortified rice

Beginning in February, low-flying planes crisscross farms across the Gulf states like crop dusters, scattering thousands of acres with a vital grain that will be harvested the following September. "The food of the world" is the number one staple for two thirds of the earth's population, and the United States is a major exporter of rice, supplied by more than 2,000 growers in Louisiana alone, plus Texas and the other Gulf states.

HAVANA-STYLE PAELLA
* *paella habana* *
SERVES 1–2

This recipe is from Columbia Restaurant in Ybor City, the historic Cuban district of Tampa. Florida's oldest and largest Spanish restaurant, founded in 1905 by Cuban immigrant Casimiro Hernandez, is still operated by his fourth- and fifth-generation descendants. The glitterati once flocked to a showroom that presented extravagant Latin revues in the 1950s. Now flamenco dancers perform six nights a week at the original location, and the family has opened several more Florida branches along the Gulf Coast (in Sarasota, St. Petersburg, and Sand Key) and in St. Augustine and the Disney World town of Celebration.

¼ cup	extra-virgin olive oil
¼ cup	chopped onion
¼ cup	chopped green bell pepper
2 teaspoons	chopped garlic
⅓ cup	cubed lean pork loin
2	ripe tomatoes, peeled, seeded, and chopped
⅓ cup	cubed cooked yuca
1	small sweet potato, peeled and cut in chunks
1	ripe plantain, peeled and sliced in 1-inch chunks
½ cup	cooked and drained black beans
	Salt and pepper
1 cup	chicken broth
½ cup	uncooked white rice
Pinch	of saffron
¼ cup	white wine
	Cooked green peas for garnish

Heat the oven to 400° F. Warm the oil in a shallow (about 3 inches deep) ovenproof skillet or casserole over medium heat. Cook the onion, green pepper, and garlic. Add the pork loin (if using) and stir until browned and tender. Add the tomatoes, yuca, sweet potato, plantain, black beans, salt, and pepper. Add the broth, rice, and saffron; stir well. Place in the oven and bake for 20 minutes. Sprinkle with the wine and garnish with cooked green peas.

Note: Leave out the pork and use vegetable broth for a colorful vegetarian paella. If you'd like to increase the number of servings, cook the same amounts of ingredients in two or more small casseroles (rather than multiplying them in a larger pan) for best results.

MEXICAN-STYLE PAELLA
* arroz a la tumbada *
SERVES 8

Similar to the paellas of Spain and the jambalayas of Louisiana, but a bit soupier, this golden cazuela from the Mexican coastal state of Veracruz is a buttery jumble of seafoods and spices. It's a carefree and unpretentious preparation, hence the name Arroz a la Tumbada, or "thrown-together rice." Join the casual spirit and toss in whatever's fresh at your seafood market.

I don't know how to credit the recipe, as it represents the contributions of at least five cooks. I obtained the original from a very kind lady, then asked another to translate it into English for me. This being the Third Coast, the translator insisted that the recipe was all wrong, and sent it to one of her aunts for correction. Of course, that version was vetoed by another aunt, who returned a fresh new copy, typed in English by her son, entitled "Rice to the Fallen Down One." He confessed that he had sneaked in a few revisions of his own. It's one of my favorite souvenirs from this book, though it loses in the translation, since I can't use such colorful interpretations as "150 grams of pig butter" or "In a mud casserole, to fry the rice with the butter without leaving gilds." Still, it sure beats my Spanish.

STOCK

2 pounds	large head-on shrimp
	Bones and head (gills removed) from the fish fillets, if available
1	unpeeled onion, quartered
1	unpeeled garlic clove, quartered
1	celery rib
2 quarts	water

For the stock: Peel, devein, and refrigerate the shrimp; rinse the heads and shells and place them in a stockpot or large saucepan with the fish bones and head (if available), the unpeeled onion and garlic, the celery rib, and water. Bring just to a boil over high heat, then reduce the heat and simmer for at least 45 minutes, skimming often to remove any scum that may collect on the surface. Strain and discard the solids. You should have about 8 cups of stock.

½ cup	lard (traditional) or unsalted butter
3 cups	uncooked rice
1	large onion, chopped
5	garlic cloves, chopped
4	ripe tomatoes, seeded and chopped
4	jalapeños, seeded and chopped
	Salt and pepper
1 pound	firm-fleshed fish fillets (such as redfish, snapper, or grouper)
	A good handful of cilantro or fresh flat-leaf parsley, chopped (about ⅓ cup)

1. To complete the dish: Melt the lard in a large clay casserole (*cazuela*) or heavy deep skillet over medium heat. Add the rice, onion, and garlic; stir and shake the pan until the rice and onion are light gold, but not browned. Stir in the tomatoes and jalapeños and 6 cups of the shrimp stock; season to taste with salt and pepper. Bring to a boil, reduce heat to low, cover the pan, and simmer for 10 minutes. Arrange the fish pieces and shrimp atop the rice, without stirring; cover and simmer until the broth is absorbed and the rice is tender, 10 to 15 minutes.

2. Heat the remaining 2 cups of stock. Serve the *Arroz a la Tumbada* in wide soup bowls, bathing each portion with a few spoonfuls of the hot stock. Top with a generous sprinkle of chopped cilantro or parsley.

JAMBALAYA

No regional specialty is more used and abused than jambalaya. It's sort of like the chicken à la king of Louisiana, the main dish of every cheapskate event and bus-tour banquet. Often produced carelessly, it can be a gluey overseasoned mess. Made right, it's pure and simple comfort food that shares Spanish roots with the paellas and arroz con pollo of Mexico and the Caribbean. As for the name, it could have sprung from a couple of sources. There's the French jambón or Spanish jamòn (ham) à la (with) the African ya (rice); also the African jambé (mixture) and ya (again, rice).

At any rate, this is the real stuff. I got the recipe from an expert, Victor Andrews, my good friend and a pillar of strong opinions when it comes to food. He's also the great-grandson of the man who founded the Louisiana town of Gonzales, home of the Louisiana Jambalaya Festival and self-proclaimed "Jambalaya Capital of the World."

"Jambalaya is a dish that was designed to be cooked in one pot," Andrews insists. "Daddy would brown the sausage very slowly and use that rendered fat to brown the chicken. Then he put in the onions, scraping up all that good gratin on the bottom of the pot. The onions brown very quickly. That's what gives the jambalaya its color and flavor. And nobody in Gonzales ever made jambalaya with tomatoes in it. That just wasn't done. Original recipes had some kind of ham, or jambon, a salt-cured ham that would be much more flavorful than the smoked ham we have now. My grandmother used to say that chicken didn't have any flavor anymore, and that the sausage you bought in the store was just not as good as the sausage you made at home. That's the secret, a good sausage. And cooking in a cast-iron Dutch oven makes all the difference in the world."

1 pound	best-quality smoked sausage, sliced ¼ inch thick
1	(3- to 4-pound) fryer, cut into 8 to 10 serving pieces
	Vegetable oil (optional)
1	large onion, chopped
6 cups	water
	Salt to taste
	Cayenne and black pepper to taste
	Tabasco sauce, if desired
3 cups	medium-grain white rice
1 bunch	scallions, chopped

1. Slowly brown the sausage over medium-low heat in a cast-iron Dutch oven (vastly preferred) or heavy deep skillet. Remove the sausage with a slotted spoon. Raise the heat to medium and brown the chicken in the rendered sausage fat, adding a bit of vegetable oil, if necessary. Set aside the browned chicken. Pour off all but 2 tablespoons of the fat.

2. Add the onion to the pan; cook over medium heat until translucent and lightly browned. Add the water, salt, cayenne, black pepper, and Tabasco (if using); raise the heat and bring the liquid to a boil, stirring to deglaze the pan. Return the chicken to the pan, reduce the heat to low, and simmer for 10 minutes. Add the rice, scallions, and sausage. Raise the heat and bring to a boil; stir, scraping the bottom well, and reduce the heat to low. Cover the pot and cook until the chicken is done, the rice is tender, and moisture is absorbed (15 to 20 minutes).

* * * go with the grain * * *

According to the USA Rice Council, some 40,000 different varieties have been cultivated around the globe, though only a small number are produced commercially. These can be divided roughly into four categories: long, medium, and short grains, plus the so-called aromatics. (Wild rice, which is native to North America, is not really a rice at all, but the seed of an aquatic grass.) Most common in supermarkets are long-grain rice (which cooks up separate and fluffy) and medium-grain, which tends to cling more. Short-grain rice is almost round and quite sticky, available in natural foods stores and Asian groceries, where it might also be labeled as pearl rice or sweet rice. Aromatics—such as India's basmati (or the Texas-grown version sometimes packaged as Texmati), wild pecan, jasmine, black japonica, Lundberg, or Wehani—have a flavor and aroma similar to that of roasted nuts or popcorn.

There are no hard-and-fast rules on which types to use in most recipes. In general, medium and short grains are best for molded dishes, such as sushi or croquettes, or for creamy desserts and puddings. Long grains and aromatics are best for pilafs and stir-fries. Usually the choice is a matter of personal preference. Most aromatics can be steamed just like regular white or brown rice, so you can stick to the basics and still experiment with new tastes and colors.

* * * * * *

good for your heart

A mainstay in nearly every food culture for more than 10,000 years, legumes have finally climbed the stalk to haute cuisine. Fashionable menus and urban markets are spilling over with obscure heirloom varieties—color-flecked beauties with evocative names like Anasazis, Appaloosas, calypsos, tongues of fire, and Maine yellow eyes. No trend here, a simmering pot of beans has always been a fixture in households up and down the Gulf Coast.

DRUNKEN BEANS
frijoles borrachos
SERVES 4–6

That Tex-Mex staple, a pot of pintos, seems downright friendly when it's spiked with beer and topped with a tequila-laced salsa for muy macho frijoles borrachos (drunken beans). If you prefer, substitute extra chicken broth or water for the beer—though most of the alcohol will dissipate during cooking. The resulting frijoles charros (cowboy beans) will still have plenty of punch from the cumin, ground chiles, and cilantro.

1 pound	pinto beans, rinsed, drained, and picked over
4 cups	unsalted chicken broth or water
2	(12-ounce) beers
¼ pound	slab bacon, cut into ½-inch pieces
1	large onion, chopped
2	garlic cloves, finely chopped
1 teaspoon	ground chipotle chiles
1 teaspoon	ground cumin
½ teaspoon	dried oregano
	Salt
¼ cup	chopped fresh cilantro

1. Combine the beans and enough cold water to cover by 2 inches in a large pot. Bring to a boil over high heat and boil for 2 minutes. Remove from the heat, cover the pot, and let stand for an hour, then drain well. Return the drained beans to the pot with the chicken broth or water and beer. Bring to a boil, then cover and simmer over low heat until the beans are just tender, about 1 hour.

2. Meanwhile, sauté the bacon pieces in a large skillet over medium-high heat until browned and crisp. Set aside and drain all but 2 tablespoons of the fat from the pan. Cook the onion in the bacon fat until translucent and lightly browned; add the garlic, ground chipotle chiles, cumin, and oregano; continue cooking for 5 minutes, until the garlic releases its fragrance.

3. Add the bacon and seasonings to the beans and continue cooking until the flavors blend and the beans are very tender, about 1 hour longer. Add salt to taste. (For a thinner broth, add more liquid as needed. For a thicker broth, purée 2 cups of the beans with a bit of their liquid and return to the pot.) Just before serving, stir the cilantro into the beans. Serve with salsa, hot flour tortillas or cornbread, and cold beer.

CUBAN BLACK BEANS and RICE
* moros y cristianos *

The Spanish name means "Moors and Christians," an old reference to the opposing complexions of the black beans and white rice. To many Cubans, they're simply "moros," the traditional accompaniment for everything from roast pork to fried fish.

2 tablespoons	olive oil
1 cup	chopped onion
½ cup	chopped green bell pepper
2	garlic cloves, minced
½ teaspoon	ground cumin
½ teaspoon	dried oregano
¼ teaspoon	ground cloves
⅛ teaspoon	cayenne pepper
1	bay leaf
3 cups	water
3 cups	cooked and drained black beans (see Note)
1½ cups	uncooked white long-grain rice
	Salt and freshly ground black pepper
	Chopped scallions for garnish
	Hot sauce

Warm the oil in a large heavy saucepan over medium heat; cook the onion, bell pepper, garlic, cumin, oregano, cloves, cayenne, and bay leaf until the onion is tender and golden brown, about 5 minutes. Add the water, beans, and rice, plus salt and pepper to taste; bring to a boil, then cover and reduce the heat to low. Do not lift the cover for 20 minutes, then check to see if all of the liquid has been absorbed and the rice is tender. If so, remove from the heat and set aside, still covered, for 5 minutes. Taste and adjust seasonings. Fluff with a fork and serve hot, garnished with chopped scallions and hot sauce.

Note: Cook the beans in water to cover by three inches, seasoned with 1 chopped onion, 1 clove of garlic, ½ teaspoon of dried thyme, a bay leaf, salt, and black pepper. They may be prepared up to 3 days in advance. Please don't use canned beans, but if you must, be sure to rinse them first.

✳ sweeten the meal ✳
fried ripe plantains

Main course or side dish, Cuban-style black beans and rice are usually edged by a sweet mound of fried ripe plantains, which are simple to prepare while the rice cooks. To serve six people, you'll need 3 black plantains. (Black skins, far beyond the yellow stage, signify ripeness.) Slit these tough and clingy skins with a sharp knife, then use it to gently pull the peel away in strips, leaving the flesh whole (like a banana). Cut the flesh on the bias into slices about ½ inch thick. Warm a few tablespoons of peanut or canola oil in a heavy skillet over medium heat and fry the slices in batches, turning to brown them well on both sides. Drain on paper towels.

For special occasions, some Cuban and Mexican families flame plantains in butter and rum, as directed in the recipe for Bananas Foster (page 333), to accompany roasted pork. Others pour beaten eggs over the fried plantains for an omelet, or braise them in sweetened coconut milk to make a simple dessert.

Unlike bananas, a close relative, plantains are seldom consumed raw. Along the Gulf Coast, as in other tropical climates around the world, they appear in many forms. The fibrous and starchy flesh may be deep-fried, pan-fried, grilled, baked, or chopped into soups or stews. Boiled and mashed, they make a nutritious main course or side dish (even a they'll-never-guess filler for meatloaf, subtracting fat and adding moisture if mixed half and half with the ground beef). No wonder these so-called cooking bananas are known in some cultures as "potatoes of the air."

✳　✳　✳　✳　✳　✳

RED BEANS and RICE

SERVES 6

*How did red beans and rice become the traditional Monday supper in Louisiana?
Some speculate that it was a thrifty use for the leftover bone from Sunday's ham.
Others say it was a no-fuss choice for laundry day, when harried mothers just added
another pot to the fire that was already stoked to boil water for washing clothes.
At any rate, it's the meal that means home to native sons, like Louis Armstrong,
who liked to sign his letters "red beans and ricely yours."
That popularity doesn't stop at the state line. Some Texans like theirs cooked with a
can or two of tomatoes, and highly spiced with cumin, ground red chiles, and oregano
(about a tablespoon of each). Mexicans make a much simpler brew, flavored only by a
chopped onion (usually sautéed in bacon fat or lard) and a large sprig of epazote,
sometimes a couple of fresh or dried chiles.
Cuban red beans are seasoned in the Creole style, like Louisiana's, but with spicy chorizo
sausage in place of the andouille, plus a small can of tomato sauce and about a teaspoon each
of cumin and oregano. About 20 minutes before the beans are done, many Cuban cooks add a
large potato (white or sweet) and a butternut squash, both peeled and diced.*

1 pound	red kidney beans
1 tablespoon	olive oil
½ pound	sliced andouille or smoked sausage or cubed ham (optional)
1	large onion, chopped
1	large green bell pepper, seeded and chopped
1	celery rib, chopped
2	garlic cloves, minced
½ teaspoon	dried thyme
1	large bay leaf
1	meaty ham bone (optional)
6 cups	boiling water, plus more if needed
	Salt, cayenne pepper, and black pepper

1. Rinse and sort the beans (sometimes you'll find tiny rocks). Place in a large saucepan or Dutch oven; cover by 2 inches with cold water. Remove any "floaters," which are too dry and will not cook properly. Soak for 4 hours. Drain in a colander.

2. Place the same pot over medium heat to dry thoroughly, then warm the oil over medium heat and sauté the sausage or ham (if using), onion, bell pepper, celery, garlic, thyme, and bay leaf until the vegetables are tender and lightly browned. Add the ham bone (if using), drained soaked beans, and 6 cups of boiling water. Bring to boil. Reduce the heat to low and simmer, covered, until the beans are tender, 2½ to 3 hours, stirring often to prevent sticking. If necessary, add extra hot water (never cold). Season to taste with salt, cayenne, and black pepper.

3. Serve over steamed rice and be sure to put out at least one bottle of hot sauce. (Many Louisiana tables are set with three or more different varieties, as everyone in the family swears by a different brand.)

Plan ahead: For creamiest results, cook the beans the day before and refrigerate overnight. Just be careful not to let the bottom scorch when reheating.

✳ ✳ ✳ cajun ketchup ✳ ✳ ✳

Restaurant and family tables in the Gulf South are usually set with at least one bottle of hot sauce, often three or more, but the diamond-shaped Tabasco logo appears in nearly every lineup. One of the most famous products on earth is produced at a quaint little country brewery, where it is packaged with labels in Japanese, Chinese, Swedish, Spanish, French, Italian, Dutch, and English for customers in more than 100 countries.

The company is still owned and operated by the family of Edmund McIlhenny, who established the brand in 1868. He cultivated the tiny *Capsicum* peppers and developed the formula where the Tabasco factory and fields now stand, on Avery Island (actually the tip of an underwater salt dome) just off the Louisiana Gulf Coast.

The ripe red peppers are picked by hand and mashed with Avery Island salt, then fermented and aged in white oak barrels for up to three years. The mash is blended with an all-natural vinegar. After about four weeks, and numerous stirrings, the pepper skins and seeds are strained out and the sauce is ready for bottling.

Meanwhile, addicts around the world can rest easy. Come hell, high water, or hurricanes, the seeds for next year's crop are stored in a bank vault.

✳   ✳   ✳   ✳   ✳   ✳

MAYAN CHILI

SERVES 6–8

Beans, pumpkin, and corn are ancient Third Coast staples that make a colorful vegetarian stew, Mayan style. Serve it with salsa and warm tortillas, Fresh Corn and Jalapeño Bread (page 253), or Sweet Potato Chips (page 26).

3 tablespoons	peanut or olive oil
1 cup	chopped yellow onion
1 tablespoon	chopped garlic
1 teaspoon	ground cumin
½ teaspoon	dried oregano, preferably Mexican
3 cups	diced uncooked pumpkin or butternut squash
3 cups	cooked and drained black beans (rinsed, if canned)
3 cups	cooked and drained pinto beans (rinsed, if canned)
1	(14½-ounce) can diced tomatoes, with juice
3 cups	chicken stock or broth, or vegetable stock
1	canned chipotle chile en adobo, finely chopped, plus 1 tablespoon of the sauce
	Kernels and juices scraped from 3 ears of fresh corn (see page 243)
	Salt and freshly ground black pepper

Warm the oil in a heavy saucepan over medium-high heat; sauté the onion, garlic, cumin, and oregano until the onion is tender and golden, about 5 minutes. Add the pumpkin and cook for 5 minutes longer. Add all remaining ingredients, with salt and pepper to taste; bring to a boil, then reduce heat to low and simmer until pumpkin is cooked, 15 to 20 minutes. Taste and adjust seasonings.

✳ ✳ ✳ the great american ✳ ✳ ✳
pumpkin

According to the International Pumpkin Association (bet you didn't know there was one), Americans bake 88 million pies straight out of the can each Thanksgiving. For most that's it—other than a strictly decorative carving on Halloween—a shame since the spectacular orange gourd is loaded with beta-carotene, vitamins A and C, potassium, iron, calcium, and other nutrients.

Seeds discovered in the high-country caves of Mexico date back to prehistoric times. The New World pumpkins were introduced to Europe by sixteenth-century explorers, then brewed into soups and beer by early colonists. Some native tribes told legends of rivers and oceans flowing from pumpkins; others claimed that they spouted precious oils, rice, gold, and silver. Africans associated them with rebirth, a good omen when plants sprang up over fresh graves.

In Mexico, pumpkin seeds (*a.k.a. pepitas*) are still a staple source of protein. Unfortunately, many commercially grown pumpkins contain seeds with thick hulls that make it difficult to free the inner core. Some groceries and natural foods stores sell roasted and hulled pumpkin seeds, which can be eaten as is or ground for thickening sauces, as for the Mayan Chicken (page 184) or Filets Mignons in Red Chile and Raisin Mole (page 216).

A sound ripe pumpkin can keep for up to seven months if it's stored in a cool dry shed or cellar at 50 to 55 degrees. Of course, cool dry sheds and cellars are out of the question on the Gulf Coast, where the best we can hope for is one month on a pantry shelf or one to four months in the refrigerator. Freshly cooked pumpkin can be refrigerated for about five days, puréed and frozen for a year.

Autumn is the best time to experiment with the real thing, when many varieties of fresh pumpkins hit the supermarkets and produce stands. The giant specimens may make the most dramatic jack-o'-lanterns, but smaller ones are less stringy, with tender flesh that's best for eating. Look for a deep orange color, a blemish-free surface, and a diameter of 12 inches or less.

✳ ✳ ✳ ✳ ✳ ✳

noodles

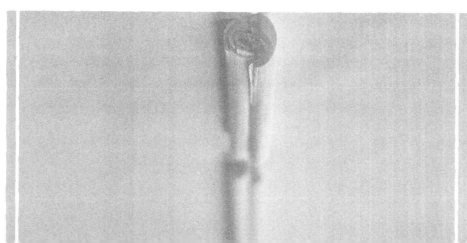

QUICK-TOSS PASTAS

Rasta Pasta * 149

Shrimp Creole Pasta * 150

Garlicky Sicilian Pasta with Shrimp * 151

Vietnamese Rice Noodles * 152

Pumpkin and Sage Pasta * 153

* ✳ *

SLOW AND EASY PASTAS

Sicilian Oven-Baked Macaroni (*Pasta al Forno*) * 155

Pasta Milanese * 156

Gulf Seafood Lasagne * 158

quick-toss pastas

Dolores Taranto Roux is the daughter of Sicilian immigrants who settled in Apalachicola, Florida, in 1904. She recalls her grandmother walking down to the dock to order crates of dry spaghetti that had to be shipped in from Italy by boat. Even after such exotica was absorbed into the typical American diet, it was limited for decades to macaroni and cheese or meatballs and red sauce.

Today pasta is almost as common as rice on Gulf Coast tables, a convenient starting point for lighter summer meals, especially during the height of shrimp season. The delicate shellfish shine in simple sautés, without rich gravies or heavy batters that can mask their briny taste. A few quick turns over medium-low heat and they'll emerge from the pan pink, but still open and relaxed, not tightly curled and tough.

RASTA PASTA

"Jamaican me hungry" is the motto at Coco Palms in Key West, where chef-owner Warren Leamard recaptures the warmth and spice of his native Montego Bay, while wife Abby creates all of the desserts. "She's in charge of everything sweet," he says, "including me."

	Shrimp stock (see page 159) or water for cooking pasta
1 pound	tricolor pasta (red, green, and gold for Jamaica)
3 tablespoons	whipped unsalted butter
1	medium onion, chopped
½	green bell pepper, chopped
2	garlic cloves, chopped
1 sprig	thyme ("must be fresh," Leamard insists)
½ cup	unsweetened coconut milk
1 tablespoon	Jamaican-style curry powder (Leamard uses Badia brand)
2 pounds	medium head-on shrimp, peeled and deveined
	Salt and freshly ground black pepper

1. Bring a large pot of stock or salted water to a rolling boil. Add the pasta and cook as directed on the package. Drain well.

2. While the pasta cooks, warm the butter in a large skillet over medium heat; cook the onion, green pepper, and garlic until the onion is soft and golden brown. Add the thyme, coconut milk, and curry powder; continue cooking until the liquid is reduced by half. Add the shrimp; cover and simmer on medium heat for about 1 minute, until the shrimp are just beginning to turn pink and curl up. ("Shrimp are supposed to be nice and plump and juicy," Leamard cautions. "Overcooking will kill them.") Season to taste with salt and pepper. Toss with the cooked pasta and serve immediately.

SHRIMP CREOLE PASTA

SERVES 4–6

Classic Creole sauces and court bouillons are infused with flavor from tomatoes and exotic spices. Though traditionally served over rice, shrimp Creole also makes a lively topping for pasta. Don't like shellfish? Use one pound of firm-fleshed fish or boneless skinless chicken breasts.

4 tablespoons	unsalted butter
1	large onion, finely chopped
1	celery rib, finely chopped
2	garlic cloves, minced
¼ teaspoon	dried thyme
¼ teaspoon	dried oregano
1	bay leaf
4 cups	peeled, seeded, and chopped ripe tomatoes, or 2 (14½-ounce) cans diced tomatoes, drained
	Grated zest of ½ lemon
½ cup	shrimp stock (see page 159) or chicken broth
	Salt, cayenne pepper, and black pepper
2 pounds	large head-on shrimp, peeled and deveined
	Shrimp stock or water for cooking pasta
1 pound	pasta
	Chopped fresh parsley and lemon slices for garnish

1. Warm the butter in a medium saucepan over medium heat and cook the onion and celery until tender and golden brown. Add the garlic, thyme, oregano, and bay leaf; continue stirring for a minute, until garlic is fragrant. Stir in the tomatoes, lemon zest, and stock or broth. Season with salt and peppers. Bring to a boil; reduce heat to low and simmer, covered, for 30 minutes, stirring occasionally.

2. Cook the pasta as directed on the package. Drain well.

3. Meanwhile, raise the heat under the sauce to medium and add the shrimp. Simmer gently until the shrimp are cooked, approximately 2 to 4 minutes, depending upon their size. Adjust the salt and peppers to taste. Serve hot or at room temperature, ladled over the cooked pasta, garnished with chopped parsley and lemon slices.

Plan ahead: Prepare the Creole sauce through step 1 and refrigerate for up to 24 hours. Just before serving, reheat it to a simmer and add the shrimp. Continue as directed in recipe.

GARLICKY SICILIAN PASTA
with shrimp

SERVES 4–6

Spaghetti with garlic and oil, a traditional Sicilian fast food, tastes even better with a little local color from Gulf shrimp. Just be sure to cook the garlic until it is golden (or it will taste raw), but not browned (or it will taste scorched). This is one dish that really benefits from the extra flavor of pasta cooked in shrimp stock.

	Shrimp stock (see page 159) or water for cooking spaghetti
1 pound	thin spaghetti
⅓ cup	olive oil
10	garlic cloves, peeled and minced
2 pounds	large head-on shrimp, peeled and deveined
1 teaspoon	salt
¼–½ teaspoon	red pepper flakes, or to taste
¼ cup	chopped flat-leaf parsley
	Lemon wedges for garnish (optional)

1. Bring a large pot of stock or salted water to a rolling boil. Add the spaghetti and cook as directed on the package. Drain well, reserving some of the cooking liquid to stretch sauce, if needed.

2. Meanwhile, warm the oil in a large skillet over medium-low heat; cook the garlic until it is softened and fragrant, about 2 minutes. Add the shrimp and continue cooking until the shrimp are just pink and the garlic is golden, but not browned (3 to 4 minutes longer). Stir in the salt and red pepper flakes. Toss with the hot spaghetti and chopped parsley. Stir in a bit of the reserved cooking liquid if you like a soupier consistency. Serve immediately, lightly sprinkled with lemon juice, if desired.

VIETNAMESE RICE NOODLES

SERVES 4

*Served at room temperature and layered with crisp vegetables, cool and spicy noodles
are a mainstay in Vietnam and a refreshing entrée for hot days on the Third Coast. Traditional
versions are made with charcoal-grilled chicken or beef, but you could substitute lean slices of
roasted pork, cooked ham, boiled shrimp, shreds of scrambled egg—whatever you have on hand.
You might also use extra-thin rice vermicelli instead of rice sticks, which are wide and
flat like fettuccine. (Just be sure to adjust cooking times according to package directions.)
The quality of imported rice noodles varies widely. Look for Number 1, Rocket,
Three Ladies, or Bun Tap Chua brands.*

½ pound	rice sticks
2 cups	shredded napa cabbage or romaine lettuce
1	small cucumber, halved, seeded, and very thinly sliced
2 cups	fresh bean sprouts
1 cup	julienned carrots
⅓ cup	chopped fresh basil leaves
⅓ cup	chopped fresh mint leaves
1 pound	peeled and deveined boiled shrimp; or slivered cooked beef, chicken, or pork
1	shallot, very thinly sliced
4 tablespoons	chopped roasted peanuts
	Fresh cilantro sprigs, basil leaves, and mint leaves for garnish
	Nuoc Cham (page 49)
	Lime wedges for garnish
	Fresh hot chiles, thinly sliced for garnish

1. Drop the rice sticks into 2 quarts of boiling water; return to the boil for 5 minutes. Drain and rinse well with cold water to prevent sticking.

2. To serve, layer cabbage or lettuce, cucumber, bean sprouts, and carrots in four large pasta or soup bowls. Top with half of the chopped basil and mint, then the drained noodles and shrimp or meat, then thin slices of shallot. Sprinkle with the rest of the chopped basil and mint. Finish each bowl with a tablespoon of chopped roasted peanuts and a sprig of cilantro. Everyone should season his own bowl to taste, so set the table with a dish of dipping sauce and a platter of extra cilantro, basil, mint leaves, lime wedges, and sliced hot chiles.

PUMPKIN and SAGE PASTA

SERVES 4–6

Though it originated in Italy, this golden sauté has a distinct Gulf Coast flavor
from the native pumpkin and crumbled queso añejo. If you can't find this hard-aged
Mexican cheese, substitute grated Sonoma dry jack or Parmesan. Look for smaller
and more flavorful pumpkins (which are cultivated for eating, not jack-o'-lanterns)
or use butternut squash.

2 tablespoons	olive oil
2 tablespoons	butter
1	small onion, halved from stem to root, then cut into thin wedges
3 cups	coarsely grated fresh pumpkin (use the shredding disk of a food processor)
2	garlic cloves, minced
¼ cup	loosely packed, finely shredded fresh sage leaves
	Salt and freshly ground pepper
1 pound	ziti or penne pasta
1 tablespoon	minced flat-leaf parsley
½ cup	crumbled queso añejo (see page 269), grated Sonoma dry jack, or Parmesan cheese

1. Warm the olive oil and butter in a large skillet over medium-high heat. Cook the onion until translucent, but not at all browned, 3 or 4 minutes. Add the shredded pumpkin and garlic; cook for a minute or so, until the garlic is fragrant, but not browned, then reduce the heat to medium-low and simmer, stirring occasionally, until the pumpkin is just tender, about 15 minutes. Add the shredded sage leaves, plus salt and pepper to taste; simmer for 1 or 2 minutes longer.

2. Meanwhile, cook the pasta in boiling salted water; drain, reserving some of the cooking liquid to stretch the sauce, if needed. Toss with the pumpkin mixture, minced parsley, and grated cheese. Adjust the salt and pepper and serve immediately.

slow and easy pastas

Fast food is no compromise on the Gulf Coast, where you can pick up a bag of spicy boiled crabs or a hot Cuban sandwich as quickly as a burger. Even so, we generally like our cooking slow and well tended. Our old favorites were born in kitchens where sauces bubble on the stove for hours and macaroni comes from the oven, rather than a microwaveable plastic bowl. Think Italian grandma food, a soothing project for an unhurried afternoon.

SICILIAN OVEN-BAKED MACARONI
* pasta al forno *

SERVES 4–6

Maria Bertucci Compagno remembers a time when all of the Usticeci (Sicilian immigrants from the town of Ustica) would dress up and gather at the New Orleans train station to greet every new arrival from their former home. She celebrated her own fifteenth birthday en route, just four days after her family landed at Ellis Island on June 22, 1950.

"We were on the ship for ten days," she said, "but it was so entertaining we hated to get off. What I really remember is when we saw the Statue of Liberty, and everyone running to one side of the deck shouting 'There it is! There it is!' Even up until today, when I think of that I can shed a tear."

Compagno contributed her mother's recipe for Pasta al Forno, which has always been a warm-weather favorite because it may be served hot or at room temperature. The hearty baked pasta is also an economical choice for large parties or potlucks. "And it is very good for a summer day," she advises. "When I was a girl in Sicily, my mother would make it for a picnic and we would all walk to the sea to go swimming, sometimes with a donkey to help carry our things."

½ pound	ground beef
1 quart	tomato-based pasta sauce, homemade or a top-quality prepared sauce
½ cup	grated Romano cheese, plus more to sprinkle top
1 tablespoon	chopped fresh basil
1 pound	ziti pasta, cooked and drained
2	hard-cooked eggs, chopped
1 cup	frozen green peas

1. Brown and drain the ground beef. Stir in about ¾ cup of the pasta sauce, the ½ cup of grated Romano cheese, and the chopped basil; mix well. Add the seasoned meat to the cooked pasta, stirring until well blended.

2. Heat the oven to 325°F. Coat the bottom of a 9-by-11-inch baking pan with a third of the remaining sauce. Top with half of the pasta mixture, then the chopped eggs and green peas. Add another coating of sauce, followed by the remaining pasta, then the rest of the sauce. Sprinkle the top with more grated Romano cheese. Bake for 20 to 25 minutes, until hot.

Plan ahead: The dish may be assembled up to a day in advance, then baked as directed.

PASTA MILANESE

SERVES 8

*Spaghetti with a slow-simmered tomato sauce, sweetened by the licorice flavor of fresh
fennel, is always the main course for the Feast of St. Joseph (see page 259). Because
the celebration falls during Lent, all of the traditional dishes are meatless.
Instead of cheese, the pasta Milanese is topped with a sprinkle of mudica
(toasted bread crumbs lightly seasoned with cinnamon and sugar) to symbolize
the sawdust of Joseph the carpenter.*

MILANESE SAUCE

¼ cup	olive oil
3	medium yellow onions, chopped
3	garlic cloves, chopped
2	(6-ounce) cans tomato paste
2	(8-ounce) cans tomato sauce
1	(18-ounce) can tomato purée
3 cups	water
2	(2-ounce) cans oil-packed anchovies, undrained
2–3 tablespoons	sugar, or to taste
2 teaspoons	fennel seeds, crushed
½ teaspoon	dried oregano
2 tablespoons	minced fresh basil leaves (or 2 teaspoons dried basil)
	Salt and freshly ground black pepper

MUDICA

2 cups	soft bread crumbs (from stale bread), finely grated
1 teaspoon	sugar
⅛ teaspoon	cinnamon
	Salt and freshly ground black pepper

PASTA

1 pound	dry spaghetti
1	bulb fennel (finocchio), trimmed and very thinly sliced
1 tablespoon	olive oil

1. Make the sauce: Warm the olive oil in a large nonreactive saucepan over low heat; cook the onions and garlic slowly, until the onions are tender, but not browned. Add the tomato paste; raise the heat to medium-low and cook, stirring constantly, until the paste loses its bright red color, about 5 minutes. Add the tomato sauce, tomato purée, water, anchovies, sugar, and crushed fennel seeds. Bring to a boil; stir well, reduce the heat to low, and cover; simmer for 1 hour, stirring often. Add the oregano, basil, salt, and pepper. Cover the pot and simmer until very thick, stirring often, 45 to 60 minutes longer.

2. For the *mudica:* Warm an iron skillet over very low heat. Add the bread crumbs and stir until golden brown. Immediately transfer to a small serving bowl. Stir the sugar together with the cinnamon; toss with the toasted bread crumbs. Season to taste with salt and pepper.

3. To finish: Add the spaghetti, fennel, and olive oil to a large pot of boiling salted water. Cook until al dente. Drain; top with Milanese sauce and *mudica.* Serve immediately.

Plan ahead: The completed sauce may be refrigerated for up to 5 days or frozen for up to 4 months. The mudica may be stored airtight at room temperature for up to 2 days. Prepare the pasta just before serving.

✳ ✳ ✳ that old goomba ✳ ✳ ✳
magic

Want to set the proper mood for a Sicilian feast, Gulf Coast style? Look for tunes by some of the great Italian-American musicians who helped blow New Orleans jazz around the globe, including Al Belletto, Sam Butera, and Sharky Bonnano. In fact, the world's first jazz recording, the original "Dixieland One-Step," was cut in 1917 by Nick LaRocca and his Dixieland Jass [sic] band. Son James LaRocca carries on the family tradition. And definitely don't forget wild man Louis Prima, whose jungle beat and crazy vocals are an instant party.

✳   ✳   ✳   ✳   ✳   ✳

GULF SEAFOOD LASAGNE

SERVES 6–8

Lasagne is an adaptable dish that can be revitalized with any ingredients you like. I like to drape the noodles with Gulf shrimp and crabmeat in a creamy béchamel, a luxurious splurge that doesn't require the usual thick layers of cheese, just a final sprinkle of Parmesan. If you have the necessary skills and equipment, sheer and eggy sheets of homemade pasta melt into the sauce for a silky texture that is well worth the extra effort. Otherwise, look for the thinnest unruffled noodles you can find.

8 ounces	dry lasagna or an equivalent amount of home-made pasta
	Shrimp stock (see page 159) or water to cook the pasta
¾ cup	unsalted butter
½ cup	finely chopped scallions
1 pound	medium head-on shrimp, peeled and cleaned
1 pound	cooked lump crabmeat
2 tablespoons	capers
4 cups	milk
½ cup	all-purpose flour
1 teaspoon	salt
Pinch	of nutmeg
	White pepper
1 cup	freshly grated Parmesan cheese

1. Heat the oven to 350° F. Cook the noodles in a large pot of boiling stock or water according to package directions (or follow your own recipe for homemade), then rinse them gently with cold water and drain on paper towels.

2. Melt 2 tablespoons of the butter in a nonstick skillet over medium heat. Add the scallions and shrimp; cook until scallions are soft and shrimp are just pink, 2 to 3 minutes; transfer to a bowl and set aside. In the same skillet, melt 2 more tablespoons of butter; cook the crabmeat and capers until just heated through, being careful not to break up the lumps of crab; transfer to another bowl and set aside.

3. Heat the milk, but do not allow it to boil. Melt the remaining ½ cup of butter in a saucepan over medium-low heat and stir in the flour, being careful not to let it brown. Gradually add the hot

milk, whisking gently to prevent lumps. Continue stirring until the sauce just comes to a boil and thickens into a smooth cream; lower the heat and stir gently for 2 or 3 minutes longer. Remove from the heat and season with 1 teaspoon of salt, plus nutmeg and white pepper to taste.

4. Spread a layer of béchamel about ¼ inch deep in the bottom of a buttered 9-by-12-inch baking dish. Lay a third of the lasagna noodles over the sauce, overlapping the strips slightly. Cover with the crab mixture and a layer of béchamel, then the second layer of noodles. Cover that with the shrimp mixture and a layer of béchamel, then the final layer of noodles. Top with béchamel, then sprinkle with the grated Parmesan. Bake for 30 minutes, or until the sauce is bubbling hot.

Plan ahead: The lasagne may be assembled and refrigerated for a few hours before baking.

∗ ∗ ∗ use your heads ∗ ∗ ∗

No getting around it—peeling shrimp is an unpleasant job, so make the most of your labor. Don't throw out those heads and shells. Simmer them into a fragrant stock, then use it to cook pasta for extra depth of flavor or to replace plain water in sauces or seafood stews. Freeze any leftovers in ice cube trays or zipper bags to season other recipes.

Just drop the shells and heads into a colander as you peel, rinse them well under cold running water, and put them in a stockpot or large saucepan with 2 or 3 quarts of water, a couple of unpeeled sliced onions, 2 halved garlic cloves, celery tops, a handful of parsley stems, and 2 or 3 bay leaves. Bring it just to a boil over high heat, then reduce the setting to low and let it simmer for 30 to 45 minutes. Strain out the solids and return the stock to a boil (if you're cooking pasta) or cool it to room temperature and freeze it for later.

∗   ∗   ∗   ∗   ∗   ∗

part 3

FISH, MEAT, and FOWL

Larger than several of the world's seas, the modestly named Gulf of Mexico stretches over 582,000 square miles and is home to a huge variety of finfish and shellfish. Coastal woods and wetlands are still rich with deer, rabbits, ducks, and quail. European colonists imported chicken, beef, and pork, then cooked up their own versions of the native turkeys, crawfish, and blue-claw crabs. All have flavored the culinary melting pot.

grilled, roasted, and stuffed

saturday cookouts

Barbecue tools see plenty of action on the Gulf Coast, where it's seldom too cold to cook outside. And we don't just go for the usual steaks and burgers. Read on to learn how you can convert your kettle grill into a clambake or use it to open oysters. But first, an authentic cowboy recipe from the Texas Gulf Coast, the birthplace of American ranching.

JOE PADILLA'S FAJITAS

Fajitas, Spanish for "belts," are simply thin strips of meat that are marinated, chargrilled, and rolled in soft flour tortillas. In Mexico they might be made with anything from pork to cabrito (that's goat to you). In Texas the meat of choice is usually beef, ideally skirt steak cut from the rib area. Ask your butcher for the more flavorful inside skirt. Otherwise, flank steak is a reasonable substitute.

This has been standard cowboy chow for generations, but recent popularity has inspired such offenses as portobello fajitas, scallop fajitas, even Thai duck fajitas. However, here is the real article from Joe Padilla, a top hand for more than forty years at the HK Ranch, which was established in 1867 in Victoria County near Placedo, Texas. Real men need only flour tortillas to complete the meal, but it's p.c. (passably cowboy) to add a hit of salsa and/or guacamole.

4 pounds	fajitas (skirt steak) or tenderized flank steak
	Juice of 8–12 limes
2	medium onions, sliced
2	garlic cloves, chopped
2	serrano chiles, minced
2 handfuls	cilantro, stems removed and leaves chopped
	Mexican beer
	Salt

1. Trim off the excess fat from the skirt steak and remove the muscle fiber. Each fajita should be ½ to ¾ inch thick in order to cook evenly. (If using flank steak, marinate and cook it whole, then slice it against the grain in narrow strips not more than ½ inch thick.) Place one layer of fajitas in the bottom of a large glass roasting pan. Squeeze lime juice over the meat. Add some of the onion slices, garlic, minced serranos, and cilantro. Add another layer of meat and continue until all of these ingredients have been used.

2. Pour enough beer over the fajitas to fill the pan halfway. Cover with plastic wrap and marinate in the refrigerator for 6 hours, basting occasionally.

3. Build a mesquite fire in your grill and let it burn until the coals are extremely hot, but not flaming. Lay the meat across the grill and cover. Turn the meat only once as it cooks. When done, remove the meat from the grill, slice it across the grain, and sprinkle with salt to taste. Serve with hot flour tortillas.

⁕ ⁕ ⁕ the birthplace ⁕ ⁕ ⁕
of american ranching

At a time when many American children were mesmerized by Western movies and TV cowboys, Carol Hoff enjoyed a life that other boys his age could only dream about. He grew up during the 1940s and '50s on his family's ranch in Goliad, just a few miles from the 1749 Mission Espíritu Santo, where Spanish missionaries established the first cattle ranch in Texas.

Say Gulf Coast and most people think seafood, but it is also a major center for beef production. The massive King Ranch, perhaps the best-known spread in America, stretches for some 825,000 acres between Corpus Christi and Brownsville. Other large operations are concentrated around Port Lavaca and Victoria, Texas. During the eighteenth and nineteenth centuries, huge cattle drives terminated at the docks of New Orleans and Tampa Bay. And ranching is still big business in central and southwest Florida.

These days we live in the age of electronic branding irons and helicopter cowboys. But Hoff remembers simpler times, when family members with herds of their own took turns working cattle, so there was always an abundance of "free" help. As a boy, he learned from his grandfathers, uncles, and cousins. They started their rounds before daylight and continued until dark, herding, calving, branding, administering vaccinations.

The noon meal was always a large affair, with many age groups represented, but the menu seldom varied. There would be a big beef roast, mashed potatoes and gravy, maybe some snapped green beans from the garden or pinto beans, thick slices of homemade bread with homemade butter, fruit cobbler for dessert, and iced tea.

"Each and every cowhand removed his hat before he came into the ranch-house," Hoff remembers, "and all of those hats would be lined up on the front porch. After a full meal, everyone took a short nap under the oak trees in the yard. Then it was back to work."

⁕ ⁕ ⁕ ⁕ ⁕ ⁕

FLORIBBEAN JERK CHICKEN

SERVES 8

*I once asked a friend from Jamaica, an excellent cook, how to make jerk chicken.
"Oh you know," he shrugged, "you make it any way you want."
There are certainly plenty of rubs and marinades on the market, but this version from
the Florida Keys is an easygoing blend of fresh tropical flavors: Gulf Coast citrus, hot chiles,
fresh ginger, allspice, cinnamon, nutmeg, and rum. Substitute 1 or 2 fiery Scotch bonnet
peppers for the jalapeños, if you dare. You could also use this jerk sauce to season steaks, ribs,
pork, or halved chickens. And while you're at it, throw some pineapple on the grill.*

½	medium onion, coarsely chopped
4	garlic cloves, coarsely chopped
3	pickled jalapeños, seeded
1 tablespoon	chopped fresh ginger
2 teaspoons	dark brown sugar
1 teaspoon	ground allspice
½ teaspoon	ground cinnamon
½ teaspoon	ground nutmeg
¼ cup	fresh lime juice
¼ cup	soy sauce
2 tablespoons	roasted peanut oil or peanut oil
2 tablespoons	dark rum
½ cup	fresh orange juice
8	boneless skinless chicken breast halves

1. Purée all of the ingredients, except for the orange juice and chicken, in a blender. Once you have obtained a smooth paste, add the orange juice and blend for a few seconds longer. Pour the jerk sauce over the chicken breast halves in a nonreactive pan or bowl; cover with plastic wrap and marinate in the refrigerator for about 3 hours, turning several times.

2. Heat a charcoal or gas grill to medium. Grill the chicken breasts until just cooked, 2 to 3 minutes per side.

THIRD COAST CLAMBAKE

SERVES 4

Dubbed "lobsters" in earlier days, probably to enhance their marketing potential, the spiny clawless crustaceans of Florida have much humbler kin. They're actually big crawfish, saltwater cousins of the Louisiana mudbug. Here they're teamed with Cedar Key clams for a little beach party that could fit into the smallest backyard.

You see, I have two categories of friends—people I like and people I like well enough to buy lobsters for—so I'm going to tell you how to downscale a clambake for a very small crowd, say around four. The traditional New England version can feed over a hundred, an all-day affair that involves digging a pit on a beach, filling it with rocks to be heated under a big fire for hours, then sweeping out the ashes with leafy branches. And that's just the beginning. I haven't even gotten to the chicken wire and tarpaulin yet.

Fortunately, the Third Coast is not known for its rocky beaches (or Protestant play ethic) and the authorities take a dim view of pits and fires. What we need here is an alternative method that doesn't require any more commitment than the average seafood boil. The directions for this kettle-grill clambake are adapted from an old issue of Cook's magazine (July/August 1989), spiced up a bit to suit Gulf South tastes. The simple setup works very well for beach or backyard. For larger groups (BYO lobster), just borrow an extra grill.

You might need to order some supplies ahead, especially the rockweed (a type of seaweed), which should be available through a good seafood market if you call several days in advance. Ditto the Florida spiny lobsters and Cedar Key clams, though it's fine to substitute Maine lobsters or New England steamer clams. Melted butter and lemons are the traditional accompaniments, but the ginger-lime butter adds a tropical flavor.

CLAMBAKE

4 pounds	Cedar Key clams or steamer clams
16 to 20	small red-skinned potatoes, about 2 pounds
16	small onions or pearl onions, about 1 pound
8	large garlic cloves
2	large sprigs fresh thyme
	Old Bay Seasoning
1 pound	andouille (cut into 4 pieces) or 4 links of chorizo or sweet Italian sausage
7 pounds	hardwood charcoal
10 pounds	fresh rockweed
4 ears	corn, silks removed and husks intact
4	Florida spiny lobsters or Maine lobsters, 1–1½ pounds each

GINGER-LIME BUTTER

1 cup	unsalted butter
3	quarter-size pieces fresh ginger, lightly crushed
½ cup	lime juice
	Salt and cayenne pepper

1. For the clambake: At least 2 hours before you're ready to begin, steam one of the clams open. If it's sandy, place all of the clams in a large bowl or bucket of salted water (⅓ cup salt to 1 gallon of water) with a handful of cornmeal to expedite the purge. Soak them for 2 hours.

2. Cover the potatoes, onions, and whole garlic cloves with water in a medium saucepan over high heat. Bring to a boil; lower the heat to a fast simmer and cook until the vegetables are barely tender, 10 to 15 minutes.

3. Meanwhile, cut six pieces of cheesecloth, each about 16 inches square. Divide the cooked potatoes, onions, and garlic cloves evenly between two of the squares; add a thyme sprig to each pile and sprinkle with Old Bay Seasoning to taste, then gather the corners of each square together to form two bags and tie the tops with string. Divide the clams between two other squares; gather those into bags and tie the tops with string. Use the final two squares to make bags for the sausages.

4. Remove both racks from a kettle-style grill and set the top rack aside. Cover the bottom rack with heavy-duty aluminum foil. Pile the charcoal into the very bottom of the grill and light the fire. When the coals burn red-hot, replace the foil-covered bottom rack and arrange half of the rockweed over the foil. Place the corn and the bags of vegetables and sausages around the outside edges. Place the bags of clams in the center, surrounded by the lobsters, tail ends out. Top it all with the rest of the rockweed. Cover the grill; open the top and bottom vents halfway. Cook until the lobsters turn bright red, the clams open, and the corn is tender, 2 to 2½ hours. (You shouldn't need to add any more charcoal.) Remove the top layer of rockweed with tongs and discard any clams that don't open.

5. For the ginger-lime butter: As soon as the clambake begins cooking, melt the butter in a small saucepan with the ginger slices. Remove from the heat and set aside until the clambake is finished. Reheat the butter with the lime juice; add salt and cayenne to taste. Remove and discard the ginger slices and serve warm.

✳ ✳ ✳ dressed to the gills ✳ ✳ ✳

Here's one of life's cruel jokes: Guy walks into a trustworthy seafood market, chooses four plump trout with clear eyes, gleaming scales, bright red gills, and no fishy odor. Back home he keeps them on crushed ice until his fire is just right, then carefully oils his grill and spaces them well apart to facilitate turning. Minutes later he shows up at the table with his prize catch, now reduced to four mangled piles of flesh and bones. (He promises to chisel the skin off the grate *mañana*.) Last time they turned out perfectly, but as any angler will tell you, fish are unpredictable creatures. What's a backyard chef to do?

natural wraps for grilled whole fish

Well, he could buy one of those long-handled metal baskets, which have also been known to stick, or resort to an unappetizing wad of aluminum foil. However, natural wrappings add eye appeal and a sense of occasion.

* Simple but attractive, fish brushed with flavored oils or seasoned rubs can be bound with a splint of long flexible twigs or woody herbs (like rosemary) that have been soaked in water, then tied with wet kitchen twine.

* Small headless fish (around 10 ounces) that are wrapped in water-soaked corn husks can be cooked right in the coals, like baked potatoes, or roasted on top of the grill. Soak the corn for a minute or two so the husks won't be too brittle, then carefully pull them back and snap the ear off the stalk, also removing the silk threads, so you're left with the leaves attached to the stalk. Gather the leaves up around the fish and tie the loose end with wet twine. (It's okay if the tail sticks out.)

* Thin slices of prosciutto make an edible wrapper that looks and tastes great, but anyone who doesn't like fish skin will also have to peel away the very expensive ham that melds to it. Wind a few slices around a small fish, leaving the head and tail free. Prosciutto is sticky enough so you can just pat it together securely (no need for string); and it should tighten and crisp as it cooks. Be sure the grill is well oiled.

* Grape leaves add a distinctive lemony flavor. Soak them in water first, if you have access to a vine. Otherwise you can buy them already cleaned and packed in jars of brine at health food stores or ethnic groceries. Like the

prosciutto, they should cling well enough without being tied, if you're careful. Again, be sure the grill is well oiled.

* Banana leaves are the biggest and easiest wrappers of all. Just plop the fish down in the center, enfold it lengthwise, and tie the whole package around the middle with wet twine. Leave the ends open to let in plenty of smoke flavor. (If you live on the Third Coast, you're probably not far from a banana tree, either in your yard or a neighbor's. Otherwise, you should be able to obtain dried leaves from an Asian grocery, or from one of the sources on page 385.) This method works especially well for firm and heavy fish, like drum or red snapper, that are dripping with marinade and need a longer cooking time. As it grills, the leaf will turn brown and crackly, adding a mild sweetness to the mix and a bit of drama to the serving platter. Just be sure to watch your fire, so it doesn't burn through the leaf.

how to grill a whole fish

If it's large (2 pounds or more), slash the thickest part of the flesh diagonally in two or three places on each side, about ¼ inch deep, so it will cook more evenly and not curl. The coals should be dusted with ash, not fiery red. The grill should be well oiled and hot before the fish is placed on it, thinnest part farthest from the heat. A cover on the grill helps the interior cook evenly and quickly before the skin burns. If the fish weighs more than 3 pounds, place the grate 6 to 8 inches from the fire; otherwise, 5 to 6 inches away will do it.

You may not want to mask the fresh taste with anything more than oil or clarified butter, salt, and pepper. You can brush on seasoned oil or marinade with a pastry brush or a small bunch of herbs, but don't ladle it on with a spoon or the overflow could cause the fire to flare up. If it does, spray the coals lightly with water, being careful not to splash ashes onto the fish. Turn the fish only once, using a wide spatula.

Test for doneness by flaking the flesh with the point of a sharp knife. Begin checking after it has cooked for about 8 minutes per 1 inch of thickness, measured at the thickest point. It will continue to cook after being removed from the heat, so take it off just before it turns completely opaque.

* * * * * *

GRILLED OYSTERS

SERVES 6

What a luxurious beginning for a cookout, and so easy! You don't even need an oyster knife. Warm lemon butter enhances the slurp factor, but you might also try Garlic-Lime Aïoli (page 29) or a simple shake of Tabasco sauce.

3 dozen	unshucked oysters
1 cup	unsalted butter
¼ cup	fresh lemon juice
¼ cup	minced fresh flat-leaf parsley
	Salt and hot sauce

1. Scrub the oysters shells with a stiff brush. Arrange them in a single layer on a grill rack about 4 inches from the hot coals and roast until the shells just begin to open, 10 to 15 minutes.

2. While the oysters are roasting, melt the butter in a small saucepan over medium-low heat; stir in the lemon juice and parsley. Season to taste with salt and hot sauce. Serve the oysters in their shells with the warm lemon butter.

✻ ✻ ✻ longnecks ✻ ✻ ✻
and lime wedges

Ancient Mayans and Aztecs fermented corn into mildly intoxicating brews, and Spanish conquistadors introduced European-style beer, but *cerveza* didn't really become popular in Mexico until refrigeration arrived in the late nineteenth century. Today breweries are a major industry, exporting such labels as Corona, Negra Modelo, Dos Equis, Tecate, and Carta Blanca. Ice down a variety of longnecks in a galvanized bucket or washtub; then balance a lime wedge atop each open bottle.

✻ ✻ ✻ ✻ ✻ ✻

SEASONED BUTTERS
for grilled seafood
EACH MAKES ABOUT 1¼ CUPS

This pair of flavorful butters will enrich grilled or broiled fish fillets, scallops, lobsters, or shrimp. The recipes are from Gulf Bay Seafood Grill in Orange Beach, Alabama.

SPICED PECAN BUTTER

1 cup	unsalted butter, softened
½ cup	finely chopped roasted pecans
1 teaspoon	finely minced garlic
1 teaspoon	cayenne pepper

FRESH HERB BUTTER

1 cup	unsalted butter, softened
1 tablespoon	chopped fresh basil leaves
1 tablespoon	chopped fresh oregano leaves
1 tablespoon	chopped fresh thyme leaves
1 tablespoon	chopped fresh parsley leaves
1 tablespoon	fresh lemon juice
1½ teaspoons	freshly ground black pepper

To make either version: Whip the butter and seasonings in a small bowl with a hand mixer until light and fluffy. Place a dollop on cooked fish or other seafood. Cover any leftover butter with plastic wrap and refrigerate or freeze.

sunday roasts

The first beef and pork on this continent arrived via the Third Coast, when Ponce de León unloaded a shipment of cattle and swine on the western shore of Florida in 1521. But attack by hostile natives forced his speedy exit to Cuba and the livestock was left to run wild in the Florida swamps. Hernando de Soto had more success a few years later, when he introduced a new herd of hogs, the predecessors of huge droves of domesticated pigs that now number more than 60 million in the United States alone.

Meanwhile, other Spanish explorers were returning to their own continent with a fine discovery: native turkeys from Mexico. In fact, cargos of New World foods gathered along the Mexican Gulf Coast had all the makings of a great Thanksgiving dinner, including sweet potatoes, corn, pumpkins, and beans that the Maya called *avacotl* (a name that would evolve into the French *haricots*).

CUBAN-STYLE PORK ROAST

SERVES 8–10

Always prepare more than you need for Sunday dinner, as thin slices of the leftover pork are an essential component of the Cuban Sandwich (page 359). The garlicky citrus marinade makes this lean roast especially moist and flavorful. A blend of regular oranges and limes can stand in for the traditional bitter orange, an extra-tart tropical fruit that is hard to find, except as an inferior bottled juice.

1½ cups	fresh juice from bitter oranges (or 1 cup fresh orange juice and ½ cup fresh lime juice)
3 tablespoons	chopped garlic
1 tablespoon	dried oregano
2 teaspoons	salt
1 teaspoon	ground cumin
1 teaspoon	freshly ground black pepper, or to taste
1	(4- to 5-pound) boneless pork loin, preferably center cut

1. Stir together the juice, garlic, oregano, salt, cumin, and black pepper. Place the pork loin in a sturdy zipper bag and pour in the marinade. Seal the bag and place it in a large bowl (in case of breaks or spills); refrigerate overnight.

2. Heat the oven to 450°F. Discard the marinade and place the pork roast in the pan. Roast for 20 minutes; lower the heat to 350°F and continue cooking until a meat thermometer placed in the thickest part of meat reads 150°F, 50 to 60 minutes. Remove the roast from the oven and allow it to sit for at least 10 minutes before carving.

* * * tough as boot leather * * *

You may yank your head backward to pull off a bite of jerky, but that's not how it got the name. Texas cowboys mangled it from *charqui*, the Spanish term for salted and sun-dried meat heavily seasoned with pepper.

* * * * * *

HERB-CRUSTED PORK TENDERLOINS
with texas red grapefruit chutney

*The big cities of the Texas Gulf Coast—Houston, Galveston, Corpus Christi,
Brownsville—have attracted residents from dozens of ethnic backgrounds, inspiring an
urban multicultural cuisine that has been branded Tex-Mix. Here's a good example:
Midwestern pork tenderloins slathered in Italian olive oil and French mustard, served on
a bed of Southern field greens, with an Indian-style chutney sparked by Rio Grande
grapefruit and Mexican serrano chiles. The recipe is adapted from TexaSweet Citrus.*

CHUTNEY

1 cup	distilled white vinegar
¾ cup	granulated sugar
½ cup	brown sugar
½ cup	fresh grapefruit juice
½ teaspoon	salt
¼ teaspoon	ground nutmeg
¼ teaspoon	ground ginger
1	medium grapefruit, sectioned and chopped
½ cup	chopped purple onion
⅓ cup	dark raisins
⅓ cup	golden raisins
⅓ cup	currants
1–2	serrano chiles, seeded and chopped

HERB-CRUSTED PORK

2	pork tenderloins
2 tablespoons	olive oil
2 tablespoons	Dijon mustard
½ cup	chopped parsley
4 tablespoons	coriander seeds
2 tablespoons	coarsely ground black pepper
½ cup	fresh orange juice
	Fresh mixed field greens
	Fresh orange and grapefruit sections

1. For the chutney: Bring the vinegar to a boil with the sugars, grapefruit juice, salt, and spices. Add the grapefruit, onion, raisins, currants, and chiles. Simmer until thickened to desired consistency.

2. For the pork: Heat the oven to 350° F. Lightly brush the tenderloins with the olive oil. Brush 1 tablespoon of the mustard on each loin, covering all sides. Mix the parsley, coriander, and pepper; spread on a cutting board and gently roll the mustard-covered tenderloins through the herb mixture.

3. Bake until the internal temperature registers 140° F on a meat thermometer (about 20 minutes per pound), basting twice with the orange juice. Remove the meat from the oven and allow to sit for 10 minutes before carving. Slice and serve on a bed of mixed greens with fresh orange and grapefruit sections and grapefruit chutney.

Plan ahead: The grapefruit chutney may be made a day or two ahead and refrigerated.

✳ ✳ ✳ the other white meat ✳ ✳ ✳

Are your family and guests bored by the same old meat and potatoes? Well, this'll really blow their hats in the creek. It's from Mama Doris Ransberger, who first served her country-fried specialty at the Texas Rattlesnake Roundup of 1959, according to *Texas on the Halfshell* by Phil Brittin and Joseph Daniel. "Get yourself a rattlesnake," her recipe begins. "Skin and clean it. Cut the snake up into three-inch lengths. Bread the meat in flour, salt, and pepper and deep fry in oil at 450 degrees until browned. Serve garnished with cholla cactus segments, small rocks, sand, and beer."

✳   ✳   ✳   ✳   ✳   ✳

BEEF TENDERLOIN
with cocoa-chile rub
SERVES 4–6

The idea of cocoa as a spice may seem strange to North American cooks who have only experienced chocolate's sweeter side, but it's a common ingredient in Mexican dry rubs and sauces. Here the earthy flavor is enhanced by the warmth of ground ancho chiles and cumin, creating an intriguing dark cloak for this unusual roast. And there's a surprise inside, too—a slender tunnel filled with garlicky herb butter that will bathe the slices as you carve.

HERB BUTTER

1 tablespoon plus 4 tablespoons	unsalted butter, softened
2	scallions, white and green parts, minced
2 teaspoons	minced garlic
¾ teaspoon	minced fresh thyme
¾ teaspoon	minced fresh oregano
¼ teaspoon	salt
	Freshly ground black pepper

ROAST

1	(2-pound) center-cut beef tenderloin roast
	Coarse salt
2 tablespoons	unsweetened cocoa
1 tablespoon	ancho powder
1 teaspoon	ground cumin
1 tablespoon	olive oil

1. For the herb butter: Melt the 1 tablespoon of butter in a small nonstick skillet over low heat and cook the scallions and garlic until the garlic is very tender but not at all browned. Stir in thyme and oregano. Cool to room temperature, then stir together with the 4 tablespoons of softened butter in a small bowl; stir in the salt and black pepper to taste. Scrape the herb butter onto parchment or plastic wrap and form it into a long thin log, about the same length as the roast; chill thoroughly, until very firm.

2. For the roast: Remove the thin strip of meat that runs along one side of the tenderloin (so the roast will have a neater appearance) and reserve it for another use. Trim the fat and silver skin from the roast, saving two of the bigger scraps for step 3.

3. Using a thin boning knife or paring knife, bore a tunnel through the middle of the roast lengthwise, twisting the knife a bit to widen the hole. (You might need to bore in from one end, and then the other, until you can poke a finger through from each side and touch your fingertips in the center.) Stuff the chilled log of herb butter into the tunnel; use meat scraps (or wads of aluminum foil) to plug the holes on each side; tie the roast securely with string. Season the outside of the roast with coarse salt.

4. Sift the cocoa powder, ancho powder, and cumin onto a work surface. Rub the roast with the olive oil, then roll it in the sifted seasonings to coat evenly. Let stand at room temperature for 30 minutes.

5. Heat the oven to 500° F. Place the tenderloin on a rack in a roasting pan and roast for 10 minutes; reduce the heat to 350° F and roast 15 minutes longer for rare, 20 minutes for medium rare. Let rest for 15 minutes before carving.

Plan ahead: Prepare the roast through step 3 and refrigerate for up to 2 days.

∗ ∗ ∗ the sincerest love ∗ ∗ ∗

"I can only compare the glorious feeling after eating a perfect chicken-fried steak," Richard West proclaimed in a *Texas Monthly* tribute, "to one remembered from years ago when I learned those were not Jane Russell's knees stuck up under her sweater."

∗   ∗   ∗   ∗   ∗   ∗

YUCATECAN TURKEY PIBIL

SERVES 12

All along the Yucatán Peninsula, fowl and pork are still steam-cooked in the ancient way, in a pib or "pit" in the ground. Often they're wrapped in banana leaves to preserve the moisture of the meat, which is marinated in a fragrant recado (seasoning paste) of bitter orange juice, achiote seeds (see page 11), cumin, cloves, and peppercorns. This recipe will help you re-create those sunny flavors in a home oven, with an added bonus: no basting. Prepared achiote paste (from a Latin grocery) simplifies the operation even further. Because the turkey steams, it will not have a crispy brown skin, but it will get a rich tawny color from the marinade, known in Mexico as recado rojo (red paste).

1	(12-pound) natural free-range turkey, giblets removed
¼ cup	unsalted butter, softened
1 cup	achiote paste (see headnote)
1 tablespoon	salt
1 teaspoon	dried oregano, preferably Mexican
¾ cup	fresh orange juice
¼ cup	fresh lime juice
2 tablespoons	unsalted butter, melted
1 tablespoon	honey
	Banana leaves, center ribs removed, or fresh corn husks
4	medium onions, sliced

1. Wash the turkey and dry it thoroughly with paper towels. Carefully lift the breast skin and spread the softened butter underneath. Mix the achiote paste, salt, oregano, orange juice, lime juice, melted butter, and honey in a bowl until well blended; spread evenly over the entire turkey, inside and out. Let stand for 30 minutes.

2. Heat the oven to 325° F. Line a deep roasting pan with banana leaves or corn husks. Place the turkey breast side up on the leaves. Place one of the sliced onions inside the turkey cavity; arrange the other three atop the turkey. Cover the turkey with banana leaves, tucking them under to completely envelop it. (If using corn husks, just overlap them across the entire surface of the turkey.) Cover the pan with aluminum foil, crimping the edges to seal it well.

3. Bake the turkey for 3 to 3½ hours, until a thermometer inserted in the thickest part of the thigh measures 180° F. Discard the leaves; transfer the turkey to a platter; let it rest for 30 minutes. Degrease the pan juices; purée in a food processor with the onions to make a sauce.

CANE CRUSHER SPARERIBS

SERVES 4–6

Steen's Pure Cane Syrup, a product of the sugar refining process, lends a dark and tangy sweetness to pork spareribs. These are baked in the oven, rather than smoked over a wood fire, but they're dripping with Old South flavor and the meat just falls from the bones. Get out the paper napkins and invite some good friends over to chew the fat.

2 racks	spareribs (5–6 pounds)
½ cup	Steen's Pure Cane Syrup (see page 301)
½ cup	prepared brown mustard
6 tablespoons	lemon juice
6 tablespoons	soy sauce
¼ cup	Worcestershire sauce
½ teaspoon	cayenne pepper

Heat the oven to 350° F. Place the ribs, meat side up, in a shallow baking pan. Whisk together the cane syrup, mustard, lemon juice, soy sauce, Worcestershire sauce, and cayenne. Brush the ribs generously with the sauce. Bake for 30 minutes, brushing frequently with the sauce. Turn the ribs and continue baking for 1 hour longer, brushing frequently with sauce.

Note: For party food, have your butcher cut each rack into three lengthwise strips (across the bones). Cut the strips into little individual ribs for out-of-hand eating, then baste and bake as directed above. Drain on absorbent paper. Serve in a chafing dish.

Plan ahead: The completed spareribs may be refrigerated for up to 3 days or frozen for up to 3 months. Reheat at 300° F until warmed through, around 40 minutes if refrigerated, 60 minutes if frozen.

nuts about . . .

Among the earliest residents of the Third Coast, the ancient Maya used nuts and pumpkin seeds to thicken stews, as did the Africans who arrived on these shores much later. French Creoles scattered butter-sautéed almonds over trout *amandine*, which inspired chefs from Texas to Florida to sizzle chicken and fish in crisp coatings of native pecans. These thoroughly modern recipes date back for centuries, but they'll require only minutes of your time.

COCOA-PEPITA FISH

SERVES 4

Like the beef tenderloin roast in the preceding section, the ancient seasoning for this fish incorporates unsweetened cocoa, along with hot chiles and toasted pumpkin seeds. The preparation is simple, yet the flavors are complex and exciting.

"I decided to use cocoa as a spice, with just enough sugar to bring out the taste," says Chef Eric Ogburn, who originally developed the recipe for a special all-chocolate menu at Vaquero's Restaurant in New Orleans. "It's subtle, not something you'd immediately recognize as chocolate. And the choice of fish is important. It needs to be flaky and mild, but with a high fat content, like grouper, redfish, sea bass, or escolar. We tried tuna, and that didn't work at all." He served the fish with mashed blue potatoes and sliced yellow tomatoes topped with Mexican queso fresca.

½ cup	cocoa powder
¼ cup	chili powder
¼ cup	sugar
2	eggs
¼ cup	water
4	(6- or 7-ounce) fish fillets (grouper, redfish, sea bass, or escolar)
	Salt
1 cup	pumpkin seeds, chopped and well toasted

1. Heat the oven to 350° F. Butter a rimmed baking dish.

2. Sift together the cocoa, chili powder, and sugar; set aside. Whisk the eggs and water to make an egg wash.

3. Season a fish fillet with salt, then dredge it in the cocoa mixture. Next, dip the fillet into the egg wash, then into the roasted pumpkin seeds. Repeat with the remaining fish. Place on a baking sheet lined with parchment. Bake for 10 to 15 minutes, until cooked through.

MAYAN CHICKEN
with pumpkin seed sauce

SERVES 4–6

Descendants of the ancient Maya still live in their ancestral homeland on the Yucatán Peninsula of Mexico, where many of the native dishes can be traced back to prehistoric times. Simple but intriguing, this modern version of a traditional Mayan stew is thickened with a toasty blend of ground native pumpkin seeds, popcorn, and cumin, as well as almonds, which were introduced by Spanish colonists. The recipe is adapted from the International Pumpkin Association.

½ cup	slivered or coarsely chopped blanched almonds
¾ cup	hulled pumpkin seeds, coarsely chopped
¼ teaspoon	cumin seeds
1 cup	popped popcorn
1	garlic clove
4	fresh green chiles (such as mild jalapeños or hotter serranos), seeded
3 cups	chicken broth
1	frying chicken, cut into 8 pieces
	Salt and freshly ground black pepper
	Peanut or olive oil to brown the chicken pieces

1. Toast the almonds in a dry skillet over low heat, shaking until golden. Add the pumpkin seeds and cumin seeds toward the end to toast them without burning. Place the nuts and seeds in a food processor or blender with the popcorn, garlic, and chiles; grind to a fine-textured paste. Heat the chicken broth to boiling and slowly stir in the paste to make a gravy; remove from heat and set aside.

2. Season the chicken with salt and pepper and brown it in the oil. Pour the sauce over the chicken; cook at a very low heat until done, 20 to 30 minutes.

PECAN-ENCRUSTED GROUPER

SERVES 6

Pecans are big business in Alabama, and they add plenty of rich crunch to this popular dish from King Neptune's Seafood Restaurant in Gulf Shores. If you can't find fresh grouper, substitute any firm-fleshed, mild-flavored fish, such as snapper, drum, sea bass, or escolar.

	Olive oil to grease baking pan, plus more for frying
6	(7-ounce) grouper fillets
	Salt and freshly ground black pepper
6 tablespoons	Dijon mustard
1 cup	roasted chopped pecans
1 cup	Italian-seasoned bread crumbs

1. Heat the oven to 350° F. Lightly oil a rimmed baking pan with olive oil.

2. Season the fish with salt and pepper. Spread one side of each fillet with 1 tablespoon of the mustard. Stir together the pecans and the bread crumbs; sprinkle over the mustard-coated side of each fillet, pressing firmly with your fingers so the crust will adhere to the fish.

3. Pour the oil to a depth of ½ inch in a large nonstick skillet; place over medium-high heat until hot, but not smoking (about 350° F). Working in two or three batches, without crowding, place the fish crust side down into the pan; fry until the pecan mixture is golden brown, 1 to 2 minutes.

4. Use a large slotted spatula to carefully turn the fish over and place it on the prepared baking pan. Bake for 10 to 12 minutes, until the fish is opaque and flaky.

*crabs: deviled, *rellenas*, and *farci**

As you can see from the name of this section, there's more than one way to stuff a crab. Whatever method you choose, it pays to clean the ugly beasts yourself because they're cheaper than ready-picked crabmeat, plus you'll have the top shells for stuffing (much more flavorful and appealing than those pointy foil things). Don't even think about using canned meat or imitation "crab sticks."

BASIC BOILED CRABS

MAKES 1 DOZEN OR MORE

Maryland crabs are steamed in Old Bay Seasoning. We "berl" ours in Zatarain's Crab Boil. East Coasters use wooden mallets, lobster picks, and the Baltimore Sun. Third Coasters use nutcrackers, table knives, and the Times-Picayune. Their blue claws come from the Chesapeake Bay. Ours come from . . . We try not to think about it.

Multiply this basic recipe for larger groups, though predicting portion amounts is a pointless exercise on the Third Coast, especially when it comes to boiled seafood. Allow at least four to six crabs per person, depending on size (of the crabs and your friends). Just remember that leftovers can always be stuffed, stewed, or forced on departing guests.

FOR EACH DOZEN CRABS

3 quarts	water
1	lemon, quartered
2	medium onions, whole and unpeeled
1	celery rib, with leaves, cut into thirds
4	garlic cloves
1 bag	commercial crab boil (Sources, page 384)
¼ cup	salt
2–3 teaspoons	cayenne pepper
1 tablespoon	whole peppercorns
1 dozen	medium or large live crabs

1. Pour the water into a large stockpot or kettle over high heat; add the lemon, onions, celery, garlic, crab boil, salt, cayenne pepper, and peppercorns; bring to a rolling boil. Cover the pot, reduce the heat to medium-low, and simmer for 20 minutes.

2. Return to a vigorous boil over high heat; add the crabs and return to a boil, then cook for 20 minutes. Remove the pot from the heat and allow the crabs to soak in the seasoned water for 5 to 15 minutes. (The longer they soak, the spicier they'll taste.)

FLORIDA DEVILED CRABS

SERVES 6

In Florida and Mississippi they're deviled; in Alabama, Louisiana, and Texas they're stuffed. Different names, same dish—the traditional fate for leftover crabs from a seafood boil, or a worthwhile treat to prepare from scratch.

6	large Basic Boiled Crabs (page 187)
3 tablespoons	unsalted butter
1 cup	finely chopped yellow onion
¼ cup	finely chopped green bell pepper
¼ cup	minced celery
2	garlic cloves, minced
¼ teaspoon	dried thyme
2 tablespoons	minced flat-leaf parsley
1 tablespoon	fresh lemon juice
1 cup plus ½ cup	soft bread crumbs (preferably French bread)
	Salt, black pepper, and cayenne pepper
1	egg, beaten
2 tablespoons	melted butter

1. Heat the oven to 375° F. Clean the crabs to yield about 2 cups of crabmeat (see opposite). Reserve and scrub top shells to hold stuffing.

2. Warm the 3 tablespoons of butter in a large skillet over medium heat; cook the onion, bell pepper, celery, garlic, and thyme until the onion is tender and golden brown. Add the parsley, lemon juice, the 1 cup of bread crumbs, and the crabmeat (being careful not to break up any lumps). Season to taste with salt, pepper, and cayenne. Stir in the egg. Stuff into the crab shells.

3. Pat the remaining ½ cup of bread crumbs over the tops of the stuffed crabs, then drizzle with the melted butter. Place in a rimmed pan and bake for 25 to 30 minutes, until the tops are well browned.

Plan ahead: Crabs may be prepared through step 2 and refrigerated for several hours or overnight.

* * * fresh crabmeat * * *
in a pinch

Whole boiled crabs (see page 187) certainly look forbidding, but those spiky shells and inhospitable claws are guarding a wealth of sweet white meat. Here's how to free it for yourself.

1. Work over a sink or several thicknesses of newspaper to catch the juices and messy innards. On the underside of each crab, you'll notice that nature has provided a convenient pull-tab. Pull it back and down to remove the top shell.

2. Turn the crab right side up; remove the feathery gills and any other spongy material with your hands or a paper towel. It's neater to clean all of the crabs to this point before proceeding, so you can clear away the biggest part of the mess and wash your hands before moving on to the finer job of extracting the meat.

3. Twist the legs and claws loose from the body, removing any meat that adheres. (We like to remove it with our mouths.)

4. Pull the papery inner shells apart with your fingers and dig out the meat, being especially careful not to break up the prized lump crabmeat around the back fins.

5. Some people crack the claws with a nutcracker, but you'll get a cleaner break if you whack them with the flat handle of a heavy table knife. Use the blade of the knife to dig out the claw meat.

* * * * * *

MEXICAN-STYLE STUFFED CRABS
· jaibas rellenas ·

SERVES 6

A favorite in the coastal states of Veracruz and Tampico, Jaibas Rellenas share more than a name with the "stuffed crabs" north of the border. The cooking technique is the same, only the seasonings differ.

6	large Basic Boiled Crabs (page 187)
3 tablespoons	olive oil, plus more for drizzling tops
1	small onion, very finely chopped
2	garlic cloves, minced
1	pickled jalapeño pepper (see page 86), seeded and minced
½ teaspoon	dried oregano, preferably Mexican, crumbled
2	fresh plum tomatoes, seeded and finely diced
1 tablespoon	minced fresh cilantro
1 tablespoon	fresh lime juice
	Salt and pepper
About ½ cup	soft bread crumbs

1. Heat the oven to 375° F. Clean the crabs to yield about 2 cups of crabmeat (see page 189). Reserve and scrub the top shells to hold the stuffing.

2. Warm the 3 tablespoons of olive oil in a large skillet over medium-high heat; cook the onion, garlic, jalapeño, and oregano until the onion is tender and golden, but not browned. Add the diced tomatoes; stir until the tomatoes are barely soft, about 30 seconds. Add the cilantro, lime juice, and crabmeat (being careful not to break up any lumps). Season with salt and pepper. Stuff into the crab shells.

3. Top each stuffed crab with bread crumbs, then drizzle lightly with olive oil. Place in a rimmed pan and bake for 25 to 30 minutes, until the bread crumbs are well browned.

Plan ahead: Crabs may be stuffed and refrigerated for several hours or overnight, then baked just before serving.

VIETNAMESE-STYLE STUFFED CRABS
cua farci
SERVES 6

The Gulf Coast has strong culinary ties that stretch all the way around the globe to
Vietnam. A shared history of French occupation and coastal living has flavored the pots in
all of our kitchens, creating many dishes in common, including spicy stuffed crabs. That
cross-cultural influence is especially evident in the Asian name: cua (Vietnamese for
"crab") farci (French for "stuffed").

6	large Basic Boiled Crabs (page 187)
¼ pound	ground pork
3	shallots, minced
2	garlic cloves, minced
¼ cup	tree ears, soaked for 20 minutes, then drained and chopped (see Note)
1 tablespoon	fresh lime juice
1 tablespoon	fish sauce (see Note)
1 tablespoon	minced fresh basil
2 teaspoons	minced fresh cilantro
Pinch	of cayenne pepper, or to taste
1	egg, beaten
3 tablespoons	peanut or vegetable oil

1. Clean the crabs to yield about 2 cups of crabmeat (see page 189). Reserve and scrub the top shells to hold the stuffing.

2. Combine the pork, shallots, garlic, tree ears, lime juice, fish sauce, basil, cilantro, cayenne, and egg. Gently stir in the crabmeat with a fork, being careful not to break up any lumps of crab. Stuff into the crab shells.

3. Warm the oil in a large skillet over medium-high heat. Place the stuffed crabs in the oil, filling side down. Fry until browned, which should take about 5 minutes. (If the filling is browning too quickly, reduce heat to medium.) Turn the crabs over and fry 6 to 7 minutes longer, until the shells are browned and the filling is fully cooked.

Note: The dried mushrooms
called "tree ears" by the
Chinese may be labeled "cat
ears" at Vietnamese markets.
Fish sauce, which is similar to
a thin soy sauce, is a salty
condiment that may be labeled
as "nuoc mam." Both are
available at Asian groceries.

Plan ahead: The crabs may be
prepared through step 2 and
refrigerated for several hours or
overnight, then fried just
before serving.

stewed and soulful

SAUCY BIRDS

Cuban-Style Chicken Creole (*Pollo Criollo*) • 195

Tex-Mex Squash with Chicken (*Calabaza con Pollo*) • 196

Campeche-Style Turkey in Dark Spice Sauce (*Chilmole*) • 197

Campeche-Style Dark Spice Paste (*Recado Negro*) • 199

* ✳ *

SLOW-COOKED AND MEATY

Greek Beef Stew (*Stifado*) • 201

Creole Beef Daube • 202

Cuban Stuffed Eye-of-Round Pot Roast (*Boliche Relleno*) • 204

* ✳ *

AROMATIC SMOTHERED FISH

Shrimp and Feta Casseroles • 207

Aunt Rosalie's Baked Fish • 208

Cajun Shrimp Stew • 210

saucy birds

Down on the Gulf we like our chicken southern fried, but we *love* it smothered in garlicky tomato sauces or simmered into dark and toothsome stews. The same goes for turkey. Roasted is all very well and good, but that's really just a formality, the prelude for greater gumbos to come. Hard to believe? Maybe you've never witnessed the spectacle of aunts tussling over the carcass from a Thanksgiving dinner.

These slow-pot standards are at the very heart of Third Coast kitchens. For richest flavor, always use homemade stock and natural free-range fowl. And don't let anyone else beat you to those turkey bones.

CUBAN-STYLE CHICKEN CREOLE
* pollo criollo *
SERVES 6

Leave out the olives, replace the olive oil with bacon drippings or rendered chicken fat, and you've got chicken Creole, Louisiana style. Both versions have strong Spanish roots, enhanced by a spicier African influence.

1	(3- to 4-pound) fryer, cut into 8 pieces
	Salt and freshly ground black pepper
⅓ cup	olive oil
2	medium yellow onions, halved lengthwise and sliced into thin wedges
2	green bell peppers, halved lengthwise, seeded, and thinly sliced
2	celery ribs, thinly sliced
½ teaspoon	dried thyme
½ teaspoon	oregano
¼ teaspoon	cayenne pepper, or to taste
2	bay leaves
4	garlic cloves
2	(14½-ounce) cans diced tomatoes, with juice
2 cups	chicken stock
1 cup	pimiento-stuffed green olives
¼ cup	minced flat-leaf parsley

1. Wash and dry the chicken. Season highly with salt and black pepper. Warm the oil in a deep skillet or Dutch oven over medium heat. Working in batches, without crowding, brown the chicken on all sides and remove to a platter.

2. Add the onions, bell peppers, celery, thyme, oregano, cayenne, and bay leaves to the hot oil in the pan; toss until the onions are browned at the edges and beginning to soften, 2 to 3 minutes. Stir in the garlic, tomatoes, and chicken stock. Bring just to a boil, cover the pan, and reduce the heat to low; simmer for 20 minutes.

3. Return the browned chicken pieces to the pan along with the olives. Stir to cover the chicken with sauce; simmer for 25 to 30 minutes, or until the chicken is cooked. Adjust the salt and pepper, if needed. Just before serving, stir in the parsley. Serve over hot steamed rice.

TEX-MEX SQUASH WITH CHICKEN
* calabaza con pollo *

Talk about comfort food! Chicken smothered in tomatoes, summer squash, and fresh corn is a sunny garden stew that is standard fare in Mexico and Texas. Serve it in wide bowls with hot cornbread or flour tortillas.

1	(3- to 4-pound) fryer, cut into 8 pieces
	Salt, freshly ground black pepper, and ground cumin
¼ cup	olive oil
1	medium yellow onion, halved and cut into medium-thick wedges
1	green bell pepper, halved lengthwise, seeded, and sliced
2	large garlic cloves, chopped
3 cups	peeled, seeded, and chopped ripe tomatoes
½ cup	chicken broth or beer
4–5	small zucchini, sliced into thick rounds
	Fresh kernels cut from 4 ears corn, plus creamy juices scraped from cobs (see page 243)

1. Wash and dry the chicken. Season highly with salt, black pepper, and ground cumin. Warm the oil in a deep skillet or Dutch oven over medium heat. Working in batches, without crowding, brown the chicken on all sides and remove to a platter. Add the onion and bell pepper; toss until browned at the edges and beginning to soften.

2. Return the chicken pieces to the pan, along with the garlic, tomatoes, and chicken broth or beer. Bring just to a boil, then cover the pan, reduce the heat to low, and simmer for 10 minutes. Stir in the zucchini, cover the pan, and continue cooking for about 15 minutes, or until the chicken is cooked and the zucchini is tender. Stir in the corn and cook until the kernels are crisp-tender, 5 minutes longer. Adjust the salt and pepper, if necessary. Serve immediately.

CAMPECHE-STYLE TURKEY
in dark spice sauce
∗ *chilmole* ∗

SERVES 6

*An offbeat and deeply flavorful brew for leftover turkey, Chilmole originated
in the Mexican coastal state of Campeche. Today it is served all over the Yucatán
Peninsula, especially around Christmas and the New Year.*
Various seasoning pastes, known as recados, *are an essential ingredient in
Yucatecan kitchens. This simple stew is transformed by a few tablespoons of Recado
Negro, a dark paste of ground chiles, garlic, citrus juice, and spices. I was
given both recipes by Karen Hursh Graber, a food writer and native New Yorker
who now lives and teaches in southern Mexico.*

2 ounces	(heaping ¼ cup) Campeche-Style Dark Spice Paste (page 199)
8 cups	turkey or chicken broth
6 cups	skinned and boned cooked turkey
	Salt
2	hard-cooked eggs, sliced

Mix the paste with a bit of broth to dissolve it, then add it to the broth and cook until the mixture is reduced to about 6 cups. (The consistency should be similar to a thin gravy.) Heat the turkey in the sauce, simmering for about 15 minutes. Taste and adjust salt, if needed. Serve in bowls, garnished with hard-boiled egg slices. Accompany with plenty of hot tortillas.

✳ ✳ ✳ global turkey trot ✳ ✳ ✳

Before Spanish explorers imported the first turkeys from the New World, Europeans celebrated special occasions with roasted peacocks, tough, stringy birds that lost most of their appeal when plucked. So you can just imagine the success of those big, fat gobblers, which had been at the center of Third Coast feasts since prehistoric times. Soon all expeditions were under orders to bring back at least five mating pairs of turkeys on every return trip.

By the late sixteenth century, that prized cargo from the Mexican coast and Yucatán peninsula had been domesticated in Italy, France, and Britain. Contrary to popular myth, the Pilgrims were already quite familiar with the main course when they celebrated the first Thanksgiving. (In fact, among the myriad historical debates about this beleaguered national holiday is the claim that the real first Thanksgiving was actually celebrated by earlier colonists at Jamestown, who probably dined on turkey as they had back in England, in observance of the traditional harvest festival.)

At any rate, for a bird that can't fly much, this Gulf Coast native has traveled far, from New World to Old World—even out of this world. When astronauts Neil Armstrong and Buzz Aldrin sat down for man's first meal on the moon, the foil packets were filled with roast turkey and all the trimmings.

Perhaps Benjamin Franklin was right when he proposed it as our national symbol. After his nominee was defeated, he wrote a letter to his daughter condemning the "bad moral character" of the bald eagle, insisting, "The turkey is a much more respectable bird, and withal a true original native of America."

✳   ✳   ✳   ✳   ✳   ✳

CAMPECHE-STYLE DARK SPICE
paste
* recado negro *
MAKES 1½ CUPS

This recipe, contributed by Karen Hursh Graber, yields considerably more than you'll need for one batch of the preceding Chilmole, but you could freeze the excess in ice cube trays to add a quick shot of complex and earthy flavor to other soups, stews, and sauces. Better yet, since everybody seems to have a surplus of turkey around Thanksgiving and Christmas, scoop some of this exotic seasoning paste into little jars to present to friends, instead of the usual cookies or fruitcake. It's a novel way to say "happy holidays" (or "I think you've had enough fudge"). One caution: This stuff stains! It will discolor rubber scrapers, plastic containers, dish towels, and your clothes. Proceed with care. The achiote seeds and ancho chiles are available in Latin markets, where you can sometimes find fresh bitter oranges.

2 tablespoons	achiote seeds
¾ cup	fresh bitter orange juice (or ½ cup orange juice and ¼ cup lime juice)
2 pounds	dried ancho chiles
2	large whole cloves
4	large whole allspice
1 tablespoon	black peppercorns
1 tablespoon	dried oregano, preferably Mexican
½ teaspoon	cumin seeds
1 head	garlic, peeled (about 10 large cloves)
	Salt to taste

Place the achiote seeds in a small bowl; pour the juice over them and allow to soak for 2 to 3 hours. Wipe the chiles with a dry cloth to remove any dust; use your fingers to pull away and discard the stems and seeds. Working in batches, toast the chiles in a dry skillet over medium-high heat until fragrant, then soak them in hot water to soften; drain well. Working in batches, process all ingredients to make a thick paste the consistency of a chilled cookie dough.

Plan ahead: Freeze the recado for up to 6 months in a single container or in ice cube trays. (Pop the cubes into a zipper bag for airtight storage.)

slow-cooked and meaty

Early Gulf Coast settlers survived hard times by living off the land and rendering poor cuts of meat into the rich and savory dishes that have since become regional trademarks. These old favorites were born of necessity, long before the word *cholesterol* was even a gleam in some Yankee scientist's eye.

To accommodate modern tastes, I've replaced the traditional bacon drippings or lard with olive oil. And all of these stews taste even better after mellowing for a day or two in the refrigerator, which will give you the opportunity to remove more of the saturated fat before you reheat them. On the other hand, those bacon drippings sure did enhance the flavor of an authentic Beef Daube.

GREEK BEEF STEW
✳ *stifado* ✳
SERVES 6

Cinnamon, cumin, and cloves spice up the Mediterranean stew known as a stifado.
It remains a popular family dish in Greek communities along the Florida Gulf Coast,
where early immigrants adapted many of their traditional lamb dishes to make way
for American beef. This thick and savory version, chunky with meat and onions,
makes a distinctive pasta sauce.

3 pounds	lean beef shoulder, cut into 2-inch cubes
	Salt and freshly ground black pepper
⅓ cup	olive oil
2	medium yellow onions, halved lengthwise and cut into thick wedges
1 tablespoon	minced garlic
2	(6-ounce) cans tomato paste
1½ cups	beef stock or broth
½ cup	dry red wine
2 tablespoons	fresh lemon juice
1 strip	lemon zest, about ½ inch wide by 2 inches long
2	large bay leaves
1	(3-inch) cinnamon stick
¾ teaspoon	ground cumin
¼ teaspoon	ground cloves
1 teaspoon	sugar

1. Season the beef with salt and pepper. Warm the oil in a heavy Dutch oven over medium heat; working in batches, brown the beef on all sides; remove with a slotted spatula and set aside.

2. Add the onions to the hot oil; stir until lightly browned, 2 to 3 minutes. Add the garlic, stirring just until it releases its fragrance, about 1 minute. Add the tomato paste and stir until it loses its bright red color. Add the stock or broth, wine, lemon juice, lemon zest, bay leaves, cinnamon stick, cumin, cloves, and sugar; stir until smooth. Return the beef to the pot. Bring the stew to a boil; reduce heat to low; and simmer until meat is tender and flavors are well blended, about 1 hour. Discard the lemon zest, bay leaves, and cinnamon stick. Adjust salt and pepper. Serve over orzo or another short pasta.

Plan ahead: Prepare up to 3 days in advance and refrigerate.

CREOLE BEEF DAUBE

A Provençal ragout, daube de boeuf is known in Louisiana as beef daube (rhymes with robe). In France it would be stewed for hours in a tall crock called a daubière, but you may use any heavy, nonreactive pot. (The acids in the wine and tomatoes do not take kindly to aluminum or cast iron.) The bell pepper is a Gulf Coast addition, while the olives are traditional in France, but not here. I've included them as an optional ingredient because they add even more taste and texture to the richly seasoned stew.

This recipe makes what my Uncle Arthur called a "long gravy," a thin and soupy sauce that is intensely flavorful. If you prefer yours thicker, just reduce it as directed in step 4. Either way, serve the daube in shallow soup bowls, over hot macaroni or steamed rice, with plenty of crusty bread for dunking.

1	(4-pound) beef shoulder or chuck roast
3 tablespoons plus 2 tablespoons	chopped garlic
1 tablespoon	salt, plus more for seasoning
1 tablespoon	freshly ground black pepper, plus more for seasoning
1 teaspoon plus ½ teaspoon	dried thyme
⅓ cup	olive oil
3	carrots, coarsely chopped
2	large yellow onions, halved lengthwise and cut into thick wedges
2	celery ribs, coarsely chopped
2	green bell peppers, seeded and coarsely chopped
1	(14½-ounce) can diced tomatoes, with juice
½ cup	dry red wine
2 cups	unsalted beef stock or broth
2	large bay leaves
1 tablespoon	fresh rosemary leaves (or 2 teaspoons dried), crushed
4	carrots, thinly sliced
½ cup	pitted and sliced Niçoise olives (optional)
¼ cup	minced flat-leaf parsley

1. Cut 1-inch-deep slits all over the roast with the tip of a sharp knife. Using a fork, mash the 3 tablespoons of garlic into a paste with 1 tablespoon of salt, 1 tablespoon pepper, and 1 teaspoon thyme. Stuff this paste into the slits. Season the outside of the roast with salt and pepper.

2. Warm the oil in a Dutch oven or extra-deep skillet over medium heat. Brown the roast well on all sides; remove it to a platter.

3. Add the coarsely chopped carrots, onions, celery, and bell pepper to the hot oil; stir until the vegetables are lightly browned, 2 to 3 minutes. Add the remaining 2 tablespoons of garlic and stir for a minute longer, just until the garlic releases its fragrance. Return the roast to the pot, settling it onto the bottom so it is covered and surrounded by the sautéed vegetables. Add the tomatoes with their juice, the wine, stock, bay leaves, rosemary, and the remaining ½ teaspoon of thyme. Bring to a boil, then reduce the heat, cover the pot, and cook at a very slow simmer for 3 hours, until the beef is fork-tender.

4. Remove the beef to a platter. Strain the stock and discard the solids. Return the stock and the beef to the pot. (If the sauce is too thin for your taste, reduce it before you return the beef to the pot.) Cool to room temperature; refrigerate, covered, for at least 1 day.

5. To serve, scrape off and discard any fat accumulated on the surface. Place the pot over medium heat; add the sliced carrots and olives (if using); bring to a full boil; then reduce the heat and simmer until the carrots are tender, about 10 minutes. Taste and adjust the salt and pepper, if needed. Stir in the parsley. Serve over hot cooked macaroni or rice.

Plan ahead: Prepare through step 4 and refrigerate for up to 3 days.

CUBAN STUFFED
eye-of-round pot roast
boliche relleno

SERVES 8

*Circular slices from the eye-of-round roast inspired the Cuban name boliche, or "ball."
It is a favorite cut of beef, sometimes baked, more often stuffed and braised for the
ubiquitous boliche relleno. The most common stuffings are chopped ham and/or spicy
chorizo, an uncooked pork sausage highly seasoned with ground red chiles and other
spices. Some cooks use whole links; others remove the sausage from its casing to help
flavor and moisturize the beef, as in this traditional recipe. Don't be alarmed by the
large amount of garlic, which is tamed and sweetened by the slow cooking, then puréed
to thicken the sauce. And be especially careful to keep your pot at a very low simmer,
as anything faster will surely dry out the extra-lean roast.*

1	(3-pound) center-cut eye-of-round roast
	Salt, freshly ground black pepper, and sweet paprika
2	uncooked chorizo sausages, casings removed and discarded
¼ pound	smoked ham, finely diced
10–12	pimiento-stuffed green olives, left whole
¼ cup	olive oil
2	large onions, halved lengthwise, then cut into medium-thick wedges
1	large red or yellow bell pepper, seeded and cut into strips
10	garlic cloves, coarsely chopped
1	(14½-ounce) can whole tomatoes, drained
2 cups	beef stock or broth
½ cup	red wine
3	large bay leaves
1 teaspoon	dried oregano

1. Trim the beef of any silver skin or excess fat. (Reserve a couple of the larger scraps to use in step 2.) Using a long sharp knife, bore a tunnel through the center of the roast, twisting the knife to make a hole about 2 inches in diameter. (Tunnel in about halfway from one end, then

from the other, until you can poke a finger through from each side to touch in the middle.) Or just ask your butcher to do it.

2. Season the roast highly, inside and out, with salt, pepper, and paprika. Use your hands to blend the chorizo, ham, and olives; force the mixture through the center of the roast. Plug each end with a scrap of the beef, then tie the roast with butcher's twine.

3. Warm the oil in a heavy Dutch oven over medium-high heat; brown the roast on all sides; remove and set aside.

4. Add the onions and bell peppers to the pot, tossing until lightly browned; stir in the garlic, tomatoes, stock or broth, wine, bay leaves, and oregano; bring to a boil. Settle the browned roast into the bottom of the pot; return the sauce just to boiling, then immediately reduce heat to a low simmer and cover the pot. Cook, turning the roast every 20 minutes or so, for 2 hours (being careful to keep the sauce at a very low simmer, never bubbling).

5. Remove the roast to a carving board. Discard the bay leaves. Strain the sauce, reserving the liquid. Purée the solids in a food processor or blender and return to the pot with the reserved liquid; if necessary, reduce sauce over medium-high heat to desired thickness.

Plan ahead: Prepare through step 4 and refrigerate for up to 3 days. Reheat before proceeding with step 5.

✻ ✻ ✱ street of dreams ✱ ✻ ✻

Spicy *boliche relleno*, stuffed eye-of-round roast, is the signature dish of Tampa's Cuban community. Aficionados head for the cafés and restaurants that line Columbus Drive, which runs through a major Latin neighborhood. It is affectionately known as Boliche Boulevard.

✳ ✳ ✳ ✳ ✳ ✳

aromatic smothered fish

It's a shame that so many Gulf Coast restaurants have abandoned their roots to sling out the usual beach fare: plain fish or shellfish, fried or broiled. By roots I mean onions, garlic, shallots, scallions, and fennel. Those little plastic cups of ketchup are no substitute for fresh tomatoes. Dill pickle chips are a poor replacement for olives or chiles. And a decorative sprig of parsley just doesn't have the power of basil, thyme, or oregano.

From classic baked redfish to rustic shrimp stew, these traditional recipes smother our great regional seafood with flavor, instead of tartar sauce or greasy batters. They represent home cooking at its best, simple and nutritious suppers with fragrances that will warm any kitchen.

SHRIMP and FETA CASSEROLES

SERVES 4

In Florida's Greek community of Tarpon Springs, I enjoyed a similar dish
served over pasta. I like it even better broiled in individual casseroles, with plenty
of crusty bread to sop up the ouzo-scented sauce and browned feta cheese. No ouzo?
You'll get a comparable sweet anise flavor from Pernod or Herbsaint. It's okay
to use canned tomatoes or dried oregano in a pinch, but fresh basil
is essential (and fresh shrimp go without saying).

¼ cup	extra-virgin olive oil
1	medium yellow onion, halved lengthwise and cut into thin half-moons
1 teaspoon	minced garlic
¼ teaspoon	red pepper flakes, or to taste
3 cups	ripe tomatoes, peeled, seeded, and chopped; or 2 (14-ounce) cans diced tomatoes, drained
¼ cup	pitted and coarsely chopped Kalamata olives
1 tablespoon	capers
2 teaspoons	minced fresh oregano, or ½ teaspoon dried oregano
2 tablespoons	ouzo, Pernod, or Herbsaint
⅓ cup	loosely packed chopped fresh basil leaves
2 pounds	large fresh shrimp, peeled and deveined
8 ounces	feta cheese, coarsely crumbled
	Minced flat-leaf parsley for garnish

1. Warm the olive oil over medium-low heat in a deep skillet; cook the onion, garlic, and red pepper flakes until the onion is translucent and pale golden, but not at all browned, 15 to 20 minutes. (The slow cooking will concentrate the sweetness of the onion and preserve its moisture.) Stir in the tomatoes, olives, capers, and oregano; raise the heat just until the mixture reaches a boil; cover the pan, reduce the heat to medium low, and simmer for 20 minutes to allow the flavors to blend.

2. Add the ouzo, basil leaves, and shrimp, then immediately spoon the mixture into four shallow individual casseroles. Top each casserole with crumbled feta and place them under the broiler until the shrimp are just pink and the cheese is browned, about 7 minutes. Sprinkle with minced parsley and serve immediately, with plenty of hot crusty bread for dipping.

AUNT ROSALIE'S BAKED FISH

SERVES 6

The first time I tasted the famous snapper Veracruz, named for its birthplace on the Gulf Coast of Mexico, I recognized the flavors immediately. It was my Aunt Rosalie's baked fish, a New Orleans Creole standard, with a slight Mexican accent from the addition of green olives, cinnamon sticks, and fresh chiles. Over the years, I have encountered the same basic dish under many different names: a Greek-style snapper with savoro sauce in Tarpon Springs, redfish Siciliano at a St. Joseph's Day feast, and a Bahamian "smudder grouper" in Key West.

Still, I'm partial to this version, which we always hoped for as we caught the ferry across the Mississippi River to my favorite aunt's big old house on Algiers Point. Her sauce is simple and delicately spiced. (Aunt Rosalie didn't approve of garlic with fish.) It's a fine complement to any firm-fleshed variety, such as redfish, drum, red snapper, or grouper. She always cooked a big one, at least 6 pounds. If you choose a smaller fish, around 3 pounds, just halve the sauce ingredients and bake it for 25 to 35 minutes. The same goes for fillets, 1 to 3 pounds, which should be seasoned with salt and pepper, then arranged in a single layer and covered with a half-recipe of the sauce. Bake the fillets for 10 to 15 minutes.

1	(6-pound) whole fish (see headnote for suggestions), head on, gills removed, scaled, and gutted
	Salt and black pepper
2	large onions, halved from stem to root and sliced into thin half-moons
2	lemons, very thinly sliced and seeded, ends discarded
4	bay leaves
½ cup plus 2 tablespoons	unsalted butter
3	celery ribs, thinly sliced on the diagonal
8 cups	peeled, seeded, and chopped fresh tomatoes (about 5 pounds) or 5 (14½-ounce) cans chopped tomatoes, drained
Pinch	of sugar (optional)
2	tablespoons chopped flat-leaf parsley for garnish

1. Wash and dry the fish; season it inside and out with salt and pepper. Place it in a large nonreactive roasting pan or casserole. (If you're squeamish, or your pan's too small, remove the head

and tail, but leave them on, if you can, for greater drama. You can always place an olive slice over the eyeball to hide the accusing stare.) Stuff the cavity with a single layer of onion slices, then a single layer of lemon slices, reserving the rest for the sauce. Place two of the bay leaves inside the cavity. Cover the pan airtight with plastic wrap and refrigerate for at least 1 hour.

2. Meanwhile, melt the ½ cup of butter in a large saucepan over medium-low heat. Cook the remaining onion slices with the celery and the two remaining bay leaves until the onions are translucent and lightly golden, but not at all browned, around 20 minutes. (The slow cooking over low heat will concentrate the sweetness of the onions.) Stir in the tomatoes and continue cooking until the tomatoes are softened, but still juicy, 5 to 10 minutes longer. Season well with salt and pepper. Stir in a pinch of sugar, if desired. Cool slightly.

3. Heat the oven to 375°F. Remove and discard the plastic wrap from the pan and spoon the tomato sauce over the fish. Arrange a single layer of lemon slices atop the fish. Dot the remaining 2 tablespoons of butter over the entire dish.

4. Cover the pan tightly with foil; bake until the flesh of the fish is just opaque, 50 to 65 minutes, depending upon the thickness of the fish. Carefully transfer the fish to a warm serving platter, spoon the sauce over it, and sprinkle on the parsley. Serve it with hot steamed rice and crusty bread.

Plan ahead: If you make the sauce well in advance and chill it before spooning it over the fish, you may prepare the dish through step 3 and refrigerate it for several hours. Add a few minutes to the baking time.

* * *and how was your* * *
thanksgiving?

Along the Florida Panhandle, a large red snapper (twenty pounds or more) stuffed with oyster dressing is known as a Panama City turkey.

* * * * * *

CAJUN SHRIMP STEW

SERVES 4–6

*Georgine Reulet Fonseca of Des Allemands, Louisiana, was born third in a big
Cajun family of nine children, but she didn't know her way around a stove until
she was married. "We had a grandma that lived right next door to us," she said.
"It was like having two mothers, but they always chased us out of the kitchen.
They didn't want us around when they were cooking. I mostly learned from my
mother-in-law and from an older sister."*

*The first thing they taught her was this shrimp stew, which can be made with
or without the potatoes, she said, depending on "how far you want to stretch it." It's a
homey preparation, closer to real-life Cajun fare than many elaborate and overspiced
restaurant concoctions. "I like to cook simple dishes with food I have in the house,"
Fonseca said. "I don't like having to run to the store for any special ingredients."
She'd rather spend her time on the water with husband, Joey, a commercial fisherman,
hauling in everything from shrimp to wild catfish. "A friend at work says 'You like to do all
that outdoors stuff,'" Fonseca said. "'You remind me of a pioneer woman.'"*

¼ cup	vegetable oil
¼ cup	all-purpose flour
1	medium onion, chopped
½	green bell pepper, seeded and chopped
1 pound	peeled and deveined shrimp
	Salt and black pepper
	Tony Chachere's Cajun Seasoning (see Note)
1½ cups	shrimp stock (see page 159) or water, plus more if needed
2–3	medium russet potatoes, peeled and quartered (optional)
	Louisiana Hot Sauce or Tabasco sauce

1. Warm the oil in a deep skillet (preferably cast iron) over medium-high heat; add the flour and stir until the roux is medium brown (darker than peanut butter). The roux can take several minutes to reach this point, but once it becomes uniformly brown, it will darken quickly. Add the onion and bell pepper, reduce heat to medium, and stir until the vegetables are smothered in roux and wilted. Add the shrimp, reduce the heat to low, and smother for about 3 minutes longer. Season to taste with salt, pepper, and Tony Chachere's Cajun Seasoning.

2. Add 1½ cups stock or water and the potatoes (if using). Bring to a boil, then turn the heat to low and simmer for about 20 minutes, or until the potatoes are tender. (Add more stock or water, if needed, for the gravy to maintain the desired consistency.) Serve over rice with Louisiana Hot Sauce or Tabasco.

Note: A round box of "Tony Chachere's" (Sources, page 384) sits near many Louisiana stoves. The ubiquitous seasoning mix contains salt, paprika, cayenne pepper, garlic powder, and other spices. As a substitute, you could sauté 1 or 2 cloves of minced garlic with the onions and add a pinch of cayenne.

* * * net income * * *

The work shrimpers do depends on the size of the vessel. The larger boats (80 to 120 feet) stay out in the Gulf for three weeks or more, storing their catch in special onboard freezers. The medium-size bay boats can go about a week at a time, dragging very near the shore or up in the bays, bringing in iced shrimp. The one- or two-person Lafitte skiffs that pull trawls or push skimmers are known as day trippers. They ply the smaller bays and bayous for a few hours at a time.

* * * * * *

from skillet
to table

SAUTÉS AND STIR-FRYS

Flash-Fried Wild Duck with Wild Mushroom
and Peppercorn Cream · 215

Filets Mignons in Red Chile and Raisin Mole · 216

Cha-Cha's Citrus Chicken · 218

Florida Spiny Lobster with Cuban Garlic Sauce
(*Mojo de Ajo*) · 219

Crawfish Stir-Fry, Indian Style (Crawfish B*huna*) · 220

* ✳ *

SOFTSHELL CRABS

Deep-Fried Softshell Crabs · 223

Pan-Fried Softshell Crabs · 224

Stuffed Softshell Crabs · 228

sautés and stir-frys

All of these recipes benefit from an inexpensive, but vital, piece of equipment that you'll find in most Third Coast kitchens, sometimes passed down for generations. A well-seasoned iron skillet (or the deeper covered version usually labeled as a "chicken fryer") is great for searing, stir-frying, sautés, and deep frying (not to mention cornbread, biscuits, jambalaya, paella, pancakes, and real old-fashioned popcorn). You can pick one up at nearly any discount mart or hardware store. Follow the seasoning and care instructions on the label and the surface will become naturally stick-resistant in no time, though it will take much longer to acquire the dull black luster that only comes with decades of hard use.

FLASH-FRIED WILD DUCK WITH
wild mushroom and peppercorn cream
SERVES 4

In the heart of Louisiana's Cajun country, at Prejean's Restaurant in Lafayette, the walls are lined with hunting trophies and display cases are jammed with some 250 culinary medals. Executive Chef Frederick Nonato developed this recipe for wild wood duck, but you could substitute domestic duck breasts. Just remember that they tend to be larger and fattier.

1 cup	all-purpose flour
2 tablespoons	Cajun seasoning (Sources, page 384)
4	(4-ounce) deboned duck breasts, pounded to a thickness of ¼ inch
¼ cup	clarified butter
½ cup	sliced shiitakes
½ cup	sliced morels
½ cup	sliced oyster mushrooms
1 teaspoon	whole black peppercorns
1 teaspoon	chicken bouillon granules
⅓ cup	French brandy
¾ cup	heavy cream

1. Stir together the flour and Cajun seasoning. Dredge the pounded duck breasts in the seasoned flour.

2. Add clarified butter to a very hot sauté pan over medium-high heat. Sauté the duck breasts for 1 minute on each side to cook medium-rare. Remove to a warm serving platter and cover to keep warm.

3. Add the mushrooms, peppercorns, and bouillon granules to the sauté pan; toss for 1 minute. Pour the brandy over the surface of the mushrooms and carefully ignite it to burn off the alcohol. When the flame goes out, stir in the cream and reduce it for 1 minute. Spoon the sauce over the duck breasts and serve immediately.

FILETS MIGNONS
in red chile and raisin mole

SERVES 6

Cowboy food goes uptown at Cafe Annie in Houston, where Chef Robert DelGrande has attracted national attention with his sophisticated makeovers of Texas and Mexican standards. Don't get skittish as you read his long list of ingredients. Once you've done the hunting and gathering (and everything is measured out and waiting by the stove), cooking proceeds swiftly. It's a showy project for those occasions when all of the guests congregate in the kitchen. And the complex smoky flavor of the mole makes it all worthwhile.

6	(6-ounce) filet mignons
	Salt and freshly ground black pepper
1 tablespoon	olive oil
2	ancho chiles (approximately 1 ounce)
6	whole allspice
12	cumin seeds
¼ teaspoon	dried oregano
2 tablespoons	unsalted butter
½ cup	raisins
½	medium yellow onion, coarsely chopped
4	garlic cloves
1	white corn tortilla, cut into eighths
3 cups	chicken stock or water
¼	fresh hoja santa leaf or 1 tablespoon fresh tarragon leaves
1 teaspoon	salt
¼ cup	hulled pumpkin seeds
¼ cup	pecan pieces
1 ounce	bittersweet chocolate, chopped
1	large ripe Hass avocado, peeled, seeded, and cut into 12 slices
18	cilantro sprigs

1. Lightly season the filets with salt and pepper. Heat the oil in a deep sauté pan (10 to 12 inches wide and 3 inches deep) over medium-high heat until very hot. Without overcrowding the pan, sear the filets quickly on each side, leaving them very rare. Transfer the seared filets to a plate and reserve. With a paper towel, wipe the sauté pan clean of any excess oil and use it for the next step.

2. Warm the pan over medium heat. Add the ancho chiles and lightly toast, turning frequently. They are done when they become aromatic and have puffed slightly. (Caution: Do not allow them to burn.) Remove the chiles; when they are cool enough to handle, remove and discard the stems and seeds. Tear the chiles into small pieces and reserve.

3. In the same pan, lightly toast the allspice and cumin seeds. Add the oregano and quickly toast. Add the butter; when it begins to sizzle, add the raisins and stir to lightly sauté. Remove approximately 2 tablespoons of the raisins and set them aside for a garnish. To the rest of the mixture remaining in the pan, add the onion, garlic, and tortilla pieces; sauté, stirring frequently, until browned and aromatic.

4. Add the chicken stock and bring to a boil. Add the hoja santa (or tarragon leaves) and salt; simmer for 15 minutes. Remove from the heat and allow to cool for at least 15 minutes.

5. In a second skillet over medium heat, stir the pumpkin seeds until they puff and pop; remove and reserve. Similarly, stir the pecan pieces until they are lightly toasted. Remove and reserve.

6. When the simmered mixture has cooled, transfer it to a blender. Reserve 1 tablespoon each of the toasted pumpkin seeds and pecans for a garnish; add the remainder to the blender. Purée the sauce until smooth.

7. Transfer the purée back to the original deep sauté pan. Bring the sauce to a simmer. Add the chocolate and stir until well mixed. (If the sauce appears very thick, add a little water to thin it.) Return the filets to the sauce. Spoon some sauce over each filet, slowly cooking them in the barely simmering sauce for approximately 5 minutes (for rare to medium-rare), or to desired doneness. Turn the filets over halfway through cooking.

8. To serve, place a filet in the center of each dinner plate. Spoon some of the chile sauce over each filet. Distribute some of the reserved raisins, pumpkin seeds, and pecans around each filet. Place two avocado slices on top of each filet and garnish with cilantro sprigs.

CHA-CHA'S CITRUS CHICKEN

SERVES 2

This speedy tropical sauté is a simple beauty from Cha-Cha Coconuts. Headquartered on the Gulf Coast, the Floribbean bistros are located in St. Petersburg, Sarasota, and Orlando.

¼ cup	fresh orange juice
2 tablespoons	fresh lime juice
2	(4-ounce) boneless, skinless chicken breast halves
	Salt and freshly ground black pepper
¼ cup	olive or vegetable oil
2	lengthwise wedges of fresh pineapple, each about 1 inch thick, peeled
2	peeled mangoes, sliced lengthwise
2	peeled bananas, cut in half crosswise, each half sliced lengthwise
2 tablespoons	guava jelly, warmed

1. Stir together the orange and lime juices; pour over the chicken and marinate at room temperature for 20 minutes. Discard the marinade and pat the chicken dry. Season it to taste with salt and pepper.

2. Warm the oil in a large skillet over medium heat. Sauté the chicken, turning it once, until browned on both sides and done. Remove to a warm plate and keep warm. Add the pineapple, mangoes, and bananas to the pan; cook, turning to heat through and lightly brown both sides of the fruit.

3. Divide the chicken and fruit between two warmed plates. Drizzle with warm guava jelly. Serve with yellow rice or Cuban Black Beans and Rice (page 140).

FLORIDA SPINY LOBSTER
with cuban garlic sauce
* mojo de ajo *

Jeannie Pierola was born in the historic Cuban neighborhood of Ybor City, where she learned to cook from her mother and grandmother. After operating three successful restaurants of her own (Tia Lena's, Cool Beans Cafe, and Boca), she brought her "new Tampa Latin" style to the venerable Bern's Steak House, and its spinoff SideBerns.

For the Cuban sauce known as Mojo de Ajo, olive oil is flavored with lots of garlic, hot chiles, lime juice, and cilantro. Don't be alarmed by the large amount of oil, as you will have plenty of the sauce left over to get your mojo workin' on other dishes. It's traditional with steamed yuca, but it's also good drizzled over grilled vegetables or pasta.

2 tablespoons plus 1 cup	olive oil
4	spiny lobster tails, split in half lengthwise
	Salt
1 head	garlic, cloves peeled and thinly sliced
2	ancho chiles, seeded and julienned
2	chipotle chiles, seeded and julienned
2	aji amarillo chiles, seeded and julienned
½ cup	fresh lime juice
3 tablespoons	chopped fresh cilantro

1. Heat the oven to 325° F. Warm 2 tablespoons of olive oil in a large sauté pan over medium heat. Season the lobster tails with salt; place them meat side down in the hot oil. Sauté the tails for about 2 minutes; flip and cook for about 2 minutes longer, until the shells are uniformly red. Place the lobsters in an ovenproof pan; bake until cooked through, 2 to 3 minutes.

2. Working quickly while the lobsters are in the oven, add the remaining cup of olive oil and the garlic to the pan. Stirring constantly, lightly toast the garlic for about 1 minute, being careful not to let it burn. Add the chiles, stirring until they are crisp, about 2 minutes. Be prepared for spattering as you stir in the lime juice and cilantro. Season with salt.

3. Place each lobster tail on a plate and top with crisped chiles and garlic, drizzling a bit of sauce over the tail. Serve immediately. Refrigerate leftover *Mojo de Ajo* for up to a week.

CRAWFISH STIR-FRY, indian style
* crawfish bhuna *

SERVES 4

We already love spicy crawfish, so it's not much of a jump to experiment with mudbugs, Indian style. This recipe is from the late Har Keswani, an Indian-born naval architect turned Louisiana chef, who claimed that exotica is in the eye of the beholder. "Cooking with your regional seafood and vegetables, even blended in unusual ways, isn't odd at all," he once told me, "but swallowing live raw oysters and sucking crawfish heads, now that is exotic!"

Keswani's wife, who finds even the steamy Gulf Coast climate cooler than her home city of Bombay, was thrilled when Har moved from the University of Michigan to a position at a shipyard in Avondale, Louisiana. "When Har came down here to see about the job, he used roll after roll of film taking pictures of banana trees and tropical plants," Anila Keswani said. "Back in Michigan, with the snow and cold weather we were having, it looked like heaven to me." The family eventually opened a string of New Orleans-area restaurants, including Taj Mahal, Shalimar, and Nirvana.

Keswani's Crawfish Bhuna will be a revelation to anyone who has never ventured beyond rich curries or heavy samosas. The word bhuna means to stir-fry. Using very little oil, fresh vegetables are cooked on a flat pan so that they retain their tenderness and coloring. You could substitute lamb or chicken for the shellfish, but either should be roasted or grilled before slices are added to the vegetables, or the meat juices will make the dish too moist to be a true bhuna. Fortunately there is no such problem when using the traditional fish or shrimp (or as in this case, crawfish tails).

2 tablespoons	corn oil
1	large onion, diced
1 teaspoon	minced fresh ginger
½ teaspoon	minced garlic
¼ teaspoon	ground cumin
¼ teaspoon	ground coriander
¼ teaspoon	garam masala
¼ teaspoon	paprika
	Salt and cayenne pepper to taste
1	large green bell pepper, seeded and cut into ¾-inch dice
1	large red bell pepper, seeded and cut into ¾-inch dice

1 pound	cooked and peeled crawfish tails
8	fresh mushrooms, quartered
1	large ripe tomato, seeded and finely chopped
1	minced jalapeño (optional; seeded for less heat)
2 tablespoons	plain yogurt
	Juice of ½ fresh lemon
1 teaspoon	minced cilantro

Warm the oil in a large frying pan over high heat, then add the onion and cook until it's softened, but still opaque (do not overcook). Add the ginger and garlic and reduce the heat to medium; stir for 1 minute. Add the dry spices and bell peppers, stirring until the bell peppers are tender, about 2 minutes. Add all of the remaining ingredients except for the lemon juice and cilantro, and sauté for 1 minute longer. Sprinkle with the lemon juice (to taste) and the cilantro. Serve with steamed basmati rice or Texmati Rice (Texas-grown basmati; see Sources, page 384).

✳ ✳ ✳ mudbugs for profit ✳ ✳ ✳

Louisiana leads the nation in crawfish farming, producing more than 90 percent of the domestic crop. The typical farmer creates his ponds by building levees around low-lying swampland, or by flooding high land, such as rice fields in the off-season (which is a great way to bring in two harvests from the same acreage). Each pond is stocked only once with crawfish, which then survive on grasses and other natural feed to reproduce at a staggering rate. One female can produce up to 800 eggs per year. A well-managed pond will yield an average of 1,500 to 2,000 pounds of crawfish per year. An extremely well-managed pond can yield up to twice that amount.

✳   ✳   ✳   ✳   ✳   ✳

softshell crabs

Sweet and briny, delicate and chewy, fresh-caught soft-shell crabs are a feast of flavors and textures. A bit of cleaning and they're ready to fry, tender enough to consume shell and all, the luxurious white flesh encased in a crackly crust of corn flour. Even more than other seafoods, they require careful handling, so read on to make the best of these strange and wonderful creatures.

DEEP-FRIED SOFTSHELL CRABS

SERVES 6

Let me tell you this right now: your stove will be a mess and the kitchen will smell like a cheap diner. So will your clothes. And your hair. That said, softshell crabs are a rare delicacy, but only when they're cooked properly, so it's best to do it yourself. First, refer to page 95 for tips on controlling odors, then roll up your sleeves and proceed fearlessly.

The temperature of the oil is vital. It must be hot, while the crabs and batter must be cold in order to sear immediately and not become saturated with grease. If you don't have an electric deep fryer, be sure to use a thermometer and a very deep pan (preferably covered with a spatter screen), as the moisture inside the crabs releases steam that bubbles up ferociously. The oil should be deep enough to float the crabs, but no more than one third up the sides of the pan.

> 6 fresh whole (uncleaned) softshell crabs, preferably live
> Salt and pepper
> Peanut oil for deep frying
> 1 egg
> 1 cup cold milk
> Corn flour (see Note)

1. Just before cooking—and no sooner—rinse and clean the chilled crabs (see page 225). Pat them dry with paper towels and season to taste with salt and pepper. Heat the oil to 365°F in an electric deep fryer or very deep pan.

2. Beat the egg together with the cold milk. Dredge the crabs in the corn flour, then the egg batter, then again in the corn flour. Immediately place in the hot oil, being careful not to crowd. They should be able to float freely on the surface of the oil. (Depending upon the size of your pan and the crabs, you may need to cook them one or two at a time.) Cook until golden brown, 5 to 6 minutes, turning once if necessary; then drain and serve immediately.

Note: Not to be confused with the much coarser cornmeal, corn flour is the same product in a much finer grind, with a powdery texture similar to wheat flour; hence the name. It is sometimes marketed as fish fry, either plain or seasoned. I prefer it plain, without the unpleasant whang of synthetic lemon and garlic powder. You could also use cornmeal, or all-purpose flour (or a mixture of the two), but corn flour will produce the lightest and most cohesive crust.

PAN-FRIED SOFTSHELL CRABS

SERVES 6

Although not nearly as messy as deep frying, this method still releases some juices from the crabs that will cause the oil to spatter, so use a heavy deep skillet and stand back.

6	fresh softshell crabs, preferably live
	Salt and pepper
¼ cup	unsalted butter
¼ cup	olive oil
1	egg
½ cup	cold milk
	All-purpose flour or whole-wheat pastry flour

1. Just before cooking—and no sooner—rinse and clean the chilled crabs (see page 225). Pat them dry with paper towels and season to taste with salt and pepper.

2. Melt the butter with the olive oil in a large skillet over medium to medium-high heat. Beat the egg together with the cold milk. Working in two batches if necessary, dredge the crabs in the flour, then the egg batter, then again in the flour. Immediately place them in the hot skillet, being careful not to crowd. Cook, turning once, until browned and crisp on both sides. Serve immediately.

* * *cleaning* * *
softshelled crabs

I'm never too sentimental to toss living crustaceans into a pot of boiling water. I'm sure they had it coming with their aggressive posture and snapping claws. But there's something more intimate about cleaning a limp and helpless soft-shell crab, cutting off its little face while its legs are still wriggling. Fresh is unquestionably best, though, and I can just hear Julia Child trilling, "Proceed fearlessly!"

If, like me, you tend to proceed squeamishly, cover the poor guys with ice for an hour or so (which will either kill them or render them totally unconscious). Then carry on with these simple instructions from the Louisiana Seafood Promotion and Marketing Board.

1. With scissors, remove the face of the crab, about ½ inch from the edge of its shell.

2. With the tip of the scissors or with your fingers, remove the hard "sand bag" that is located behind the mouth.

3. Lift the back of the shell at its pointed ends and cut away the feathery gills on each side.

4. Lift and snip off the "apron" from the bottom of the crab, near the back end.

Soft crabs should always be cleaned just before cooking, so that they won't lose their natural juices and delicate flavor. For highest quality, avoid buying crabs that are already cleaned. They may be purchased fresh (alive) or frozen. Freezing fresh soft crabs is very easy and produces excellent results. However, don't clean them before freezing (which will drain away their natural juices). Simply rinse with cold water and wrap with freezer paper or plastic wrap, folding the legs and claws near the body.

* * * * * *

* * * soft shells, hard labor * * *

The next time you're lucky enough to dine on softshell crabs, think about Ethel Smith. She was up every two hours last night, as always, monitoring the progress in her backyard shedding tanks. She probably wore her white rubber boots, although she sometimes forgets, only to be reminded by a sharp pinch on the toe from some scrabbling escapee who made it over the wall. During one semi-conscious dawn patrol, she was startled wide awake by a slender green snake that had wound around her ankle.

"I almost had a heart attack," she said. "That's when I quit coming out here in flip-flops."

Her husband, Anthony, works the day shift, running their traps on Bayou Barataria in South Louisiana. After he ties up the boat, he fills the giant underwater pen alongside their dock with hard crabs bound for local wholesalers or restaurants. Together, the Smiths sort out the "busters" (crabs that show signs of molting), which are transferred to the shedding tanks. Then he usually takes the afternoon watch, checking the tanks every two hours while Ethel naps.

Meltingly sweet taste and chewy-tender texture aside, softshell crabs were originally prized because they had to be captured at the peak of a natural process. In order to grow, the blue crab occasionally sheds its rigid shell. Underwater the new shell remains soft for just a few hours, allowing the crab to stretch to a bigger size before hardening again.

Thanks to modern aquaculture, commercial producers can now control those fleeting conditions to maximize their harvest. The Smiths designed and built their own shedding system, with research materials from the Louisiana Cooperative Extension Service and plenty of trial and error. Today their 8,000-gallon ecosystem can hold up to 4,000 busters at a time, using filtered saltwater and fresh-caught crabs from the bayou behind their house.

At the earliest sign of molting (a red line along the back paddles) the crabs are placed in the first holding tank, then moved to different tanks as they pass through progressive stages. During the last hours, they gradually crack loose under the points of their shells and begin to back out.

"That's when they go to jail," Anthony said, tossing one into the final tank, which is divided by a grid into single cells, each just large enough for one occupant. "They're at their most vulnerable now. If you don't separate them, the other crabs could kill them."

"Crabs will always fight," Ethel said. "You might have just two of them in this huge tank and they'll pull each other's claws off. They're worse than kids."

While in this period of solitary confinement, the crabs are kept under the closest watch, ready to be placed on ice soon after they back out of their old shells, before the new ones have time to harden. Most are still alive, though in a state of suspended animation, when they're sold no more than 24 hours later.

And so it goes, every two hours, seven days a week. This labor-intensive operation remains in full swing for about eight months each year, as crabs rarely molt during the coldest weeks of winter.

"This works like a big aquarium," Anthony said of their setup, which rambles through their former boathouse and a couple of adjoining structures. The water in the tanks is kept around 75°F, the optimum temperature to encourage quick shedding. It is also sparkling clear and odorless, thanks to an elaborate filtration system.

With such a steady supply, the Smiths can afford to experiment in their own kitchen. They prefer to season cleaned softshell crabs simply (with lemon juice, salt, pepper, garlic powder, and onion powder), then sauté them in butter to serve over pasta. They also like them cut in half, then wrapped with bacon and charcoal grilled. Either way, cook the crabs for 4 to 5 minutes on each side.

*   *   *   *   *   *

STUFFED SOFTSHELL CRABS

SERVES 6

To my mind, this is gilding the lily, but the seasoned crabmeat stuffing plumps up the cleaned bodies (sort of like taxidermy) for an even more impressive entree that has become quite popular on restaurant menus in recent years. Ditto the final drizzle of hollandaise, which is really over the top, though it's kind of late to worry about your arteries by this point. Be sure to read the preceding recipe for fried softshell crabs, as all of the same warnings apply here.

CRABMEAT STUFFING

⅓ cup	minced onion
¼ cup	minced green bell pepper
¼ cup	minced celery
1 teaspoon	minced garlic
Pinch	of dried thyme
3 tablespoons	unsalted butter
½ pound	white crabmeat
1 tablespoon	minced fresh flat-leaf parsley
	Salt and pepper
	Soft bread crumbs

CRABS

6	fresh whole (uncleaned) softshell crabs, preferably live
	Salt and pepper
	Vegetable oil for deep frying
1	egg
1 cup	cold milk
	Corn flour (see Note, page 223)
	Hollandaise sauce (optional)

1. For the stuffing: Sauté the onion, bell pepper, celery, garlic, and thyme in the butter in a small skillet over medium heat until the onion is tender and golden, but not browned, about 5 minutes. Stir in the crabmeat and parsley; season to taste with salt and pepper. Remove from the heat and add just enough bread crumbs to bind the mixture, about 1 cup. Cool completely before stuffing the crabs.

2. To finish the crabs: Just before cooking—and no sooner—rinse and clean the chilled crabs (see page 225). Pat them dry with paper towels and season to taste with salt and pepper. Place the stuffing between the body and upper shell of the cleaned crabs. Heat the oil to 365° F in an electric deep fryer or very deep pan.

3. Beat the egg together with the cold milk. Dredge the stuffed crabs in the corn flour, then the egg batter, then again in the corn flour. Immediately place in the hot oil, being careful not to crowd. The crabs should be able to float freely on the surface of the oil. (Depending upon the size of your pan and the crabs, you may need to cook them one or two at a time.) Cook until golden brown, 6 to 8 minutes, turning once if necessary, then drain and serve immediately. Drizzle with hollandaise, if desired.

* * * grading on the curve * * *

Softshell crabs, sorted by size from the biggest to the littlest, are officially graded as whales, jumbos, primes, hotels, and mediums. Of course, as these are fishermen's measurements, there are no smalls. However, extra-light specimens, with a skimpy ratio of meat to shell, are rejected as "kites."

* * * * * *

part 4

GARDEN and HEARTH

Try to imagine the cuisines of the world without tomatoes, bell peppers, hot chiles, sweet potatoes, squashes, corn, beans, and avocados. All are native to the Gulf Coast. They were scattered around the globe by European explorers, who in turn provided America with its first wheat, rice, and dairy products. Citrus and olives arrived with Spanish missionaries, okra with African slaves. These are the tastes of sunny days, warm earth, and stone ovens.

vegetable
centerpieces
and sides

GET STUFFED

* ✳ *

ALL FIRED UP

* ✳ *

HOT POTATOES

get stuffed

One of the most prolific fruits of the Gulf Coast is also among the most—well, tasteless. Like zucchini, chayotes are much more exuberant on the vine than on the plate. Faced with thousands of bumper crops, dating all the way back to the Aztecs, regional cooks have learned to make the best of the mild-flavored gourds.

At the other end of the flavor spectrum, hot chiles are tamed by creamy fillings of rice, seafood, or cheeses. The spicy bite is just one of the complex flavors of *chiles rellenos* (stuffed chiles), an enduring favorite in the kitchens of Mexico and Texas.

PUMPKIN STUFFED
with *picadillo*

SERVES 8

*Old World meets New World in this dramatic autumn dinner, a Third Coast pumpkin stuffed
with Spanish-influenced* picadillo. *The ground meat is seasoned with a Moorish blend of
tomatoes, onions, bell peppers, cinnamon, cloves, raisins, ripe olives, and almonds. In Mexico
it would also be used (sans egg) as a stuffing for crisp corn tacos or soft wheat tortillas.*

1	(4-pound) pumpkin
3 tablespoons	olive oil
1 pound	lean ground beef or a blend of lean ground beef and lean ground pork
1	large onion, finely chopped
1	red bell pepper, seeded and finely chopped
2	garlic cloves, minced
1 cup	tomato sauce
2 tablespoons	lemon juice
1 tablespoon	dark brown sugar
1 teaspoon	ground cinnamon
$\frac{1}{2}$ teaspoon	ground cumin
$\frac{1}{4}$ teaspoon	ground cloves
$\frac{1}{2}$ cup	sliced ripe olives
$\frac{1}{2}$ cup	raisins
$\frac{1}{2}$ cup	blanched slivered almonds
2	eggs, lightly beaten

1. Cut the top from the pumpkin and reserve, scoop out the seeds and fibers, and wash it inside
   and out. Place it in a large stockpot and cover with salted water; bring to a boil over high heat;
   reduce heat and simmer gently until just barely tender, about 25 minutes. Drain.

2. Warm 2 tablespoons of oil in a nonstick skillet over medium heat; brown the beef with the
   onion and bell pepper; add the garlic and cook a minute more. Transfer to a large bowl. Stir in
   the tomato sauce, lemon juice, sugar, cinnamon, cumin, cloves, olives, raisins, and almonds.

3. Heat the oven to 350°F. Stand the pumpkin upright in a roasting pan. Stir the beaten eggs into
   the *picadillo* and stuff it into the pumpkin. Replace the pumpkin lid and brush it all over with
   1 tablespoon of oil. Bake for 1 hour. Let stand for 10 minutes; cut into wedges.

SHRIMP and TEXMATI-STUFFED
poblanos

SERVES 6

Texmati (Sources, page 384) is a Texas-grown version of India's basmati rice, a long and slender aromatic that is available in either polished white or unrefined brown versions. The delicate grains add yet another texture to roasted poblanos stuffed with corn and shrimp in a creamy cheese sauce. Instead of fried batter, these enlightened chiles rellenos are crisped in a sheath of toasted bread crumbs. The recipe is from the USA Rice Council.

8 ounces	queso fresco (see page 269) or a mixture of ½ cup cottage cheese and ½ cup feta cheese
1 cup	corn kernels, preferably fresh (see page 243)
2 cups	cooked Texmati rice, or any long-grain white or brown rice
1 cup	chopped cooked shrimp
½ cup	(2 ounces) shredded Cheddar cheese
¼ cup	(1 ounce) shredded Monterey Jack cheese
¼ cup	chopped onion
¼ cup	sour cream
1 teaspoon	salt
12	poblano peppers, approximately 2–3 ounces each, roasted and peeled (see opposite)
2 cups	fresh bread crumbs
½ cup	grated Parmesan cheese
3 tablespoons	unsalted butter, melted
4	eggs
1 tablespoon	water
1 cup	all-purpose flour

1. Heat the oven to 350° F. Combine the queso fresco and corn in a food processor or blender, and process just until corn is no longer visible. Transfer the cheese mixture to a large bowl. Add the rice, shrimp, Cheddar, Monterey Jack, onion, sour cream, and salt; set aside.

2. Cut a small slit in one side of each poblano pepper and carefully remove the seeds, leaving the stems intact. Pat the peppers dry. Stuff each with approximately ¼ cup of the shrimp mixture. Secure with a wooden pick, if necessary.

3. Combine the bread crumbs, Parmesan, and melted butter in a medium bowl and stir until blended; set aside. Beat the eggs with the water in a medium bowl.

4. Roll the stuffed peppers in the flour, dip in the egg wash, then coat with bread crumb mixture. Place in a shallow baking dish, allowing a little space between each pepper. Bake for 30 minutes or until golden brown and thoroughly heated. Serve immediately.

✳ ✳ ✳ fresh hot chiles ✳ ✳ ✳
roasted and peeled

Roasting chiles adds a smoky depth of flavor, tenderizes the flesh, and makes peeling easier. Place fresh whole chiles under a broiler element or in a dry skillet over medium heat, or hold them directly over a gas burner with a long-handled fork. Turn them until the skin is blistered all around and slightly charred.

Wrap each hot chile in a paper towel and set it aside to cool for 10 to 15 minutes. The trapped steam will loosen the skin, then you can use the paper towel to help peel it away.

Make a lengthwise slit along one side of each peeled chile and pull out the stem, seeds, and ribs (being careful not to tear the softened flesh). And remember to wash your hands afterward, scrubbing under your fingernails, so you won't spread residue from the hot oils to your eyes or other sensitive areas.

✳ ✳ ✳ ✳ ✳ ✳

CREOLE MIRLITONS
stuffed with shrimp

SERVES 6 AS A MAIN COURSE, 12 AS A FIRST COURSE OR SIDE DISH

In many Louisiana families, shrimp-stuffed mirlitons are a traditional side dish for Thanksgiving and Christmas dinners. Also known as chayotes, the vegetable pears have a mild flavor, similar to cucumbers or zucchini, which melts into the buttery sautéed seasonings and sweet shrimp.

6	mirlitons (chayotes)
¼ cup plus 3 tablespoons	unsalted butter
¼ cup	all-purpose flour
1 cup	hot milk
1	medium yellow onion, finely chopped
½ cup	finely chopped red bell pepper
¼ cup	finely chopped celery
2	garlic cloves, finely chopped
½ teaspoon	dried oregano
¼ teaspoon	dried thyme
⅛ teaspoon	cayenne pepper, or to taste
1 pound	medium shrimp, peeled, deveined, and coarsely chopped
4	scallions, white and green parts, thinly sliced
¼ cup	minced fresh flat-leaf parsley
	Salt and freshly ground black pepper to taste
3 cups	plain soft bread crumbs, preferably from French bread

1. Cut the mirlitons in half lengthwise. Place in a large pot; cover with salted water, bring to a boil, and reduce heat to a lively simmer. Cover the pot and cook until mirlitons are fork-tender, about 45 minutes.

2. Meanwhile, melt ¼ cup butter in a saucepan over medium-low heat; whisk in the flour and cook, stirring, until sizzling and pale gold, but not browned. Whisk in hot milk until smooth; simmer, stirring constantly, for 2 or 3 minutes. Set aside to cool.

3. Scoop out pulp from the cooked mirlitons, leaving the shell intact. Coarsely chop the pulp.

4. Heat the oven to 375° F. Melt the remaining 3 tablespoons butter in a large skillet over medium heat. Sauté the onion, bell pepper, celery, garlic, oregano, thyme, and cayenne pepper until the vegetables are tender, but not browned. Stir in the chopped mirliton pulp, shrimp, scallions, and parsley; continue cooking for 3 or 4 minutes longer, until most of the moisture is absorbed and shrimp have just begun to turn pink. Stir in reserved cream sauce. Season to taste with salt and black pepper. Stuff the shrimp mixture into the mirliton shells.

5. Sprinkle each stuffed shell with about ¼ cup of the bread crumbs, pressing lightly with your hands so the crumbs will adhere. Arrange the stuffed mirlitons in a lightly greased baking pan. Bake for 25 to 35 minutes, until the stuffing is bubbly and bread crumbs are toasted.

Plan ahead: Complete recipe through step 5 and refrigerate for up to 1 day, or freeze for up to 2 months.

✳ mock applesauce ✳

Some Third Coast cooks use mirlitons in place of apples for making pies, coffeecakes, or quick breads. Mirliton "applesauce" tastes surprisingly like the real thing, a fun novelty if you're a gardener with a bumper crop. Just add two tablespoons of lemon juice for each cup of cooked mirliton puree; then season it to taste with brown sugar, ground cinnamon, and vanilla. It tastes best warm and makes a good accompaniment for roast pork.

all fired up

These colorful vegetables need not be relegated to the
sidelines. Each would make a delicious centerpiece for a
light lunch or summer supper. Just add a glass of wine and
a loaf of crusty bread (and a big chocolate cake) and you'll
have a very satisfying meal.

Lulu's L.A. Caviar *(page 36)* and a pile of tasty saltines for serving

Little Shrimp Cakes on Sugarcane Skewers *(page 48)*
and Lemongrass Beef Skewers *(page 47)*

ABOVE: Veracruz-Style Sauces for Fresh Seafood *(page 29)*,
with a sampling of oysters and a Mojito *(page 365)* with a sugarcane swizzle stick
BELOW: Marinated Crab Fingers *(page 42)*

Gulf Shrimp "Martini" with Cioppino Sauce *(page 62)*

Spinach and Fried Oyster Salad *(page 96)*

ABOVE: Jamie Shannon's Watermelon and Summer Vegetable Salad *(page 78)* and a refreshing Watermelon Cooler *(page 379)*
BELOW: Creole Filé Gumbo *(page 110)*; a pile of filé for serving in the background

Chilled Avocado and Crabmeat Soup *(page 128)*

Beef Tenderloin with Cocoa-Chile Rub *(page 178)* and a side of Brabant Potatoes *(page 247)*

Creole Grillades and Grits *(page 281)*

A selection of ingredients for Aunt Rosalie's Baked Fish *(page 208)*

ABOVE: Tex-Mex Squash with Chicken *(page 196)*
BELOW: Cha-Cha's Citrus Chicken *(page 218)*, served with your basic yellow rice

Big Bruce's Ultimate Prickly Pear Grande Margarita *(page 370)* and, in the
background, Sangrita *(page 375)* and a shot of tequila

Grilled Vegetable Muffuletta *(page 361)*

ABOVE: Fresh Orange Cake *(page 294)*
BELOW: Mango Chiffon Pie *(page 312)*

The Blue Margarita *(page 369)*

Pumpkin Flan *(page 316)*

GRANDPA LOCICERO'S
sicilian eggplant
MAKES ABOUT 12 CUPS

Chef Duke LoCicero worked at several Houston restaurants before returning home to New Orleans to open Cafe Giovanni in the French Quarter. He agreed to share an old family recipe, which was brought to this country by his grandfather, Innocenzio "Charles" LoCicero, a native of Trabia, a Sicilian seaside village near Palermo.

Eggplant can add a meaty texture to many vegetarian dishes, but it has a special affinity for Italian sauces and seasonings. It is the main ingredient in this rich and chunky ragout that may be served either hot or cold, as an appetizer with toasted bread or as a sauce for pasta. It is also good as a side with seafood or meat.

1 cup	extra-virgin olive oil
2	medium to large eggplants, peeled and cut into small cubes
2	medium red onions, diced small
2	large heads garlic, roasted and peeled
2 cups	sliced black olives
1 cup	diced canned pimientos
1 cup	sweet Marsala wine
1½ cups	sliced fresh basil leaves
¾ teaspoon	red pepper flakes
2 tablespoons	sugar
2 cups	tomato-based red pasta sauce (homemade or best-quality commercial)
2 tablespoons	balsamic vinegar
½ cup	capers
1 tablespoon	anchovies, puréed
1 cup	sliced green olives

Heat the olive oil in a large pot over medium heat and cook the eggplants, onions, and garlic until soft. Add all remaining ingredients and continue to cook at low to medium heat until 80 percent of liquid has evaporated. Cool to room temperature, then refrigerate for 6 hours. Serve cold or reheat.

MEXICAN SQUASH
and corn sauté
* calabacitas *

SERVES 4–6

A rustic side dish or light vegetarian entree, this summery sauté could also be enriched by Mexican-style crème fraîche for calabacitas con crema. Just add a few tablespoons of Crema (page 267) with the corn. Either way, it's a big favorite along the coast of Texas and Northern Mexico.

2 tablespoons	olive oil
1	medium yellow onion, chopped
2 pounds	yellow crookneck squash or zucchini (or a mix), thinly sliced
2	mild chiles, such as Anaheims, roasted, peeled, and chopped (see page 237), or a 4-ounce can of chopped green chiles, drained
	Kernels and creamy juices from 3 ears of fresh corn (see opposite)
	Salt and freshly ground black pepper

Warm the oil in large deep nonstick skillet over medium-high heat; cook the onion until golden brown. Add the squash and green chiles; continue stirring until squash is lightly browned around edges. Cover pan and reduce heat to medium low; continue cooking, stirring often, until squash is tender, 10 to 15 minutes. Raise heat to medium and stir in corn; cook uncovered until kernels are just crisp-tender, 1 to 2 minutes. Season to taste with salt and black pepper.

ROASTED CORN
with two mexican rubs

For corn roasted in its natural wrapping, pull back the husks without detaching them; remove all of the silks, then rewrap the husks, securing at the top with string. Thus prepared, soak the ears in cold water for 20 minutes, then grill over hot coals, turning occasionally, for 20 minutes. The corn will be steamed to tenderness with a pleasant hint of smokiness.

If you like a more pronounced smoky flavor (though the kernels will be slightly tougher), corn can also be roasted directly on the grate. Shuck and oil the ears, then cook them on a covered grill for about 15 minutes, turning occasionally.

And if you really want to go all out, the traditional method for a beach corn roast is similar to a clambake. Build a fire in a hole in the sand, allowing it to burn until the sand is very hot. Remove the coals and fill the pit with corn (desilked, husks tied at the top), then seal the pit with wet burlap sacks covered in sand. The corn is left to steam in its husks for about 20 minutes. Then again, there's always the microwave . . .

Mexican street vendors in the northern coastal states of Tamaulipas and Tampico dip whole ears of roasted corn into Crema (page 267) or mayonnaise, then cover them in crumbled Queso Blanco (page 267) and ground red chiles. You could substitute feta or Parmesan cheese.

For a lighter Tex-Mex rub, stir salt together with ground ancho or chipotle chiles, spicing it as hot as you like. Dip a lime wedge in the mix and rub it over a cooked ear of corn. Chomp!

✳ ✳ ✳ shuck that corn! ✳ ✳ ✳

Now that fresh corn is available in supermarkets year-round, there's no excuse to use canned or frozen kernels, when the taste and texture of the real thing is so much better. You can't even argue convenience because the whole process of shucking and scraping takes only a minute per ear.

After pulling off the leaves, use a clean brush or dish towel to wipe away the clingy silks. Rinse and dry the corn, then stand it on end in a large shallow bowl and slice downward with a sharp knife to cut off the kernels. And be sure to scrape the cob with a spoon to release the creamy juices left behind. Each ear will yield about 1 cup of kernels.

✳ ✳ ✳ ✳ ✳ ✳

ENLIGHTENED GREENS

*Collards and turnip greens are old Southern favorites that many people find
unappealing, mainly because they're traditionally stewed with gobs of pork fat.
However, when properly prepared, they're among the most nutritious vegetables
you can eat, packed with a wealth of vitamins and minerals. Collards, for
instance, contain more available calcium than cow's milk.*

*Dr. Bob Randall, Ph.D., is the executive director of Urban Harvest Community
Gardens and Orchards, a Houston organization that helps city dwellers and schoolchildren
learn to grow their own food. He offered these simple instructions for preparing collards,
one of his favorite crops. He said the same method would also work with kale or turnip
greens. And here's an old Southern trick for minimizing odor as they cook: add two or
three unshelled pecans to the boiling water.*

1	large bunch of collards, kale, or turnip greens
2 tablespoons	olive oil
3	garlic cloves, minced
	Kelp powder
	Black pepper
	Balsamic vinegar

1. Wash the greens. Place the whole leaves in a large pot, cover them with water, and boil until tender, about 15 minutes. Drain the leaves well, then coarsely chop them.

2. Warm the oil over medium heat in a wok or large skillet. Stir-fry the garlic until it releases its fragrance, about 30 seconds. Add the drained and chopped greens; toss until heated through and evenly coated with the garlic and oil, about 1 minute. Season well with kelp powder and black pepper, tossing to get the seasonings all over the greens, then sprinkle with the vinegar, tossing to coat evenly. Serve immediately as a vegetable or a hot salad.

IRON-SKILLET SQUASH

SERVES 4–6

It just doesn't get more Southern than this. Tender yellow squash, smothered with onions in an iron skillet, appears on summer supper tables from the Florida Panhandle to the tip of Texas. I got the recipe from Margaret Warr, a food columnist for the Pensacola News Journal.

4–5	slices bacon
2 pounds	(4–5 medium) sweet onions, such as Vidalias, chopped
2 pounds	yellow squash, sliced
	Salt and pepper

Heat the oven to 350° F. Cook the bacon in a large iron skillet over medium heat until crisp. Crumble and set aside. Add the onions and squash to the bacon drippings in the pan. Place in the oven; bake for 1 hour, stirring every 15 minutes. Top with the crisp crumbled bacon.

✳ ✳ ✳ snappy dinner ✳ ✳ ✳
music

The frenetic Cajun–R&B–Caribbean sound of Louisiana's French-speaking black Creoles gets its name from—of all things—string beans. Musician Clifton Chenier recalls jam sessions on his grandmother's front porch, where some family members would syncopate on washtub and floorboards, while others were snapping beans for Sunday dinner. They called it *les haricots* music, pronounced *zydeco*.

✳ ✳ ✳ ✳ ✳ ✳

hot potatoes

Little red or white potatoes are well used on the Gulf Coast, where they're essential ingredients for seafood boils, salads, cottage fries, and big pots of smothered green beans. They're not really "new potatoes," though that's what everybody calls them. It's just a catch-all name for any variety that is harvested young, during spring or early summer, when the flesh is extra-sweet and the skins are still thin and tender.

Coasters also like their potatoes big and orange. At their best, baked sweets need only a pat of butter to enhance their rich and toasty flavor, but read on for a couple of meal-size casseroles that place them at the center of the plate.

BRABANT POTATOES

SERVES 6–8

*Simple and succulent, these little potatoes crisped in butter have been a
fixture in the Creole dining palaces of New Orleans for generations.
If you prefer, replace half of the butter with olive oil.*

2 pounds	small red or white potatoes, scrubbed and halved
1	large bay leaf
	Chicken stock or broth
	Salt
6–8 tablespoons	unsalted butter
	Freshly ground black pepper

1. Place potatoes and bay leaf in a medium saucepan and cover by 1 inch with stock. Season to taste with salt. Bring to a boil over high heat; reduce heat to medium-low and simmer, covered, until potatoes are barely tender, but still firm, about 12 minutes. Drain well.

2. Melt butter in a large, well-seasoned iron skillet or nonstick skillet over medium-high heat. Add potatoes, season to taste with salt and pepper, and toss until browned and crisp on all sides, about 5 minutes. Serve immediately.

Plan ahead: Prepare through step 1 and hold at room temperature for a few hours.

✳ ✳ ✳ precious cargo ✳ ✳ ✳

Spanish conquistadors were digging for gold during the sixteenth century when they first came across potatoes in South America and carried them back to Europe. The English name is derived from *batatas*, the West Indian word for sweet potatoes, though the two species are completely unrelated.

✳   ✳   ✳   ✳   ✳   ✳

ORANGE SWEET POTATO SOUFFLÉ

*Candied sweet potato casseroles, crowned by a sticky mass of melted marshmallows,
always provoke cries of outrage from nutritionists—just one of the reasons Southerners
enjoy this enduring holiday tradition. However, here is a more (or is it less?) civilized
alternative that replaces the goo with the fresh Third Coast tang of oranges and allspice.*

1 pound	sweet potatoes, baked and peeled (see page 303)
3 tablespoons	unsalted butter, at room temperature
½ cup	warm cream or milk
1 tablespoon	frozen orange juice concentrate, at room temperature
2 teaspoons	finely grated orange zest
¼ teaspoon	ground allspice
2 tablespoons	orange liqueur, optional (or an additional tablespoon of thawed orange juice concentrate)
	Salt and freshly ground black pepper
4	egg yolks
6	egg whites

1. While the potatoes are still warm, purée them in a food processor until smooth. Add the butter, warm cream, thawed orange juice concentrate, orange zest, and allspice. Add the orange liqueur, if using. Season highly with salt and pepper; process briefly to blend. Add the egg yolks; process until smooth. Transfer to a large mixing bowl.

2. Heat the oven to 375° F. In a separate bowl, whip the egg whites until stiff but not dry; gently fold into the puréed potatoes. Turn into a buttered 6-cup soufflé dish and bake until well-puffed and brown, about 20 minutes. Serve immediately.

SWEET POTATO and CORNBREAD
dressing

SERVES 6 AS A MAIN COURSE, 8–10 AS A SIDE DISH

*Mississippi-style cornbread dressing gets a boost of flavor and regional color from
bright orange sweet potatoes. And there's no need to wait for Thanksgiving.
Serve this hearty side with pork roast or baked chicken, or make it with
vegetable broth for a meatless main course.*

6 tablespoons	unsalted butter
3 cups	peeled and diced raw sweet potatoes
1	large onion, chopped
2	ribs celery, chopped
2 teaspoons	grated fresh ginger
1	large bay leaf
⅓ cup	minced fresh parsley
1 tablespoon	chopped fresh sage or ½ teaspoon dried
1 teaspoon	fresh thyme leaves or ¼ teaspoon dried
5 cups	crumbled cornbread
½ cup	coarsely chopped roasted pecans
	Chicken or turkey broth
	Salt and freshly ground black pepper
1	egg, beaten

1. Melt the butter in a large skillet over medium heat and cook the sweet potatoes, onion, celery,
ginger, and bay leaf until the potatoes are just tender and the onions are translucent and light
gold, 5 to 7 minutes. Scrape into a large mixing bowl. Stir in the parsley, sage, thyme, cornbread, and pecans. Toss gently to coat.

2. Heat the oven to 375° F. Remove and reserve the bay leaf. Add enough broth to moisten the
dressing well, season it highly with salt and pepper, and stir in the beaten egg. Turn the stuffing into a buttered casserole and place the reserved bay leaf on top.
Bake uncovered for about 45 minutes, or until the surface is crisp
and browned and the stuffing is hot through.

*Plan ahead: Prepare through
step 1 and refrigerate for up to
2 days.*

breads, grains, and cheeses

FRESH HOT BREADS

Fresh Corn and Jalapeño Bread • 253

Aunt Burma's Angel Biscuits • 254

Foolproof Food-Processor Biscuits • 255

Sweet Potato Biscuits • 256

Rich Sicilian Flatbread (*Sfincione*) • 258

* ✳ *

MUSH!

Basic Microwave Polenta or Grits • 261

Fried or Baked Polenta or Grits • 262

Sweet Potato Polenta with Salsa • 263

Nassau Grits • 265

* ✳ *

EASY HOMEMADE CHEESES

Crema • 267

Queso Blanco • 267

Creole Cream Cheese • 268

fresh hot breads

The earliest residents of the Third Coast pounded corn for tortillas that they griddled atop hot rocks. European colonists added the eggs and milk to turn it into cornbread. They also introduced the wheat flour for biscuits, which natives adapted into Indian frybread and Mexican *sopaipillas*, cousins of the pillow-shaped *beignets* sold at the sidewalk cafés of New Orleans. City bakeries developed the crackly yard-long loaves known as po-boy bread in Louisiana or Cuban bread in Florida. Sicilian delis imported crusty muffuletta buns that inspired the sandwich of the same name. But nothing evokes home and hearth like bread fresh out of the oven, and these simple comforts are within the range of the busiest cooks.

FRESH CORN and JALAPEÑO
bread

SERVES 12

*Texas community cookbooks are big on jalapeño cornbread made with canned creamed
corn, which turns out cloyingly sweet and kind of gummy. This version has a much
fresher taste and lighter texture from creamy corn juices grated right off the cob, along
with a handful of crisp kernels. It's not too spicy, but you can cut the heat even more by
leaving out the fresh jalapeños and/or substituting Cheddar cheese for the pepper jack. For
authentic flavor, grease the pan with bacon drippings. For extra-crisp edges, heat a greased
cast-iron skillet in the oven, then pour the batter into the sizzling hot pan to bake.*

1 cup	buttermilk
1 cup	yellow cornmeal
1 cup	flour
2 tablespoons	sugar (optional)
1 teaspoon	baking powder
¾ teaspoon	salt
½ teaspoon	baking soda
2	eggs, beaten
¼ cup	unsalted butter, melted
1 cup	grated corn (use the large holes of a box grater)
1 cup	fresh corn kernels cut from the cob
1 cup	grated pepper jack cheese
⅓ cup	sliced scallions
2–3	fresh jalapeño peppers, seeded and minced

1. Combine the buttermilk and cornmeal in a mixing bowl and set aside for 30 minutes.

2. Heat the oven to 400° F. Stir together the remaining dry ingredients and add to the cornmeal
mixture, along with beaten eggs and melted butter. Mix gently just until everything is incorporated. Add the corn, grated cheese, scallions, and minced jalapeños, then spoon into a
greased 12-inch iron skillet (or a 9-by-12-inch pan) and bake for 25 to 30 minutes. Let sit for 5
minutes before cutting. Serve hot with butter and salsa.

AUNT BURMA'S ANGEL BISCUITS

MAKES ABOUT 5 DOZEN

Feather-light angel biscuits are a standard in Texas kitchens. This version was passed along by Houstonian Jan Fenner Masson, the daughter of a veterinarian who served the Gulf Coast ranches around Port Lavaca for more than forty years. The recipe is from Masson's late aunt, Burma Wood Fenner, a fine cook who was also famous in the family for her vast experience with cow pies. It seems Aunt Burma lost her diamond wedding ring while baling hay, and convinced that it must have been fed to the cattle, spent weeks poking around the pasture hoping to find it. Alas, no luck.

Five dozen is a lot of biscuits, but they may be cut and individually frozen on cookie sheets, then transferred to zipper bags so you can pull out as few or as many as you need. Just thaw, then let rise and bake as directed. The cooked biscuits also freeze well.

5 cups	all-purpose flour, preferable a soft winter-wheat flour such as Martha White or White Lily
⅓ cup	sugar
1 teaspoon	baking soda
1 teaspoon	salt
2	(¼-ounce) packages active dry yeast
4 tablespoons	warm water
¾ cup	vegetable shortening
2 cups	buttermilk
	Melted butter

1. Sift the flour, sugar, baking soda, and salt into a mixing bowl. Set aside. Dissolve the yeast in the warm water; add to the dry ingredients. Cut in the shortening. Gently pour the buttermilk into the flour mixture, stir to incorporate, then turn onto a floured surface, kneading and working the mixture for 2 or 3 minutes until it forms a nice dough.

2. Roll the dough out on a floured board to a thickness of ¼ inch. Cut with a biscuit cutter. Dip the tops in melted butter and fold biscuits over halfway, buttered side in. Place on a lightly greased cookie sheet and let rise until doubled, about 1 hour. Bake at 400°F for 15 minutes.

Plan ahead: Rolled and cut biscuits can also rise overnight in the refrigerator. Return to room temperature before baking as directed.

FOOLPROOF FOOD-PROCESSOR
biscuits

MAKES 12–14 BISCUITS

Butter (in place of the usual shortening) and the nutty taste of whole-grain wheat give an extra depth of flavor to these easy biscuits. Be sure to look for the pastry flour, rather than regular whole wheat flour, for lightest results.

2 cups	whole wheat pastry flour
1 tablespoon	baking powder
½ teaspoon	salt
¼ teaspoon	baking soda
1 stick	unsalted butter, cold
⅔ cup	cold buttermilk, plus more if needed

1. Heat the oven to 450° F. Place the flour, baking powder, salt, and baking soda in the bowl of a food processor. Process briefly (about 15 seconds) to blend. Cut the chilled butter into 8 slices and distribute around the surface of the flour mixture. Pulse in five to ten short bursts until the mixture resembles coarse meal with several chunks of butter about the size of small peas. Add ⅔ cup buttermilk; pulse in four or five short bursts, just until a dough comes together. (Add a few more tablespoons of buttermilk if the mixture remains too dry to form a dough.)

2. Drop dough by heaping tablespoons onto an ungreased cookie sheet to make 12 to 14 biscuits. Bake for 10 to 12 minutes, until golden brown.

SWEET POTATO BISCUITS
MAKES ABOUT 20 DROP BISCUITS

Two great comfort foods come together in these soft buttery biscuits flavored
by sweet potatoes, a colorful indulgence in Louisiana, Mississippi, and Alabama.
Drop biscuits require less handling (for airy texture) and no extra flour for rolling
(useful here, as the lower fat content, plus the added weight of the puréed potatoes, could
make the dough pasty). However, if you have what Southerners call "a light hand,"
these are especially pretty when rolled and cut. Use a 1-inch cutter to make about
four dozen mini-biscuits for tea sandwiches or hors d'oeuvre, to be filled with
country ham and honey mustard or smoked turkey and chutney.

2½ cups	unbleached all-purpose flour or whole wheat pastry flour, plus more if necessary
1 tablespoon	baking powder
1 tablespoon	sugar (optional)
1 teaspoon	salt
¼ teaspoon	baking soda
4 tablespoons	unsalted butter, chilled
1½ teaspoons	grated orange zest
½ cup	buttermilk
1 cup	puréed cooked sweet potato

1. Heat the oven to 400°F and butter a large baking sheet. Place the flour, baking powder, sugar if using, salt, and soda in the bowl of a food processor and process for a minute to blend well. Cut the chilled butter into 8 pieces and add to the bowl with the grated orange zest, then pulse several times until the mixture resembles coarse meal with bits of butter the size of small peas. Scrape the mixture into a large mixing bowl. (If you don't have a food processor, sift the dry ingredients into a bowl, then cut in the butter quickly with a pastry cutter or two knives. Stir in orange zest.)

2. In a separate bowl, mix the buttermilk with the sweet potato purée until thoroughly blended. Add to the dry ingredients and stir just until moistened, being careful not to overblend.

   For drop biscuits: Drop by tablespoons onto the baking sheet and bake for 12 to 15 minutes, or until bottoms are lightly browned and centers are cooked through.

   For cut biscuits: Use your hands to gently knead the dough for five or six turns, just until it holds together. (If the dough is very wet, add flour by teaspoons until it's workable.) Roll out to a thickness of 1 inch on a lightly floured board, then sprinkle the top with additional flour and cut into desired shapes. Place on the baking sheet and bake until the bottoms are lightly browned and centers are cooked through, 12 to 15 minutes (if using a 2- or 3-inch cutter) or 7 to 10 minutes (for 1-inch mini-biscuits).

· ∗ ∗ the gentle art of biscuits ∗ ∗ ·

Sometimes the simplest homestyle foods, like apple pie and fried chicken, can take longer to master than the flashy stuff, and good biscuits definitely require a special touch. Handle the dough as little as possible, mixing lightly and quickly just until it's blended, so the pockets of moisture will turn to steam in the oven, producing flaky layers. Add only enough buttermilk so the dough is soft, yet workable.

Most recipes call for a brief period of kneading before the biscuits are cut, but don't smash the dough down. Instead, fold it and pat it for five or six turns to build up several layers (like puff pastry). After that, roll or pat the dough gently to a thickness of ½ inch. Be even more gentle as you reroll the scraps. Don't twist the cutter, or the biscuits will be lopsided.

Mine have risen much higher lately since I've learned how to arrange them in the pan. I was spacing them out like cookies (which the finished product resembled), but they should be a little crowded, sides barely touching, to support each other as they rise.

Southern flours (Martha White, White Lily) are milled from soft winter wheat produced in mild climates for a softer blend that's best for biscuits. And always be sure that your baking powder is fresh.

∗   ∗   ∗   ∗   ∗   ∗

RICH SICILIAN FLATBREAD
sfincione
SERVES 8–12

*Italian Americans who have settled along the Gulf Coast continue to honor the
patron saint of Sicily every March 19, St. Joseph's Day, by creating elaborate food-laden
altars decorated with handmade breads and cookies (see opposite). One of the traditional
holiday treats is this luxurious flatbread with a soft and cakelike texture similar to
brioche. The lightly sweetened dough is enriched by eggs and olive oil; topped with
sardines, black olives, and fresh tomatoes; then sprinkled with grated pecorino
cheese after baking. It's adapted from an old family recipe that was given to
me by Giovanni DiCaccamo, a native of Palermo.*

1 cup	lukewarm water
3 tablespoons	active dry yeast
3½ cups	all-purpose flour
½ cup	olive oil
2	eggs
2 teaspoons	sugar
1 teaspoon	salt
3	fresh tomatoes, sliced very thin
1	can sardines, packed in olive oil, drained
1 cup	sliced black olives
1 cup	grated pecorino cheese

1. Stir the water and yeast together in the bowl of an electric mixer until the yeast dissolves. Add
   the flour and mix briefly to blend, then add the olive oil, eggs, sugar, and salt. Beat with the
   mixer on medium speed for 3 minutes. The dough will be very soft and sticky. Cover the bowl
   and leave the dough in a warm place to rest for 45 minutes. It will triple in volume.

2. Heat the oven to 450° F. Grease a 12-by-17-inch rimmed baking pan with olive oil. Deflate the
   dough (it will still be very soft and rather sticky) and turn it out onto the greased pan. Use your
   fingers and a rubber scraper to spread the dough evenly into the pan, reaching into the corners.
   Cover the top with a single layer of sliced tomatoes, then scatter on the sardines and olives.
   Bake on a lower shelf for 15 to 20 minutes, until the crust is golden. Remove from the oven and
   sprinkle with cheese. Slice and serve.

✳ ✳ ✳the feast day of st. joseph ✳ ✳ ✳

Many visitors are surprised by the real New Orleans accent, which sounds more like Joe Pesci than Blanche Dubois. That's because this old French colony was flooded during the nineteenth century by a new wave of settlers from the same Sicilian villages that helped to populate Brooklyn. Everyone knows about our Gallic roots, but "the Paris of the Americas" is also home to a huge community of Italian Americans, who have played a major role in creating our distinctive cuisine, jazz, architecture, hand gestures (and strangely un-Southern speech patterns). One of their liveliest contributions to the regional culture has been the annual celebration of the Feast Day of St. Joseph on March 19.

The custom dates back to the Middle Ages, when the people of Sicily petitioned their patron saint to deliver them from a famine. The rains finally fell and crops of fava beans flourished, so they showed their gratitude by building a spectacular food-laden altar in his name.

From the Florida Panhandle to Galveston, but especially in Louisiana, the faithful continue to erect fantastic "St. Joseph altars" in private homes and churches, even some commercial buildings. The multi-tiered extravaganzas are covered with sculpted breads, stuffed artichokes, fruit and vegetables, bottles of wine, decorated cakes, and huge mounds of colorful Sicilian cookies. Donations are collected for the poor, who will also receive much of the food when the altars are "broken" at day's end. Meanwhile, every visitor is handed a dried fava bean for luck. Italian or not, he'll tuck it inside his wallet, a cheerful superstition that protects each of us from going broke during the coming year.

"I've worked on altars ever since I was a young child and I'm sixty now," says Marilyn Macaluso Ortalano of Marrero, Louisiana. "My aunt is in her nineties and she's still helping out. Family and friends, we all get together. We've even got two stoves going in the garage. The women are making sauces and breads and cookies. The men are mixing the dough and manning the ovens. It's nothing for us to go through 250, 300 pounds of flour.

"One year they had me working on five different altars," she says. "It's a tradition that you don't refuse anyone who asks for help. This is meant to be an act of penance, but there's also a feeling of joy and camaraderie. There's always a lot of cutting up. And a lot of jokes you don't expect to hear when you're working for St. Joseph."

✳ ✳ ✳ ✳ ✳ ✳

mush!

Creamy polenta is a stylish partner for Creole stews and ragouts, Italian sausages and peppers, beans, grilled vegetables, or sautéed wild mushrooms. Meanwhile, under the plain old American name of cornmeal mush, it can be a nutritious hot cereal or a Deep South indulgence with fried chicken and cream gravy.

The same corn, in a coarser grind, produces grits. Both grits and polenta may be served hot and soft, or chilled and cut into firm slices for frying or broiling.

Unfortunately, busy modern cooks may have been discouraged by traditional Italian recipes for polenta, which call for slowly scattering cornmeal into boiling water by handfuls (a process that can take upwards of 20 minutes), then stirring constantly for 30 to 45 minutes longer (depending on the source) until the spoon stands upright in the pot. Oh, and I forgot to tell you—the stirring must always be in one direction only. I'm not sure why. Right about now you're probably thinking, "give me a break," so here it is.

BASIC MICROWAVE POLENTA
or grits

SERVES 4 AS A MAIN COURSE, 6–8 AS A SIDE DISH

Coasters know plenty of ways to dress up a bowl of mush, from Cajun Shrimp Stew (page 210) to Ranch-Style Eggs (page 279), and this method gets it on the table with minimal fuss. Optional additions include red pepper flakes, shredded fresh basil leaves, sun-dried tomatoes, roasted red peppers, wild mushrooms, chopped jalapeños, toasted pine nuts, roasted garlic, or fresh corn kernels. For a homestyle Italian touch, pour the hot polenta onto a board or platter at the table, dot with butter, and sprinkle generously with freshly grated Parmesan, then cut into serving wedges with string or dental floss.

4 cups	water
1 cup	yellow cornmeal (preferably coarse and stone-ground) or 1⅓ cups stone-ground grits
1 teaspoon	salt
1–3 tablespoons	unsalted butter
	Black pepper to taste
¼ cup	grated Parmesan, crumbled gorgonzola, or other cheese (optional)

1. Pour the water into an 8-cup measure or deep microwaveable bowl. Slowly pour in the cornmeal or grits while whisking. Stir in the salt.

2. Microwave uncovered on full power for 6 minutes. Whisk, then microwave on full power for another 6 minutes until the liquid is absorbed and the texture is smooth. (Grits may take 2 or 3 minutes longer.)

3. Stir in the butter along with the pepper and cheese (if desired). If not using cheese, you may want to add more salt and butter. Let stand for 3 minutes, then serve.

FRIED OR BAKED POLENTA
or grits

SERVES 4 AS A MAIN COURSE, 6–8 AS A SIDE DISH

That warm and sludgy quality that makes polenta and grits such satisfying
comfort foods also makes them stiffen into a cakelike substance as they cool—
all the better for cutting into slices.

Butter a small loaf pan (7 by 4 inches), then pour in hot polenta or grits (see preceding recipe) and bang sharply on the counter to pack down. Cover the pan and refrigerate it for at least an hour, until firm. (You may prepare the recipe up to this point one or two days in advance, or you could use leftover polenta or grits, cut into odd shapes.) Cut into ½-inch slices and let dry on a rack for about 20 minutes.

To fry polenta or grits: Dust with flour (if desired) and sauté lightly in clarified butter or olive oil until golden and crisp, about 4 minutes per side.

For Southern-fried grits: Dip slices in beaten egg and sauté in butter or bacon drippings until golden and crisp, 3 to 4 minutes per side.

To broil polenta or grits: Brush with olive oil or clarified butter and brown for 2 to 3 minutes on each side.

For polenta au gratin: Arrange slices, slightly overlapping, in a buttered baking dish or pizza pan. Sprinkle with grated Parmesan cheese and bake at 400°F for 20 to 25 minutes, or until lightly browned.

SWEET POTATO POLENTA
with salsa
SERVES 8–10

*I got this recipe a few years ago from the Texas-based natural foods chain Whole
Foods Market for a newspaper article on Thanksgiving for vegetarians, but it would make
a fine main course or side dish at any time of year. You could also cut the firm polenta
into small triangles for hors d'oeuvre. Serve with one of the salsas in the book
(pages 85–87 and 90–91) or your favorite.*

5½ cups	vegetable stock
1	small chipotle pepper, stemmed, seeded, and chopped
1 teaspoon	salt
2½ pounds	sweet potatoes, peeled and cut into 1-inch pieces
¾ cup	finely chopped yellow onion
1½ teaspoons	minced fresh garlic
½ teaspoon	fresh rosemary, minced
1 tablespoon	olive oil
1¾ cups	stone-ground yellow cornmeal
6 tablespoons	honey
2 cups	corn kernels (fresh or frozen)
	Salt and pepper to taste

1. Bring the stock, chipotle, and salt to a boil in a pot over high heat. Add the sweet potatoes; simmer until tender. Strain, reserving the broth, and purée with 2 cups of the liquid.

2. Cook the onion, garlic, and rosemary in the olive oil in a saucepan over medium-high heat for 2 minutes. Add the remaining cooking liquid and the sweet potato purée. Bring to a boil and whisk in the cornmeal in a steady stream. Reduce the heat slightly and cook until the polenta pulls away from the sides of the pan, stirring constantly, about 20 minutes.

3. Remove from the heat. Stir in the honey and corn; season with salt and pepper. Pour into a lightly oiled 13-by-9-inch pan. Cover with plastic and refrigerate for at least 1 hour (or up to 1 day) until firm.

4. Heat oven to 350° F. Cut firm polenta into squares and place on a lightly greased baking sheet. Bake for 15 minutes. Serve with salsa.

✷ ✷ ✷ the old island ways ✷ ✷ ✷

I encountered lots of people on my long drives to research this book, but Anne O'Steen best exemplified the Third Coast spirit. I met her on the remote island of Cedar Key, in the Big Bend area just below Florida's Panhandle. The widow of a professional fisherman, she continues to harvest from her own clam lease, and swears by the grits she gets from her brother, who grows and grinds the corn. Meanwhile, she delivers the daily mail and operates a small waterfront restaurant, Anne's Other Place.

"I wanted to call it 'Shut Up and Eat It,' but my daughter wouldn't let me," she explained.

She treated me to a vivid example of the old island ways, recalling the day that a long-time adversary rushed over to fetch her when a family member was injured in a car accident. After years on nonspeaking terms, this fellow islander took O'Steen's place at the stove and insisted she go straight to the hospital, promising to mind the restaurant until closing time.

"She stayed in here the rest of the afternoon, then all the way through dinner," O'Steen marveled, "cooking, washing dishes, cleaning the kitchen. . . . And the next day she was right back to normal, not speaking to me again."

✷   ✷   ✷   ✷   ✷   ✷

NASSAU GRITS

SERVES 6

A specialty of the Florida Panhandle, particularly around Pensacola, this spicy brunch or side dish is seasoned Bahamian style (with tomatoes, onion, and garlic), hence the name. Some cooks prepare the sauce and grits separately, then stir them together. Others use shrimp or firm-fleshed fish instead of ham. (If so, add them during the final few minutes of cooking.) The bacon seems to be a constant, though you could sauté the seasonings in olive oil and stir up a vegetarian version.

4	strips bacon
½ pound	ham, finely cubed
1	yellow onion, chopped
1	green bell pepper, chopped
1–2	garlic cloves, chopped
1	(14-ounce) can chopped tomatoes, with juice
1 cup	uncooked quick grits
3½ cups	water
	Salt and freshly ground black pepper

1. Fry the bacon in a large heavy sauce pot until crisp; drain on paper towels, then crumble and set aside. Drain off all but 2 tablespoons of the bacon fat. Add the ham, onion, and bell pepper; cook over medium heat until the vegetables are soft and browned. Stir in the garlic and tomatoes; reduce heat to low; cover the pot and simmer for 30 minutes, stirring occasionally and mashing the tomatoes with a spoon.

2. Add the uncooked grits and water. Bring to a boil, then reduce the heat to low and cover the pot. Simmer very slowly, stirring occasionally, until nearly all of the liquid is absorbed and the grits are soft and creamy, 15 to 20 minutes. Season to taste with salt and pepper. Serve hot, topped with the crumbled bacon.

✶easy homemade cheeses✶

Handcrafting cheeses is an art, but these elementary projects require no talent or experience. Just follow the directions to create traditional dairy products that are part of our cuisine and available in our shops, but are also simple to make in case you can't find them in your neighborhood.

You'll need very little in the way of special equipment. Cheesecloth is available at natural foods stores and some supermarkets, as well as in fabric departments and specialty cooking shops. I had fine results using a standard candy/deep-fry thermometer to measure the temperature of the cream or milk, but you could mail-order dairy thermometers through the source for cheesemaking supplies listed on page 385.

CREMA

Mexicans call it Crema. The French say crème fraîche. Either way, the commercial version (when you can find it) might trigger a case of sticker shock. It's strange that something so easy to make at home should be so expensive. Lighter and tangier than whipped cream as a dessert topping, it is also great as a substitute for heavy or sour cream in cooked sauces because it won't curdle when heated.

1 cup	heavy cream, preferably not ultra-pasteurized
2 tablespoons	cultured buttermilk, or plain yogurt with active cultures

Warm the cream to 95°F in a nonreactive saucepan, then stir in the buttermilk or yogurt. Pour into a clean glass jar and cover with a double thickness of cheesecloth. Allow to stand undisturbed until thickened, 16 to 20 hours. Refrigerate for at least 1 hour before serving. (Crema will keep in the refrigerator for up to 10 days.)

QUESO BLANCO

MAKES 1½ POUNDS

Raw or unpasteurized milk, available at some health food stores, will produce a firmer queso blanco, according to Bob Carroll, editor of Cheesemaker's Journal. Because this traditional Mexican cheese will not melt, it can even be stir-fried with vegetables. It also holds its shape and texture when crumbled over hot soups and sauces.

1 gallon	milk (preferably raw)
¼ cup	distilled white vinegar

Warm the milk in a stainless-steel pot over medium heat until it reaches 175°F. Remove from the heat and slowly add the vinegar, stirring gently. A curd with a greenish yellow whey should quickly form. Drain the curd into a cheesecloth-lined colander. Tie the four corners of the cheesecloth together and hang the curd from the handle of a wooden spoon placed across a bowl. Set aside to drain for 1 hour. Refrigerate for up to 1 week.

CREOLE CREAM CHEESE

MAKES ABOUT 1½ POUNDS

Before they were swallowed up by national corporations, many of the old
Louisiana dairies used to sell this regional delicacy, as well as the much-beloved ice
cream known as Frozen Creole Cream Cheese (page 327). Now very few commercial
sources remain, but local cooks have always produced their own versions of this simple
luxury, which is easy to make and hard to resist. Traditionally eaten with sugar for
breakfast, it's like cottage cheese, but with a single round curd. It was originally
packaged in pint containers with the cakelike curd floating in heavy cream, perhaps
one reason for its near extinction in the age of nonfat yogurt.

The recipe is adapted from a version written by the late Myriam Guidroz, a
cookbook author and food columnist, and my predecessor at the Times-Picayune. As for
special equipment, you'll need to punch holes in the bottom and sides of plastic margarine
tubs (or similar containers) for the liquid to drain out. A cœur à la crème mold should work
as well, if you want to get fancy about it. The liquid rennet (sometimes labeled as rennin)
is an organic enzyme that curdles milk for cheese. It is available at many natural foods
stores, also from the source for cheesemaking supplies listed on page 385.

1 gallon	skim milk (may be made with reconstituted dry skim milk powder)
½ cup	cultured buttermilk
½ teaspoon	liquid rennet
	Half-and-half or heavy cream to serve
	Sugar to serve

1. Place the milk in a large container and bring it to room temperature, no cooler than 70° F and no warmer than 80° F. Add the buttermilk; stir well. Pour in rennet and stir vigorously for 1 minute. Cover the container and let it stand at room temperature for 12 to 15 hours. (Do not stir again or you will disturb the formation of the cheese.) The rennet will convert the milk solids to a "caked" cheese. The longer it stands, the firmer the cheese will be.

2. Meanwhile, punch holes in the bottom and sides of two 16-ounce plastic margarine tubs (or similar containers) to allow any residual liquid to drain out. After the cheese has set, ladle it into the perforated tubs to drain. Place these molds on a rack in a large roasting pan and refrigerate for at least 4 to 6 hours, until curds are completely solid and no more water drips out. Transfer to clean containers and store in the refrigerator for up to 1 month.

3. To serve, spoon about ¼ cup of cheese into a small bowl and cover with light or heavy cream. Sprinkle with sugar.

✳ ✳ ✳ say queso! ✳ ✳ ✳

Tex-Mex and Taco Bell aside, Mexican cuisine is generally rather sparing in its use of cheese. True regional varieties are much milder and lower in fat than the shredded Cheddar that blankets tacos and enchiladas north of the border. The most common Mexican cheeses are now available in U.S. supermarkets, especially those in urban areas. Otherwise, you should find a good selection at any Latin grocery.

✳ *Crema* ✳ The Mexican version of crème fraîche is a delicate substitute for sour cream, also a cool and tangy drizzle for tropical fruit salads. It is particularly useful for enriching hot sauces or soups, as it will not curdle when heated. Crema is easy (and economical) to make at home, following the simple directions on page 267.

✳ *Queso fresco* ✳ A cross between ricotta and soft farmer cheese, the rustic and smooth-flavored "fresh cheese" is crumbled atop everything from refried beans to desserts. Feta makes a good substitute, especially if you soak it in water for an hour or so to tame the salty bite.

✳ *Queso blanco* ✳ You'll find directions on page 267 for making this simple but intriguing "white cheese." Similar to queso fresco, it has an almost rubbery texture, which is not unpleasant, plus an unusual quirk. It won't melt, so you can use it in stir-fries and sautés.

✳ *Queso añejo* ✳ Similar in taste and texture to Parmesan, this "aged cheese" is slightly softer, so you can crumble it with your hands. Great with wine and fresh fruit, try it when you want a more pronounced flavor.

✳ *Queso asadero* ✳ Like the name says, this "grilling cheese" melts luxuriously into quesadillas or enchiladas without dissolving into goo. It's also used in the northern border states to make *queso fundido* (that's fondue to you).

✳ *Queso Chihuahua* ✳ It's named for the state where it is produced. The mild Cheddar was introduced to the region by German Mennonites.

✳ ✳ ✳ ✳ ✳ ✳

breakfast
and brunch

HOT HOT HOTCAKES

Fresh Corn and Sage Griddle Cakes * 273

Yuca Pancakes * 275

Pumpkin-Chipotle Waffles * 276

Creole Rice Fritters (*Calas*) * 277

* ✳ *

MORNING LUXURIES

Ranch-Style Eggs (*Huevos Rancheros*) * 279

Creole Grillades and Grits * 281

Cedar Key Shrimp and Grits * 282

hot hot hotcakes

These lively cakes will wake you right up on a Saturday morning, especially when they're topped with pepper jelly or with sour cream and salsa. Even on the darkest winter night, you'll be warmed by the sunny Gulf flavors of corn, sage, pumpkin, ground chiles, and oranges.

FRESH CORN
and sage griddle cakes
SERVES 4

*A big hit with my tasters, soft little griddle cakes get a crisp edge from cornmeal
and a pleasant crunch from crumbled bacon and fresh corn kernels. They're also a treat
at dinnertime, an unexpected stand-in for rice or potatoes, a savory bed for roasted
duck or grilled shrimp. If you like, skip the scallions and spices to make sweet
flapjacks drizzled with maple syrup or tupelo honey.*

¾ cup	yellow cornmeal
¾ cup	all-purpose flour
1 teaspoon	baking powder
¼ teaspoon	baking soda
½ teaspoon	salt
2	large eggs, beaten
1½ cups	buttermilk
¼ cup	unsalted butter, melted
2 cups	fresh corn kernels
5	slices bacon, cooked very crisp and crumbled
2 tablespoons	minced fresh sage
2 tablespoons	minced scallion
	Freshly ground black pepper
	Clarified butter, bacon fat, or vegetable oil for frying

1. Whisk together the cornmeal, flour, baking powder, baking soda, and salt in a mixing bowl
until blended; make a well in the center. Beat the eggs with the buttermilk and butter until
smooth; pour all at once into the well, stirring just until incorporated (a few lumps are okay).
Add the corn kernels, crumbled bacon, sage, scallion, and three or four grinds of black pepper.

2. Heat a griddle or large cast-iron skillet over medium heat (350° F for an electric griddle) and
lightly grease it with clarified butter, rendered bacon fat, or vegetable oil. Spoon about ¼ cup
of batter onto the griddle for each pancake, spacing well apart and spreading corn kernels
evenly in a single layer. Turn when the edges look dry and crisp; then cook for about 30 seconds on the other side.

* * * sweet as tupelo honey * * *

Ben Lanier may have spent his life in the small town of Wewahitchka, Florida, but the world has come to him. Along with his father and grandfather, he has been the subject of dozens of magazine and newspaper features. The late Shah of Iran had a standing order for L.L. Lanier and Sons Tupelo Honey (Sources, page 385), which has also found its way into the kitchens of the Bush family, Robert Redford, and other notables. Hollywood came knocking (literally) when director Victor Nunez drove out to the house in search of someone to teach Peter Fonda how to handle bees for his role in *Ulee's Gold*. Later the cast and crew returned to shoot the film on location in Lanier's stomping grounds.

Still, he goes about his work, tending some 900 hives in the Apalachicola River swamps, where the family of founder Lavernor Laveon Lanier has harvested pure tupelo honey for three generations. In fact, they brought in their hundredth annual crop in 1998.

The process begins with nectar from the spring blossoms of the tupelo gum trees that flourish in northwest Florida, the only place that tupelo honey is produced commercially. It is prized for its distinctly delicate flavor, but also for a unique property. It will never granulate because of an exceptionally high ratio of levelose (44.03 percent) to dextrose (29.98 percent), prompting some physicians to okay moderate consumption for their diabetic patients, Lanier claims.

Pure tupelo honey is relatively expensive because it requires more labor and equipment than other varieties. In order to get a fine, unmixed product, the colonies must be stripped of all stores just as the white tupelo bloom begins. During April and May, the bees are moved to special elevated platforms at the river's edge, so they can fan out through the blossoming swamps. They must have clean combs in which to place the new honey; then the crop must be removed before it can be contaminated from lesser honey sources. The timing is critical, requiring years of specialized beekeeping experience, but the end result is a rare treat indeed.

* * * * * *

YUCA PANCAKES

*Bland and slightly sweet yuca (a.k.a. cassava or manioc) is a starchy potato-like
tuber that is a staple in Cuba and along the Mexican coast. It's available in many
U.S. supermarkets and Latin groceries. The safest way to attack the gnarly brown
root is to cut it in half crosswise, then stand it upright on its level cut surface,
slicing downward with a sharp knife to peel the skin away.*
*Crisper than hash browns, these golden cakes are great topped with Papaya Salsa
(page 56). Ladle the batter out with a teaspoon (instead of a tablespoon) for crunchy
little mini-cakes that make good finger food on their own, or an offbeat
bed for more elaborate hors d'oeuvre.*

2	eggs
2 cups	peeled and grated yuca (use the large holes of a box grater)
¼ cup	thinly sliced scallions
1	small garlic clove, minced
1 tablespoon	seeded and finely minced pickled jalapeño
	Salt and white pepper to taste
	Peanut or canola oil for frying

1. Beat the eggs in a mixing bowl until smooth; stir in the yuca, scallions, garlic, and jalapeño, plus salt and white pepper to taste.

2. Warm 2 tablespoons of oil in a nonstick skillet over medium-high heat. Working in batches, without crowding, drop yuca batter into the hot oil by rounded tablespoons, then immediately use the back of the spoon to gently flatten and spread the mixture into thin patties about 3 inches in diameter. Cook until the edges are well browned, then flip and brown the other side. Drain well on paper towels. Before spooning out each subsequent batch, add more oil to the skillet (if necessary), and stir the batter well.

PUMPKIN-CHIPOTLE WAFFLES

SERVES 5

*Butter-toasted pecans and a bit of cornmeal add crisp texture to luxurious sour
cream waffles warmed by the ancient coastal flavors of pumpkin, cinnamon, and smoky
chipotle chiles. Serve them sweet and simple, with a drizzle of maple syrup or honey.
Even though most waffle irons will accommodate about 1 cup of batter, I prefer to
use ½ cup, so there's plenty of room for a full rise. The lighter texture and craggy uneven
edges are more appealing, plus the smaller size is plenty when waffles are as rich as this.*

4 tablespoons	unsalted butter
⅓ cup	finely chopped pecans
¾ cup	all-purpose flour
2 tablespoons	yellow cornmeal
1½ teaspoons	baking powder
¼ teaspoon	baking soda
¼ teaspoon	salt
¾ teaspoon	chipotle powder
½ teaspoon	ground cinnamon
2	eggs
½ cup	unsweetened solid-pack pumpkin (not pie filling)
½ cup	sour cream
½ cup	milk
	Grated zest of 1 orange
3 tablespoons	brown sugar

1. Warm the butter in a small skillet over medium heat; cook the pecans just until lightly browned. Set aside to cool slightly. Sift the flour, cornmeal, baking powder, soda, salt, chipotle powder, and cinnamon into a mixing bowl and make a well in the center. Whisk the eggs in another bowl until lightly beaten, then stir in the pumpkin, sour cream, milk, orange zest, and brown sugar until smooth. Stir in the butter and pecans. Pour the pumpkin mixture into the well in the dry ingredients and stir just until blended (a few lumps are okay).

2. Spoon about ½ cup of the batter onto a preheated waffle iron for each waffle. Close the lid and bake until crisp.

CREOLE RICE FRITTERS
* calas *

*Well into the 1940s, vendors still roamed the streets of the French Quarter, calling out
"Calas! Hot and sweet!" Though not so common today, the Creole rice fritters were once a
morning tradition in South Louisiana, where they were dusted with confectioners' sugar
and served with a drizzle of cane syrup (Sources, page 384). They're still a fine treat for
breakfast or brunch because you can mix the yeast sponge before you go to bed and it will
rise overnight for the lightest puffs. Don't forget to brew a pot of chicory coffee.*

1½ cups	hot steamed white rice, cooked very soft
1½ teaspoons	active dry yeast
½ cup	warm water
1¼ cups	sifted flour
¼ cup	granulated sugar
½ teaspoon	salt
¼ teaspoon	ground cinnamon
¼ teaspoon	grated nutmeg
3	eggs, at room temperature, beaten
	Canola oil for deep frying
	Confectioners' sugar
	Cane syrup (optional)

1. Place the rice in a mixing bowl and mash it to a coarse paste with a fork; cool to lukewarm. Sprinkle the yeast over the warm water and let sit for 5 minutes, then pour it into the lukewarm rice and stir to blend well. Cover the bowl with plastic wrap and leave it in a warm spot for several hours or overnight.

2. Sift the flour, granulated sugar, salt, cinnamon, and nutmeg onto a sheet of waxed paper; add the dry ingredients to the rice sponge, along with the beaten eggs, and stir lightly just until smooth. Cover and let stand in a warm place for 30 minutes.

3. Pour the oil to a depth of 3 inches in a deep iron skillet, or fill an electric deep fryer according to manufacturer's directions; heat to 350° F. (Use a thermometer to maintain the correct temperature.) Drop the dough by tablespoons into the hot oil and fry until golden brown, about 3 minutes. The calas should turn over by themselves as they cook, but it's okay to give them a nudge. Drain on paper towels, dust with confectioners' sugar, and serve hot with cane syrup.

morning luxuries

We're talking about the luxury of time because these indulgences are too complicated for a busy Monday morning, but great for a leisurely weekend brunch. That's a modern name for a Third Coast tradition that was popular long before it was packaged by fern bars in the 1970s. Though the practice is not so common nowadays, some Mexicans still supplement their early coffee and bread with a later meal of tortas or tacos for brunch, which they call *almuerzo*. Generations of Louisiana Creoles also clung to that old European custom, starting off with café au lait and rolls, then dining again at mid-morning. Many were Catholics, who abstained from food or drink before Sunday Mass, enjoying an elaborate breakfast afterward. Meanwhile, ranchers and farmers all along the coast still attend to chores at dawn, then sit down later for a hearty meal, maybe even the *Huevos Rancheros* that follow.

RANCH-STYLE EGGS
✷ huevos rancheros ✷

SERVES 4

Mexican "ranch-style eggs" are served sunny-side up, either on or under an earthy red chile sauce. They may be additionally garnished with shredded cheese, sliced jalapeños, or chopped cilantro. For even more color, finish each plate with black beans, yellow grits, and avocado slices.

The fiery huevos were a mainstay for Joan Crawford, according to biographer Bob Thomas. The actress once proclaimed, as she offered brunch to a visiting reporter from Ladies' Home Journal, "Only a couple of dames like us, who were born in Texas, could eat this food for breakfast and not die."

2 tablespoons	olive oil
1 cup	chopped onion
1	garlic clove, minced
3 cups	peeled, seeded, and chopped ripe tomatoes; or 2 (14-ounce) cans diced tomatoes, drained
4 teaspoons	chipotle paste (see page 37), or to taste
	Salt
8	eggs
	Canola or olive oil for frying eggs
	Crumbled queso fresco or grated cheese, sliced jalapeños, and/or chopped cilantro (optional)

1. Warm the olive oil in a nonreactive skillet over medium heat and cook the onion until very lightly browned, 5 to 7 minutes, then add the garlic and cook for a minute or two longer until garlic is soft, but not brown. Stir in the tomatoes and chipotle paste. Cook over medium-low heat until the flavors blend and the sauce thickens to the consistency of chunky ketchup, about 15 minutes. Add salt to taste. Keep it warm while frying the eggs.

2. For each serving, spoon about ½ cup of the sauce on each warmed serving plate and top it with two fried eggs. Garnish with crumbled or grated cheese, sliced jalapeños, and/or chopped cilantro, if desired.

Plan ahead: Prepare through step 1 and refrigerate the sauce for up to 3 days. Prepare and refrigerate garnishes the night before.

* * * unscrambling * * *
mexican eggs

After several days spent navigating the trendiest bistros on Galveston Island, we found our favorite meal at an old neighborhood restaurant known as Apache Mexican Food. For more than forty years, Ildefonso and Frances Ochoa have operated the little *tortillería*, where they still produce their own tortillas and housemade chorizo sausage for simply wonderful breakfasts.

For the weary traveler or exhausted cook, what could be more soothing than a warm plate of scrambled eggs? It makes a cozy brunch, of course, but also an undemanding supper or midnight snack. Follow these directions to start your morning like they do in Mexico and Texas.

* *Migas:* This is one of those dishes that is definitely more than the sum of its parts, comfort food for the ages. Sauté chopped yellow onion in olive oil, butter, or bacon drippings. When the onion is tender and golden, add corn tortillas that have been cut into thin strips (one tortilla for every egg). When the tortillas are soft and lightly browned, stir in the beaten eggs. If you like, top the hot scramble with a bit of crumbled queso fresco.

* *Machacado con huevos:* Unlike the chemically processed and brightly colored "chipped beef" in jars at the supermarket, Mexican-style *machacado* is flavorful air-dried beef, about the color and texture of pipe tobacco. (Also known as *carne seca*, or "dried meat," it's available in 1-ounce packets at Latin groceries, or from the Sources, page 385.) When you sauté the dry shreds in butter or oil—with or without chopped onion—they make a crisp seasoning for scrambled eggs. A final sprinkle of shredded Cheddar or crumbled queso fresco is optional. The resulting *machacado con huevos* (often billed simply as *machacado*) is a hearty meal. It is usually served with beans, warm flour tortillas, and slices of avocado and tomato.

* Breakfast tacos: Eggs scrambled with mild green chiles (roasted, peeled, and chopped) are also regionally correct, especially stuffed into warm flour tortillas. Set out fresh tomatoes, chunked avocado, cilantro sprigs, salsa, crumbled queso fresco, cooked chorizo, or other garnishes for guests who like to roll their own.

* * * * * *

CREOLE GRILLADES and GRITS

SERVES 6

Thin scallops of pork, beef, or veal are simmered in a rich tomato gravy and
served for brunch throughout French Louisiana, where the old Creole/Cajun standard
is known as grillades (pronounced GREE-yods) and grits.

6	boneless center-cut pork chops, about 3 ounces each, trimmed of fat and pounded thin
	Salt and black pepper
3 tablespoons	unsalted butter
3 tablespoons	olive oil
3 tablespoons	all-purpose flour
1	medium onion, thinly sliced
1	green bell pepper, seeded and finely chopped
½ teaspoon	dried thyme
1	bay leaf
2	garlic cloves, minced
1	(14½-ounce) can diced tomatoes, with juice
1 cup	chicken stock or broth
2 tablespoons	chopped fresh flat-leaf parsley
4 cups	cooked grits

1. Season the pork with salt and pepper. Warm the butter and olive oil in a large nonreactive skillet over medium-high heat; brown the pork lightly on both sides; remove to a plate.

2. Add the flour to the hot pan, whisking constantly to make a medium-brown roux. Add the onion, bell pepper, thyme, and bay leaf; reduce the heat to medium and continue cooking, stirring constantly, until the onion is soft and lightly browned, 4 to 5 minutes. Add the garlic and stir for a minute longer. Add the tomatoes and the stock or broth; stir until sauce is smooth. (Don't be concerned if there are small bits of undissolved roux; they'll disintegrate as the sauce simmers.) Cover the pan, reduce the heat to low, and simmer for 20 minutes, stirring occasionally.

3. Return the browned pork to the pan, spooning the sauce over the pieces to cover them completely; simmer for 10 minutes. Sprinkle with the parsley and serve immediately with hot grits.

CEDAR KEY SHRIMP
and grits

SERVES 8 AS A MAIN COURSE, 16 AS A SIDE DISH

*Far from the more famous Florida Keys, the secluded community of Cedar Key is
a peaceful time warp in the "Big Bend" area, where the Gulf Coast veers south from
the Panhandle. The Island Hotel, established in 1859, is still a prime destination for fine
dining. This is one of the house specialties, on the menu for both breakfast and dinner.
The oven-crisped slices of creamy cheese grits are studded with shrimp, drizzled with a
slightly smoky cream sauce. Since most of the elements are best prepared in advance, it's a
practical (but ultra-rich) centerpiece for a weekend brunch.*

SHRIMP GRITS

½ pound	medium shrimp, shelled and deveined
2 cups	stone-ground white grits (not quick-cooking)
4 cups	chicken broth
1 cup	heavy cream
4	scallions, cut into ¼-inch slices
½ cup	(2 ounces) grated sharp Cheddar cheese
	Salt and pepper

BACON GRAVY

½ pound	sliced bacon, chopped
1	large onion, chopped
2 cups	heavy cream
2 cups	whole milk
2 teaspoons	Creole seasoning mix or Paul Prudhomme's Seafood Magic spice mix
1	chicken bouillon cube
3 tablespoons	all-purpose flour

TO COMPLETE DISH

1 tablespoon	vegetable oil
1 tablespoon	unsalted butter

1. For the grits: Coarsely chop the shrimp and chill. Wash the grits in cold water in a large bowl, letting the grits settle to the bottom of the bowl and carefully draining off as much water as possible.

2. Bring the broth and cream to a boil in a heavy 4-quart saucepan over high heat. Whisk the drained grits into the boiling broth mixture and return to a boil, whisking. Reduce the heat to low and continue cooking, uncovered, for 30 minutes, stirring frequently with a wooden spoon. (Mixture will be thick enough to hold spoon upright.) Stir in the shrimp, sliced scallions, and Cheddar; stir until the shrimp are cooked through, 8 to 10 minutes. Season with salt and pepper.

3. Oil a 9-by-5-inch loaf pan and spoon the grits into the pan, spreading evenly. Cool the grits in the pan on a rack, then chill uncovered in the refrigerator until firm, for at least 4 hours and up to 2 days.

4. For the gravy: Sauté the bacon and onion over moderately high heat in a 4-quart heavy saucepan or Dutch oven, stirring until the bacon is crisp and the onion is golden, about 10 minutes. Do not drain the fat.

5. Meanwhile, heat the cream, milk, spice mix, and bouillon cube in a saucepan to a bare simmer, stirring occasionally until the cube is dissolved.

6. Add the flour to the bacon and onion and cook over moderately low heat, stirring, for 1 minute. Whisk in the hot cream mixture and simmer, whisking until thickened, about 5 minutes. (The gravy will keep, covered and chilled, for up to 2 days.)

7. To complete the dish: Run a thin knife around the edges of the loaf pan and invert the solidified grits onto a cutting board. Cut crosswise into 16 half-inch slices. Heat the broiler and arrange an inverted large baking pan on the broiler rack so that the pan with the grits will be 1 to 2 inches from the heat.

8. Place ½ tablespoon of oil and ½ tablespoon of butter in a large shallow baking pan; heat under broiler just until butter melts, about 30 seconds. With a pastry brush, spread the oil and butter evenly over the pan bottom and arrange eight slices of grits on the pan. Broil until browned, 3 to 4 minutes, then turn and brown the other side, 3 to 4 minutes more. Broil the remaining slices in the same manner using the rest of the oil and butter. Serve with hot gravy.

part 5

SUGARCANE and SPICE

Indulge your sweet tooth at the very source. Sugarcane farms still thrive in the region that also gave the world a taste for chocolate, vanilla, molasses, sweet potatoes, pecans, peanuts, and tiny key limes. French and Spanish colonists introduced almonds, citrus, candies, and pastries to the Gulf Coast. Germans planted coffee in the Mexican coastal highlands of Chiapas, Tabasco, and Veracruz. Colorful Sicilian cookies and gelati were an immediate hit, especially in Louisiana. And bananas made their North American debut in 1874, when longshoremen unloaded 250 bunches from Colón at the Port of New Orleans.

cakes, pies, and flans

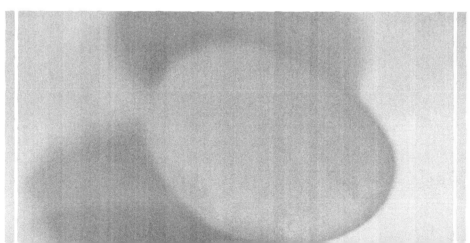

SCREEN-PORCH SPECIALS

Key Lime Pound Cake * 289

Almond Strawberry Cake * 290

Hummingbird Cake * 292

Fresh Orange Cake * 294

* ❋ *

SIMPLE PLEASURES

Café au Lait Blondies * 297

Rum Pecan Cake * 298

Cajun Cane Syrup Cake (*Gâteau de Sirop*) * 300

* ❋ *

SWEETER THAN YAMS

Sweet Potato Pie * 303

Apple and Sweet Potato Turnovers

(*Empanadas de Manzana y Camote*) * 304

Sweet Potato Muffins * 305

Sweet Potato Rum Bars with Browned Butter Frosting * 306

* ❋ *

ICEBOX PIES

Mayan Dude Ranch Margarita Pie * 309

Black-and-White Chocolate Banana Cream Pie * 310

Mango Chiffon Pie * 312

Key Lime Pie * 313

* ❋ *

NEW WORLD FLANS

Mocha Flan * 315

Pumpkin Flan * 316

Caramelized Orange Flan * 317

✳screen-porch specials✳

Company coming? Want a dessert that'll really stick to their ribs (and other regions a lady would never mention)? Then tackle one of these towering extravaganzas that our mothers and grandmothers baked before Betty Crocker in a box, before Sugar Busters, before well-meaning nutritionists tried to convince us that puréed prunes could ever replace butter. That is to say, these old cakes are a lot of trouble and achingly sweet, loaded with bad cholesterol and trans-fats. Like me! Now where's my big knife?

KEY LIME POUND CAKE

SERVES 16–24

This is your grandmother's pound cake, dense and slightly chewy, with an eggy spring and a melting texture from plenty of butter and sour cream. The tart citrus glaze dissolves into the hot cake, intensifying the flavor all the way through. If you can find key limes, great, but regular (a.k.a. Persian) limes are fine. Just be sure to use fresh-squeezed lime juice, never bottled. Try to wait at least 24 hours before you cut into it for the best taste and smoothest grain. And keep the slices thin, because this is a rich one.

1½ cups	unsalted butter, softened
1	(3-ounce) package cream cheese, softened
2¾ cups	granulated sugar
1 tablespoon	finely grated lime zest
1 teaspoon	pure vanilla extract
6	eggs
3 cups	all-purpose flour
½ teaspoon	salt
¼ teaspoon	baking soda
1 cup	sour cream
1½ cups	confectioners' sugar
½ cup	fresh lime juice

1. Heat the oven to 350° F. Grease and flour a 12-cup tube pan.

2. In the bowl of an electric mixer, beat the butter, cream cheese, and granulated sugar until light and fluffy. Beat in the lime zest and vanilla. Add the eggs, one at a time, beating well after each addition.

3. Sift together the flour, salt, and baking soda; add to the batter gradually, alternating with the sour cream, beating well after each addition. Pour the batter into the tube pan and bake for 55 to 60 minutes, or until toothpick inserted in center comes out clean.

4. Meanwhile, whisk the confectioners' sugar with the lime juice until smooth. As soon as you remove the hot cake from the oven, poke the entire surface with a skewer at one-inch intervals. Spoon half of the glaze over the hot cake. Let the cake stand upright in the pan for 10 minutes; then invert it onto a serving plate. Spoon the remaining glaze over the cake slowly, allowing it to sink in. Cool the cake completely before serving.

ALMOND STRAWBERRY CAKE

SERVES 12–16

A fondness for almond sponge cake traveled to the New World with Portuguese and Spanish colonists. In the Yucatán, torta de cielo (almond "cake of heaven") is still served at wedding celebrations. To many Cubans, it's known by the rather unappetizing name of tocino del cielo, or "bacon of heaven," because of its rich almond flavor and ethereal texture.

Classic recipes are tricky, as they contain little or no flour or leavening. This chiffon version from Softasilk Cake Flour is easy and dependable, if not strictly traditional. In Latin homes it might be served with a simple dusting of confectioners' sugar, maybe a sprinkle of sherry or rum. However, if you split it horizontally, the delicate almond layers make an enlightened substitute for an Old South shortcake.

We have such an abundance of fresh Louisiana strawberries each spring that we can afford to experiment with sorbets and salads, congratulating ourselves over wholesome bowls of sparkling red fruit with just a sprinkle of balsamic vinegar and chopped mint. Of course, a few weeks of this and we're forced to admit that our mothers and grandmothers were right. Such bounty calls for a celebration. This is no time to skimp on the whipped cream.

2 pints	fresh strawberries
1¼ cups	sugar, divided
6	eggs, separated
8 ounces	almond paste
¼ cup	vegetable oil
½ teaspoon	almond extract
⅛ teaspoon	cream of tartar
⅔ cup	cake flour (not self-rising)
1 teaspoon	baking powder
2 cups	heavy cream, well chilled

1. Hull and halve 1 pint of the strawberries; then mix with ½ cup of the sugar; let stand at room temperature for at least an hour.

2. Heat the oven to 325°F. Beat the egg yolks, almond paste, oil, and almond extract in a large bowl on medium speed until well blended. Beat the egg whites and cream of tartar in another large and perfectly clean bowl on high speed until foamy. Beat in ½ cup of the sugar, 1 tablespoon at a time, until stiff peaks form. Stir about one quarter of the egg whites into the yolk batter. Mix the flour and baking powder; stir into the batter. Fold the remaining egg whites into the batter; spread the batter into a greased springform pan, 9 by 3 inches.

3. Bake until the top is brown and the cake springs back when touched lightly in the center, 35 to 40 minutes. Immediately invert onto a wire rack; cool completely. Remove from pan.

4. Beat the chilled cream and remaining ¼ cup sugar in a chilled bowl on high speed until stiff. Split the cake horizontally to make two layers. Spread half of the whipped cream on the bottom layer. Reserve 12 small strawberries from the unsweetened pint. Slice the remaining strawberries; arrange over the whipped cream on the cake. Top with the second cake layer; spread with the remaining whipped cream. Garnish with the reserved strawberries. Serve with the sweetened strawberries.

Plan ahead: Prepare the recipe through step 3 and refrigerate the cake, wrapped airtight, for up to 1 day, or freeze for up to 2 months.

✻ ✻ ✻ and colette claimed ✻ ✻ ✻
they added weight to the breasts

Sugared almonds wrapped in tulle are a common wedding favor, especially among Latino and Greek-American families. It's an old European custom that symbolizes children, happiness, romance, and good fortune.

✻ ✻ ✻ ✻ ✻ ✻

HUMMINGBIRD CAKE

SERVES 12–16

Dolores' Sweet Shop is a cheery meeting spot in the beautiful little port
town of Apalachicola, Florida. Since we were on vacation, my sister and I ordered
cake for breakfast. It was so good, we went back for more at lunch. Later that afternoon,
Dolores passed us on the street and called out, "I just made you another
hummingbird cake for tomorrow."
"This is sad," my sister said. "We've only been in town for one day and they
already know us at the bakery."
Dolores Taranto Roux was born in Apalachicola, the daughter of Sicilian immigrants.
Her mother and grandparents came through Ellis Island in 1904; her father arrived in 1914.
"My family settled here because it reminded them so much of their homeland," Roux
says. "It's very much like Sicily—the same climate, the same plants, everything. My
grandmother made wine and sold it to local restaurants. She had a brick oven in her backyard, where she made bread. She put my mother through college selling that bread."
Dolores's hummingbird cake is not an old Taranto family recipe, but it is one of the most
popular desserts in community cookbooks throughout the South. The name was probably
inspired by the nectar sweetness of the pineapple and bananas.

CAKE

3 cups	sifted all-purpose flour
1 teaspoon	baking soda
1 teaspoon	salt
2 cups	sugar
1 teaspoon	ground cinnamon
3	eggs, beaten
1 cup	vegetable oil
2 teaspoons	vanilla extract
1	(8-ounce) can crushed pineapple, with juice
2 cups	mashed ripe banana
1 cup	chopped pecans

FROSTING

1	(8-ounce) package cream cheese, softened
½ cup	butter, softened
1 pound	confectioners' sugar
1–2 teaspoons	vanilla extract
½ cup	chopped pecans

1. For the cake: Heat the oven to 350° F. Butter and flour three 9-inch round cake pans or coat them with cooking spray.

2. Sift together the flour, baking soda, salt, sugar, and cinnamon. Set aside.

3. Beat the eggs with the vegetable oil and vanilla in a mixing bowl until smooth. Add the egg mixture to the dry ingredients, stirring just until moistened. Fold in the pineapple with juice, mashed banana, and pecans. Divide the batter among the baking pans. Bake for 25 to 30 minutes, or until a toothpick inserted near the center comes out clean. Cool in the pans for 10 minutes; then remove to racks to cool completely.

4. For the frosting: Beat the cream cheese and butter until fluffy; beat in the confectioners' sugar and vanilla until smooth and fluffy. ("Add a few drops of water if it's too stiff," Roux says. "If it's too thin, add a little more sugar.")

5. Spread the frosting between the layers and all around the top and sides of the cake. Sprinkle the chopped pecans on top.

Plan ahead: Refrigerate the completed cake, wrapped airtight, for up to 2 days. Bring to room temperature before serving.

* * * going bananas * * *

The so-called banana trees that shade porches and patios all over the Gulf Coast are not really trees at all. They're the world's largest herbs, growing up to two stories high in a single season.

* * * * * *

FRESH ORANGE CAKE

SERVES 12–16

*Fresh citrus adds plenty of sunny flavor to a buttery sweet-tart cake from the Florida
Gulf Coast. The orange curd makes a rich and tangy filling, but there's plenty of
frosting to go around if you choose to skip that step.*

CAKE

3 cups	sifted cake flour
2 cups	sugar
1 tablespoon	baking powder
½ teaspoon	baking soda
½ teaspoon	salt
1 cup	unsalted butter, softened
1 cup plus ¼ cup	buttermilk
4	eggs
1 tablespoon	finely grated orange zest

ORANGE CURD

4	egg yolks
½ cup	sugar
¼ cup	unsalted butter, softened
¼ cup	strained fresh lemon juice
2 tablespoons	strained fresh orange juice
1 tablespoon	finely grated orange zest

ORANGE FROSTING

1 pound	confectioners' sugar, minus ¼ cup
½ cup	unsalted butter, softened
1 tablespoon	strained fresh orange juice, plus more if needed
1 tablespoon	strained fresh lemon juice
1 tablespoon	finely grated orange zest

1. For the cake: Heat the oven to 350° F. Butter and flour two 9-inch round cake pans. Place the flour, sugar, baking powder, baking soda, and salt in the bowl of an electric mixer; beat on low speed for 30 seconds to blend. Add the butter and 1 cup buttermilk; beat on low speed until incorporated; increase speed to medium and beat for 1½ minutes.

2. Whisk the remaining ¼ cup buttermilk, the eggs, and orange zest in a separate bowl until smooth. Add to the mixing bowl in 3 batches, beating for 20 seconds after each addition and scraping down the sides as needed. Turn the batter into the pans and bake for 30 to 35 minutes, until a toothpick inserted in the center comes out clean. Cool the cake layers in the pans for 10 minutes, then remove them to racks to cool completely.

3. For the orange curd: While the cake is baking, combine all of the ingredients for the orange curd in a small, heavy nonreactive saucepan over medium-low heat. Stir constantly until the curd has thickened to the consistency of cooked pudding, about 10 minutes, being careful not to let it boil or it will curdle. Immediately pour it into a heatproof bowl, place plastic wrap directly over the surface, and refrigerate until it is well chilled and thickened enough to spread between the cake layers, 45 minutes to 1 hour.

4. For the frosting and assembly: Beat all of the frosting ingredients with an electric mixer until smooth and fluffy; add extra orange juice, if needed, to reach a spreadable consistency. Spread the orange curd evenly over the top of the first layer, place the second layer on top, then swirl frosting over the top and sides of the entire cake. Store any leftovers in the refrigerator.

simple pleasures

Ask us to name the fragrances that evoke the Third Coast and most of them will stir our taste buds, as well: roasting coffee, molasses from the sugarcane refineries, rum, citrus, spices, and vanilla. (We'll just forget about eau de Bourbon Street.) These old-fashioned desserts will capture those kitchen memories, a soothing antidote for work-jangled nerves, a homey welcome for visiting friends.

CAFÉ AU LAIT BLONDIES

A soft jolt of coffee energizes chewy chocolate-free brownies. The creamy color and flavor, with just a hint of cinnamon, will remind you of a fragrant cup of café au lait. Like yours stronger? Use espresso powder and scatter the frosting with chocolate-coated coffee beans.

CAKE

1½ cups	firmly packed light brown sugar
½ cup	unsalted butter, softened
2½ teaspoons	instant coffee (or espresso powder), dissolved in 2 teaspoons warm water
1 teaspoon	vanilla extract
2	eggs
1½ cups	all-purpose flour
1 teaspoon	baking powder
½ teaspoon	cinnamon
¼ teaspoon	salt

FROSTING

¾ teaspoon	instant coffee (or espresso powder)
1 tablespoon	cream or milk, plus more if needed
⅓ cup	unsalted butter, softened
2 cups	confectioners' sugar
½ teaspoon	vanilla extract

1. For the cake: Heat the oven to 350° F; grease a 9-by-11-inch baking pan. Cream the brown sugar with the butter in a mixing bowl until light and fluffy. Beat in the dissolved coffee, vanilla, and eggs. Sift or whisk together the dry ingredients, then add to the wet ingredients, beating just until blended. Spread the batter in the pan. Bake for 25 to 30 minutes, or until edges are browned and center is set. Cool completely.

2. For the frosting: Dissolve the instant coffee in 1 tablespoon of cream or milk in a small deep bowl. Add all of the other ingredients and beat until blended, adding up to 1 additional tablespoon of cream or milk, if necessary, to reach spreading consistency. Spread the frosting over the cooled cake layer, then cut into 36 bars.

Plan ahead: The blondies are best the day after baking. Refrigerate uncut bars for up to 1 week, wrapped airtight. Freeze uncut bars for up to 3 months.

RUM PECAN CAKE

SERVES 12–16

*Meltingly tender and slightly spicy, this simple beauty is imbued with the
Gulf Coast flavors of brown sugar, rum, oranges, and chopped toasted pecans. I have
also replaced part of the flour with ground pecans, an idea inspired by the rich almond
taste of the "golden Grand Marnier cake" in Rose Levy Beranbaum's Cake Bible.
Like many fans, I have adopted her method of beating the butter with the sour cream
and all of the dry ingredients (rather than creaming it first with the sugar, then the eggs).
The result is a velvety texture with an extra-fine grain.*

CAKE

2½ cups	sifted cake flour
½ cup	finely ground toasted pecans
¾ cup	granulated sugar
¾ cup	firmly packed light brown sugar
1 tablespoon	grated orange zest
1 teaspoon	baking powder
1 teaspoon	baking soda
½ teaspoon	salt
½ teaspoon	ground cinnamon
¼ teaspoon	ground cloves
1 cup	unsalted butter, softened
⅔ cup	sour cream
3	large eggs
⅓ cup	dark rum
1 cup	finely chopped toasted pecans

GLAZE

¼ cup	unsalted butter
3 tablespoons	orange juice
½ cup	sugar
2 tablespoons	dark rum

1. For the cake: Heat the oven to 350° F. Combine the flour, ground pecans, sugars, zest, baking powder, baking soda, salt, cinnamon, and cloves in the bowl of an electric mixer. Beat for a minute to blend. Add the butter and sour cream; beat for 2 minutes. Add the eggs, one at a time, beating well after each addition. Add the rum, beat for 2 minutes longer. Fold in the chopped pecans.

2. Turn the batter into a greased and floured 10-inch Bundt pan or tube pan; smooth the surface. Bake for 1 hour, or until a toothpick inserted near the center comes out clean.

3. Cool the cake in the pan for 10 minutes, then carefully invert onto a large plate. Prick the surface all over with a bamboo skewer.

4. For the glaze: Melt the butter in a small saucepan; add the orange juice and sugar; boil for 5 minutes, stirring constantly. Remove from the heat; stir in the rum. Brush the glaze evenly over the top and sides of the cake until the glaze is fully absorbed. Cool completely, then store airtight for at least 1 day before serving.

Plan ahead: This cake actually tastes much better the second day, after the flavors have mellowed, and it may be wrapped airtight and stored at room temperature for up to 4 days. It also freezes well.

* * *the all-american nut* * *

Pecan trees are prized throughout the Gulf South, and not just because of the shade. They're a major cash crop in Alabama, Louisiana, Mississippi, and Texas. Sixteenth-century explorers from Spain and France first encountered the native American nut in coastal Mexico, where it grew wild along the riverbanks, a primary food source for indigenous peoples since prehistoric times.

*   *   *   *   *   *

CAJUN CANE SYRUP CAKE
* gâteau de sirop *

SERVES 9

With a darker molasses flavor and a bit less spice than gingerbread, this uncomplicated old cake is still common in Louisiana's country kitchens. Here vegetable oil replaces the more traditional lard. Some cooks add chopped pecans and/or raisins to the batter. Others bake it in a deep iron skillet or muffin tins. This version comes straight from the source, Steen's Pure Cane Syrup.

1½ cups	Steen's Pure Cane Syrup (Sources, page 384)
½ cup	vegetable oil
1	egg, beaten
2½ cups	sifted all-purpose flour
1 teaspoon	ground cinnamon
1 teaspoon	ground ginger
½ teaspoon	ground cloves
½ teaspoon	salt
1½ teaspoons	baking soda
¾ cup	hot water

Heat the oven to 350° F. Grease and flour a 9-inch square pan. Combine the syrup, oil, and beaten egg; stir until blended. Sift the flour with the spices and salt. Dissolve the baking soda in the hot water. Add the flour mixture to the syrup mixture, alternating with the soda water, beginning and ending with the flour mixture. Pour into the pan. Bake for 45 minutes, or until center springs back when pressed lightly with a fingertip. Serve warm or at room temperature.

✳ ✳ ✳ from cane field ✳ ✳ ✳ to sugar bowl

In November on the back roads of the Third Coast, it's common to see tractor-drawn wagons overflowing with sugarcane bound for nearby refineries, or to drive over dried stalks littering the pavement. More than 500,000 acres are planted in Louisiana, which leads the nation in cane cultivation.

At the refineries, the juice is squeezed from the cane and repeatedly boiled down, producing sugar crystals and a syrupy residue known as molasses. Light molasses is the more delicate product from the first boiling. Dark molasses, richer and less sweet, is obtained during the second boiling. Thick and bitter blackstrap molasses comes from the third go-round, and despite claims by health food enthusiasts, is only marginally higher in nutrients (iron, calcium, phosphorus) than the other two. Coasters feed it to their cattle.

The commercial brown sugar sold today, whether light or dark, is actually granulated sugar flavored with molasses. It is meant to replicate the taste and texture of the so-called raw sugar before it is processed to the ultimate state of purity and whiteness. However, authentic raw sugar often contains molds and other contaminants, so the only versions marketed in the United States must be specially treated, an operation that also removes most of the residual minerals. The same is true of turbinado sugar, which is steam-cleaned of any real nutritional superiority to regular white sugar, though it does have a richer cane flavor.

Confectioners' sugar is granulated white sugar milled into a fine powder. It is blended with a bit of cornstarch to prevent lumps, but still needs sifting for most recipes (or to dust over French Market *beignets*).

Steen's Pure Cane Syrup is actually a type of molasses, though it is thinner (to pour more easily) and slightly milder in flavor. One of the last of its breed, it is still produced at a small sugarcane mill in Abbeville, Louisiana, and is a great favorite throughout the state as a topping for biscuits, pancakes, and the Creole rice fritters known as *calas* (page 277). Cane syrup is also an essential ingredient for an old-timey "French bread float." (Cut off the "nose" from a loaf of French bread and dig out the fluff from the center, then spread butter generously around the well and fill it with the syrup.)

✳ ✳ ✳ ✳ ✳ ✳

sweeter than yams

The Gulf South may not have brilliant fall foliage, but we see plenty of seasonal color each autumn, when mountains of deep orange sweet potatoes hit the stands. And that beauty is more than skin deep. The world's most nutritious vegetable is even better for you than spinach or broccoli—just the sort of news that makes me want to cream it with sugar and eggs and whip it into a dessert.

SWEET POTATO PIE

SERVES 8

Quite similar to pumpkin pie (and its Latin version, pastel de calabaza), this Deep South classic combines the same spices with the denser texture of sweet potatoes, especially earthy and countrified when it's made with dark brown sugar and a whole wheat crust. Bake it in a clear glass pan to ensure a flaky golden bottom.

1½ cups	mashed cooked sweet potato
⅔ cup	firmly packed brown sugar
1 cup	light cream or evaporated milk
1 teaspoon	ground cinnamon
½ teaspoon	ground ginger
¼ teaspoon	ground nutmeg
½ teaspoon	salt
½ teaspoon	grated orange zest (optional)
2	eggs, slightly beaten
2 to 3 tablespoons	bourbon whisky
1	9-inch pastry shell, unbaked

Place a cookie sheet on the lowest rack and heat the oven to 425° F. Combine all of the filling ingredients in a food processor or blender and process until smooth. Pour into the pastry shell; place the pie on the heated cookie sheet. Bake for 15 minutes, then lower the heat to 350° F and continue baking until the filling is set in the center, 35 to 40 minutes. Serve warm or at room temperature.

✳ ✳ ✳ baked-in goodness ✳ ✳ ✳

You could start these recipes with canned sweet potatoes, though taste and texture are sure to suffer. Fresh is definitely best. And be sure to bake the potatoes in a conventional oven to concentrate their caramel sweetness, as boiling or microwaving tend to make them starchy and unappealing.

Just place the potatoes, unpeeled and scrubbed, on a cookie sheet or heavy-duty aluminum foil, pierce them several times with a fork, and bake at 400° F for 15 minutes, then reduce the heat to 375° F and continue baking until they are soft, but not mushy, 40 to 60 minutes, depending upon size and shape.

✳ ✳ ✳ ✳ ✳ ✳

APPLE and SWEET POTATO
turnovers
* empanadas de manzana y camote *

MAKES 1 DOZEN

Like Cajun "hand pies," and other old-timey turnovers baked north of the border, Mexican empanadas are stuffed with a wide variety of sweet or savory fillings. Apples and sweet potatoes are among the traditional favorites, so I've combined both for a warm autumn snack that's enhanced by the woodsy flavor of toasted pine nuts.

2 cups	peeled and diced tart apples, such as Granny Smith
1 cup	diced cooked sweet potato
¼ cup	lightly toasted pine nuts
⅓ cup	sugar
1 tablespoon	all-purpose flour
¾ teaspoon	ground cinnamon
¼ teaspoon	grated nutmeg
⅛ teaspoon	salt
1 tablespoon	fresh lemon juice
1	recipe empanada dough (see page 32)
	Confectioners' sugar for dusting

1. Heat the oven to 400° F. Toss the apples, sweet potato, and pine nuts with the combined dry ingredients, then toss lightly with the lemon juice until well coated.

2. Divide the dough into 12 balls and roll each into a 5-inch circle on a floured surface. Scoop about 2 tablespoons of the apple mixture into the center of each round; fold over and seal the edges completely by pressing with a fork. Prick the tops of the empanadas with the tines of the fork to allow steam to escape.

3. Place on a lightly buttered baking sheet and bake for 15 to 20 minutes, until golden brown. Serve warm or at room temperature, dusted with confectioners' sugar.

Plan ahead: Prepare recipe through step 2 and refrigerate the unbaked empanadas for up to 24 hours.

SWEET POTATO MUFFINS

MAKES 1 DOZEN

Rich and spicy, these soft Southern goodies are delicious warm or at room temperature, a
fine treat for dessert, breakfast, or coffee breaks. They also make unusual tea sandwiches,
split and spread with chutney and slices of smoked turkey or ham.

⅓ cup	unsalted butter, at room temperature
½ cup	sugar
2	eggs
1 cup	puréed cooked sweet potato
⅓ cup	fresh orange juice
2 teaspoons	grated orange zest
1¾ cups	all-purpose flour
2 teaspoons	baking powder
½ teaspoon	baking soda
½ teaspoon	salt
½ teaspoon	ground cinnamon
¼ teaspoon	ground cloves

1. Heat the oven to 375°F. Grease a 12-cup muffin tin.

2. Using an electric mixer, cream the butter and sugar until fluffy. Blend in the eggs, sweet potato
   purée, orange juice, and orange zest.

3. In another bowl, whisk together the flour, baking powder, baking soda, salt, cinnamon, and
   cloves. Add to the sweet potato mixture, stirring by hand just until incorporated.

4. Spoon the batter into the greased muffin tin, filling each cup two-thirds full. Bake until lightly
   browned and toothpick inserted in center comes out clean, about 20 minutes. Cool in pan for
   5 minutes; then turn out onto rack to cool completely.

SWEET POTATO RUM BARS
with browned butter frosting

MAKES 48 BARS

Browned butter intensifies the nutty taste of the rum-spiked frosting, a tawny finish for rich golden bars colored by the autumn flavors of the Gulf Coast: sweet potatoes, oranges, and toasted pecans.

BARS

½ cup	golden raisins
¼ cup	good-quality dark rum
1 cup	all-purpose flour
1 cup	stone-ground whole wheat flour
1½ cups	firmly packed brown sugar
1 tablespoon	finely grated fresh orange zest
2 teaspoons	baking powder
1 teaspoon	baking soda
1 teaspoon	ground cinnamon
1 teaspoon	ground nutmeg
½ teaspoon	ground cloves
½ teaspoon	salt
4	eggs
2 cups	puréed baked sweet potato
¾ cup	vegetable oil
¼ cup	fresh orange juice
½ cup	finely chopped toasted pecans
2 heaping tablespoons	minced crystallized ginger

FROSTING

¾ cup	unsalted butter
4 cups	confectioners' sugar
2–4 tablespoons	good-quality dark rum
1 teaspoon	finely grated orange zest
½ cup	chopped, toasted pecans

1. For the bars: Soak the raisins in the rum until soft and plump, at least 30 minutes. Heat the oven to 350° F. Grease and flour a 15-by-10-inch baking pan.

2. Combine all of the ingredients—except the raisins, rum, pecans, and crystallized ginger—in a large bowl. Beat with an electric mixer at low speed until the dry ingredients are moistened, then beat at medium speed for 2 minutes. Fold in the rum-soaked raisins (plus any remaining soaking liquid), pecans, and crystallized ginger. Spread the batter evenly in the pan and bake for 25 to 35 minutes, or until a toothpick inserted in the center comes out clean. Cool completely.

3. For the frosting: Melt the butter in a heavy saucepan over medium heat, stirring constantly, until light brown. Remove from the heat; add the sugar, rum, and orange zest. Beat until smooth and creamy, adding extra rum, if needed, to reach spreading consistency. Spread over the cooled sweet potato layer and sprinkle with chopped toasted pecans. Cut into 48 bars.

Plan ahead: Flavors mellow and the bars taste best the day after baking. Refrigerate the uncut bars for up to 1 week, wrapped airtight. Freeze the uncut bars for up to 3 months.

∗ ∗ ∗ food of the world ∗ ∗ ∗

Here in the Gulf South, we have always made good use of our most popular native vegetable. Botanists believe the sweet potato was domesticated more than 5,000 years ago in Central America and Mexico. Beginning in the sixteenth century, European explorers spread it around the world, a cinch due to an unusually broad adaptability. The plants multiply rapidly from a few roots and have few natural enemies, growing well in poor soils with little fertilizer. In fact, this dependable foodstuff is a staple on the semiarid plains of East Africa, where it is known as *cilera abana*, or "protector of the children."

∗ ∗ ∗ ∗ ∗ ∗

icebox pies

Long after the arrival of electric refrigeration, we still call them icebox pies. A favorite summer dessert in the South for generations, they're ingrained in our collective memory, along with ceiling fans, porch swings, backyard picnics, and church suppers. Down here, homestyle favorites like lemon meringue and coconut cream will never go out of style, but there's always something new under the sun.

MAYAN DUDE RANCH
margarita pie

SERVES 8

*Some time ago I got this recipe from the boss lady at the Mayan Dude Ranch,
who signs her letters, "Friendly like, Judy Hicks." For more than fifty years she and her
husband, Don, have welcomed visitors to their spread in Bandera, Texas, where
they also raised twelve children of their own.*

PRETZEL CRUST

1½ cups	crushed pretzels
¼ cup	packed brown sugar
½ cup	unsalted butter, melted

FILLING

1 envelope	unflavored gelatin
½ cup	fresh lemon juice
5	egg yolks
1 cup	sugar
¼ teaspoon	salt
¼ cup	tequila
¼ cup	Triple Sec
1 teaspoon	grated lemon zest
5	egg whites

1. For the crust: Heat the oven to 400°F. Combine all of the ingredients and press into the bottom and up the sides of an 8- or 9-inch pie pan. Bake for 5 minutes. Cool, then chill.

2. For the filling: Soften the gelatin in the lemon juice. In the top of a double boiler, beat the egg yolks well with ½ cup of the sugar and the salt. Stir in the gelatin mixture. Cook over boiling water, stirring constantly, until the mixture starts to thicken, about 5 minutes. Pour into large bowl. Stir in the liquors and lemon zest. Chill, stirring frequently, until the mixture begins to thicken, about 45 minutes.

BLACK-AND-WHITE CHOCOLATE
banana cream pie

SERVES 6–8

This newfangled comfort food stars that coastal favorite, bananas. However, crumbled dark chocolate wafers replace the traditional graham cracker crust, and white chocolate enriches James Beard's classic vanilla custard filling. Even more white chocolate is shaved into big curls and mounded atop the whipped cream.

Beware of bright white chips and bars, which are typically a blend of shortening, milk solids, sugar, lecithin, and artificial flavorings (translation: unpleasantly sweet and greasy). Names such as "baking chips" or "confectionery bar" or "summer coating" are a dead giveaway that these inferior products can't be labeled as "white chocolate," because they don't contain any cocoa butter. That's what gives the right stuff its soft ivory hue.

CHOCOLATE COOKIE CRUST

1¼ cups	chocolate cookie crumbs
¼ cup	sugar
¼ cup	unsalted butter, melted
2 ounces	good-quality white chocolate, such as Tobler Narcisse, melted

FILLING

⅔ cup	sugar
7 tablespoons	all-purpose flour
¼ teaspoon	salt
2	eggs
2 cups	whole milk
1 cup	light cream or half-and-half
2 ounces	good-quality white chocolate, such as Tobler Narcisse, finely chopped
1 teaspoon	vanilla extract
4	bananas
1 cup	heavy cream, whipped
	Good-quality white chocolate, such as Tobler Narcisse, for garnish

1. For the crust: Heat the oven to 300° F. Mix the crumbs with the sugar and stir in the melted butter until combined. Press the crumbs into the bottom and up the sides of a 9-inch pie pan. Bake for 10 minutes. Cool completely, then brush surface evenly with melted white chocolate. Cool completely before filling.

2. For the filling: Whisk together the sugar, flour, salt, and eggs until smooth. Scald the milk and cream in a medium saucepan; slowly stir the hot milk into the egg mixture, then return the custard to the pan and cook over medium-low heat, stirring constantly, until it thickens and just begins to bubble. Reduce the heat to a simmer and continue stirring for 2 minutes. Add the chopped white chocolate, stirring until the chocolate is completely melted and the custard is smooth, 1 to 2 minutes. Remove from the heat; add the vanilla. Cool to room temperature.

3. Peel 3 of the bananas and slice ½ inch thick. Spread a thin layer of cooled custard in the pie crust. Cover with a layer of sliced bananas. Add another layer of custard, followed by bananas, then a final layer of custard. Chill thoroughly.

4. Just before serving, peel and slice the last banana; arrange the slices atop the chilled pie; top with whipped cream. Using a vegetable peeler, shave wide curls of white chocolate and scatter generously over top of pie.

Plan ahead: Complete the pie through step 3 and refrigerate for up to 24 hours.

MANGO CHIFFON PIE

SERVES 8

Fresh mango purée and Italian meringue give it a silky texture, but this pie is relatively
low in fat. Use a good-quality, mild-tasting yogurt for creamiest results.

GINGERSNAP CRUST

1½ cups	gingersnap cookie crumbs
¼ cup	unsalted butter, melted

FILLING

1 envelope	unflavored gelatin
¼ cup	fresh orange juice, strained
2 tablespoons	fresh lime juice, strained
1½ cups	mango purée, pushed through sieve to remove any tough fibers, if necessary
½ cup	plain yogurt
1¼ cups	sugar
⅓ cup	water
2	egg whites
¼ teaspoon	salt

1. For the crust: Heat the oven to 300°F. Combine the crumbs and melted butter. Press firmly into the bottom and up the sides of an 8- or 9-inch pie pan. Bake for 10 minutes. Cool completely before filling.

2. For the filling: Sprinkle the gelatin over the orange and lime juices in a small saucepan; set aside for 5 minutes, until the gelatin is softened, then stir over medium heat until the gelatin is completely dissolved. Add the mango purée and yogurt; stir until smooth. Pour into a large bowl and chill, stirring occasionally, until mixture is slightly thickened and mounds when dropped from a spoon, 30 to 45 minutes.

3. Bring the sugar and water to a boil in a small saucepan, stirring until the sugar dissolves. Continue boiling until the syrup reaches 238°F on a candy thermometer (soft-ball stage).

4. Meanwhile, beat the egg whites with the salt until stiff peaks form. Slowly pour the hot syrup into the beaten whites, beating until stiff and glossy, about 5 minutes. Gently fold into the mango mixture. Mound into the prepared pie shell and chill until firm.

Plan ahead: Complete and refrigerate pie up to 24 hours in advance.

KEY LIME PIE

SERVES 8

Aficionados insist on the kumquat-size key limes, which are great if you do your grocery shopping in Miami or grow your own. If your market doesn't import the real thing, regular (a.k.a. Persian) limes are fine. Either way, freshly squeezed juice (not bottled) is essential.

CRUST

1½ cups	graham cracker crumbs
2 tablespoons	sugar
¼ cup	unsalted butter, melted

FILLING

4	egg yolks
1 tablespoon	finely grated lime zest
1 can	sweetened condensed milk (not evaporated milk)
½ cup	fresh lime juice (see headnote)
1	9-inch graham cracker crust, preferably home-made, cooled completely
	Whipped cream

1. For the crust: Heat the oven to 300° F. Combine the crumbs, sugar, and melted butter. Press firmly into the bottom and up the sides of an 8- or 9-inch pie pan. Bake for 10 minutes. Cool completely before filling.

2. For the filling: Beat the egg yolks with the lime zest until the mixture is frothy and tinted pale green. (If you prefer the traditional pale yellow color, add the lime zest when you beat in the juice.) Beat in the condensed milk until smooth, then beat in the lime juice. Set aside for 15 minutes to allow the mixture to thicken slightly.

3. Heat the oven to 325° F. Pour the filling into the crust and bake for 15 minutes, until filling is set, but still wobbly. Refrigerate until well chilled, at least 4 hours. Garnish with whipped cream.

new world flans

The most famous Latin American dessert, imported by Spanish settlers, is a soothing end for rich and spicy Third Coast meals. In Cuban or Mexican communities, flans might be flavored with plain vanilla, cinnamon, coconut, grated lemon rind, ground almonds, rum, or brandy. Baked as directed in the recipes that follow, at a medium-low temperature in a simmering *baño de María* (water bath), the custards will be especially smooth and creamy, with little chance of curdling or overcooking.

MOCHA FLAN

Cocoa and coffee—two dark beauties from the Mexican coastal highlands—are the perfect partners for a cinnamon-scented custard. As it chills, the bittersweet chocolate adds extra body to this flan, creating a rich texture that is almost as dense as ice cream.

¾ cup plus ¼ cup	sugar
2 cups	half-and-half
4 ounces	best-quality bittersweet chocolate, coarsely chopped
1 teaspoon	instant coffee powder or espresso powder
4	eggs, lightly beaten
1 teaspoon	vanilla extract
¼ teaspoon	ground cinnamon
⅛ teaspoon	salt

1. Heat the oven to 325° F. Place the ¾ cup of sugar in a large heavy skillet over medium-high heat. Cook, without stirring, until the sugar begins to melt. Reduce the heat to low and cook and stir until it turns a golden brown. Quickly pour the caramel into a 1-quart flan dish or shallow round casserole (or a 10-inch deep-dish pie plate), tipping to coat the bottom and sides. You must work fast, as the caramel will harden immediately, but it will turn into a thick syrup after the flan bakes and chills.

2. Combine the half-and-half with the chopped chocolate and espresso powder in a small heavy saucepan over medium heat, stirring until they are completely dissolved. Cool slightly.

3. Whisk the eggs with the remaining ¼ cup sugar, the vanilla, cinnamon, and salt. Whisk in the chocolate mixture. Strain the custard into the caramel-lined flan dish. Place in a large baking pan and add steaming (but not quite boiling) water halfway up the side of the flan dish. Bake for 50 to 60 minutes, or until set in the center when gently shaken. Remove from the hot water; cool, then chill for at least 4 hours or overnight.

4. To serve, loosen the edges of the custard with the tip of a knife. Place a platter on top and quickly turn over. Hold in place until the caramel flows out.

Variations: Delete the espresso powder for a chocolate flan. For a coffee flan, increase the coffee powder to 1½ teaspoons and add an extra ¼ cup of sugar to the custard.

Plan ahead: Prepare through step 3 and refrigerate for up to 3 days.

PUMPKIN FLAN

SERVES 6

This deep golden flan, draped in a glossy amber syrup, is a jewellike finale for an
autumn dinner. Even so, it's a simple dessert that doesn't overpower the delicate
pumpkin flavor with the usual Thanksgiving pie spices, just toasty caramel,
vanilla, and a shot of sugarcane rum.

¾ cup plus ½ cup	sugar
4	eggs, lightly beaten
1½ cups	cooked pumpkin or winter squash purée (see Note), sieved to remove any fibers
1 cup	light cream
3 tablespoons	dark rum, preferably sugarcane rum, such as Mount Gay
1 teaspoon	vanilla extract
⅛ teaspoon	salt

1. Heat the oven to 325°F. Place the ¾ cup sugar in a large heavy skillet over medium-high heat. Cook, without stirring, until the sugar begins to melt. Reduce the heat to low and cook and stir until it turns a golden brown. Quickly pour the caramel into a 1-quart flan dish or shallow round casserole (or a 10-inch deep-dish pie plate), tipping to coat the bottom and sides. You must work fast, as the caramel will harden immediately, but it will turn into a thick syrup after the flan bakes and chills.

2. Beat the eggs with the remaining ½ cup sugar. Stir in the pumpkin purée, cream, rum, vanilla, and salt. Strain the mixture into the caramel-lined flan dish. Place in a large baking pan and add steaming (but not quite boiling) water halfway up the side of the flan dish. Bake for 50 to 60 minutes, or until set in the center when gently shaken. Remove from the hot water, cool, then chill for at least 4 hours or overnight.

3. To serve, loosen the edges of the custard with the tip of a knife. Place the platter on top and quickly turn over. Hold in place until the caramel flows out.

Note: Please don't use canned pumpkin. Fresh pumpkin or winter squash has a brighter golden color and more delicate taste. Just be sure to bake or steam it, rather than boiling, or the purée will be too watery. If you don't have the time to start fresh, use frozen squash purée rather than canned pumpkin. (Birds Eye packages a very good winter squash purée in 12-ounce frozen boxes, exactly the right amount for this recipe.)

Plan ahead: Prepare through step 2 and refrigerate for up to 3 days.

CARAMELIZED ORANGE FLAN

SERVES 8

Sort of a cross between flan and cheesecake, the sweetness and density of this
custard is somewhat relieved by the acidity of the citrus. It's based on the traditional flan
de queso crema (cream cheese flan) served in Mexican and Cuban homes. (To make
the authentic version, replace the orange juice with undiluted evaporated milk,
or with whole milk; delete the lemon juice, orange zest, and nutmeg.)

¾ cup	sugar
1	(8-ounce) package cream cheese, softened
5	eggs
1	(14-ounce) can sweetened condensed milk
1 cup	fresh orange juice, strained
2 tablespoons	fresh lemon juice, strained
2 scant teaspoons	finely grated orange zest
1 teaspoon	vanilla extract
¼ teaspoon	nutmeg
⅛ teaspoon	salt

1. Heat the oven to 325° F. Place the sugar in a large heavy skillet over medium-high heat. Cook, without stirring, until the sugar begins to melt. Reduce the heat to low and stir until it turns a golden brown. Quickly pour the caramel into a 1-quart flan dish or shallow round casserole (or a 10-inch deep-dish pie plate), tipping to coat the bottom and sides. You must work fast, as the caramel will harden immediately, but it will turn into a thick syrup after the flan bakes and chills.

2. Beat the cream cheese with an electric mixer until smooth; add the eggs, one at a time, beating well after each addition. Beat in the condensed milk until smooth; stir in the orange juice, lemon juice, orange zest, vanilla, nutmeg, and salt. Pour into the caramel-lined flan dish. Place in a large baking pan and add boiling water halfway up the side of the flan dish. Bake for 50 to 60 minutes, or until set in the center when gently shaken. Remove from the hot water and chill for at least 4 hours or overnight.

3. To serve, loosen the edges of the custard with the tip of a knife. Place a platter on top and quickly turn over. Hold in place until the caramel flows out.

Plan ahead: Prepare through
step 2 and refrigerate for up to
3 days.

ices, cookies,
and candies

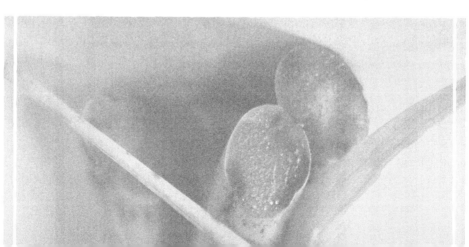

COOL IDEAS

* ❋ *

HOT FINALES!

* ❋ *

A LITTLE SOMETHING SWEET

* ❋ *

ESSENTIAL PRALINES

cool ideas

Now that home machines and food processors have simplified the process, the most colorful fruits of the season are an inspiration to create your own sorbets, sherbets, ice creams, and gelati. You could also experiment with the frozen purées of exotics, such as passion fruit or guava, that are sold at Latin markets. Good fresh candidates include figs, mangoes, papayas, melons, peaches, nectarines, pears, oranges, tangerines, kiwi, and strawberries.

The following basic formulas may be endlessly modified with different fruits, even blends of several at once. You might need to adjust the amount of sugar, depending upon the quality and natural flavor of the fruit. Just remember that it will not taste as sweet when frozen. And if you use berries with tough seeds or skins, you'll need to strain the purée before chilling it. Use any sort of ice cream maker for the recipes in this section. Just follow the manufacturer's instructions.

BASIC FRUIT SORBET
MAKES ABOUT 1 QUART

Pure fruit essence is smoothed out and chilled into a refreshing sparkler that melts on your tongue. It's the perfect treat for a steamy summer afternoon, or an elegant finale for a Third Coast meal. Timing is important, since sorbets don't keep as well as ice creams. Ideally, they should be served within 8 hours of freezing.

1 quart	fresh fruit purée
2 tablespoons	fresh lemon or lime juice
⅔ cup	superfine sugar (see Note), or to taste

Stir all of the ingredients together until they're well blended and the sugar is dissolved. Chill thoroughly, then freeze in an ice cream machine according to manufacturer's directions. (If you don't have a machine, see below.)

Note: If superfine sugar, also known as bar sugar, isn't on the shelves in your grocery, check a liquor store.

✳ ✳ ✳ no cranking required ✳ ✳ ✳

If you don't own an ice cream maker, you can still get by the old-fashioned way, with a sturdy whisk and a large, nonreactive metal bowl. (Glass is a poor conductor that retards the process.) First, turn your freezer to its coldest setting. Pour the chilled blend for your frozen dessert into the bowl and freeze until it's ringed with about a half inch of crystals. This takes an hour or so. Whisk it, repeating the process every 30 to 40 minutes thereafter, until it is frozen through, then freeze it for an additional 15 minutes before serving.

A food processor cuts the labor. Just stash the mixture until it's frozen solid (the center might still be soft), then break it up and process quickly until smooth, but not melted. Pour it back into the metal bowl and return it to the freezer to "ripen" for about 15 minutes.

These still-freeze methods will always produce a coarser, grainier texture than a machine. Even machine-made sorbets and sherbets will never be as smooth as ice creams, but they'll make up for that with brilliant color and intensity of flavor.

✳ ✳ ✳ ✳ ✳ ✳

BASIC FRUIT ICE CREAM

MAKES ABOUT I QUART

*Ripe and sweet Louisiana figs, Mississippi blackberries, Alabama peaches,
Florida mangoes, Tex-Mex prickly pears—they all scream for ice cream.
Pick a basketful, call some good friends, and get cranking.*

3	egg yolks
¾ cup	sugar, or to taste
1½ cups	heavy cream
2 cups	fresh fruit purée
1 tablespoon	vanilla extract

1. Whisk together the egg yolks, sugar, and ¼ cup of the cream until well blended. Place the remaining 1¼ cups of the cream in a heavy saucepan and heat just to a simmer. Gradually add the warm cream to the egg mixture, whisking constantly; return the custard to the saucepan over medium-low heat. Cook, stirring constantly, for about 5 minutes, until the custard thickens enough to coat the spoon. Be very careful not to let it boil, or the eggs will curdle.

2. Strain the custard; allow it to cool to room temperature; stir in the fruit purée and vanilla extract. Chill until cold, for at least 1 hour. Freeze in an ice cream machine according to manufacturer's directions (or see page 321).

∗ ∗ ∗ will work for ice cream ∗ ∗ ∗

Variety once meant vanilla, chocolate, or strawberry. But that was before Angelo Brocato Ice Cream & Confectionery introduced New Orleans to a whole rainbow of brilliant Italian ices and gelati in 1905. Armed with his recipes from Palermo, the Sicilian immigrant and his hardworking family churned out their products the old-fashioned way, with ice and salt, well into the 1950s.

"We used that last machine until it wore out and we couldn't get any more parts for it. But at least it was electric," said Angelo Brocato III, one of six grandchildren who operate the business today. "Before that, my grandfather would give neighborhood boys ice cream to help him turn the two-handed cranks. Even when I was growing up, if my friends came in, my father would put them to work. I used to get embarrassed, but they kept coming back for more."

∗ ∗ ∗ ∗ ∗ ∗

QUICK FRUIT ICE CREAM

MAKES ABOUT 1 1/2 QUARTS

*Many traditional Gulf Coast desserts incorporate sweetened condensed milk.
It was a practical alternative to fresh dairy products in the steamy Southern climate
before refrigeration became common. Now we've just learned to like the taste.
Versions of this recipe, usually made with puréed mango or mashed banana,
are a favorite in regional community cookbooks.*

3 cups	half-and-half
1	(14-ounce) can sweetened condensed milk
1 cup	puréed or mashed fruit
1 tablespoon	vanilla extract

Stir together until all ingredients are well blended. Freeze in an ice cream machine according
to manufacturer's directions.

Note: To prepare in your freezer, delete the half-and-half. Whisk together the condensed milk, fruit, and vanilla. Whip 2 cups of heavy cream to stiff peaks and fold in gently until smooth. (Do not use nondairy whipped topping.) Pour into a 9-by-5-inch loaf pan (or another 2-quart container). Cover tightly and freeze until firm, about 6 hours.

ITALIAN-STYLE CITRUS
and herb sherbet
SERVES 8

This tart and refreshing treat, further cooled by fresh mint, begins with a cooked Italian meringue that makes it both fluffier and more stable. If you like, use oranges instead of grapefruit and 2 tablespoons of fresh rosemary leaves in place of the mint, especially striking if you can find red-streaked blood oranges.

4	tree-ripened grapefruit, preferably Texas Reds
1¼ cups	sugar
⅓ cup	water
3	egg whites
¼ teaspoon	salt
1 tablespoon	minced fresh mint, preferably spearmint

1. Juice the grapefruit to measure 3 cups of juice and pulp; set aside. Bring the sugar and water to a boil in small saucepan, stirring until the sugar dissolves, then continue boiling until the syrup reaches 238° F on a candy thermometer (soft-ball stage).

2. Meanwhile, beat the egg whites with the salt until stiff peaks form. Slowly pour the hot syrup into the beaten whites, beating until stiff and glossy, about 5 minutes. Fold in the reserved grapefruit juice and pulp and minced mint. Freeze in an ice cream maker according to manufacturer's directions (or see page 321).

SICILIAN CHOCOLATE CHIP
gelato
✴ stracciatella ✴
MAKES ABOUT 1 QUART

Gelati were introduced to the Third Coast by immigrants from Sicily, where the colorful Italian-style ice creams originated. The silky texture comes from a cooked custard that's extra rich in egg yolks. This flavor is named for its "little rags" of shredded chocolate. You could also use the basic custard as your starting point, then stir in anything you like, from fruit purées to liqueurs and nuts. You'll find a few ideas in the notes that follow the recipe.

2 cups	whole milk
5	egg yolks
¾ cup	sugar
2 tablespoons	light corn syrup
2 cups	whole milk, heated to a simmer
1 teaspoon	pure vanilla extract
½ cup	shredded semisweet or bittersweet chocolate

1. Warm the milk in a heavy saucepan over medium heat until it just reaches a simmer. Whisk together the egg yolks, sugar, and corn syrup until smooth. Gradually add the hot milk, whisking constantly. Return the custard to the saucepan and cook, stirring constantly, over medium-low heat until the custard thickens enough to coat a wooden spoon, about 6 minutes. Do not boil.

2. Strain into a clean bowl and stir in the vanilla. Refrigerate until very cold, at least 2 hours. Transfer to an ice cream maker and freeze according to manufacturer's instructions. When the gelato is partially frozen, but still rather soft, stir in the shredded chocolate.

Note: For fruit gelato, *delete the vanilla and chocolate. When the custard has cooled to lukewarm, add 1 cup of puréed fruit (such as fresh figs, berries, peaches, nectarines, mango, cantaloupe, or honeydew melon) mixed with 1 tablespoon of fresh lemon juice. Stir until well blended.*

For espresso gelato, stir 1 to 2 tablespoons espresso powder and ¼ teaspoon ground cinnamon into the hot custard. Delete the chocolate (or leave it in for espresso-flavored stracciatella).

TRIPLE COCONUT ICE CREAM

*The triple shot of flavor comes from coconut, toasted coconut, and cream
of coconut. Top this rich and easy ice cream with bittersweet chocolate sauce,
fresh tropical fruit, grilled pineapple, or Bananas Foster (page 333).*

2 cups	sweetened flaked coconut
1	(16-ounce) can sweetened cream of coconut, such as Coco Lopez
1½ cups	heavy cream
1 cup	milk
¼ teaspoon	pure almond extract
Pinch	of salt

1. Heat the oven to 350°F. Spread 1 cup of the coconut on a baking pan in a single layer; bake until lightly browned, 8 to 10 minutes. Cool.

2. Stir together the cream of coconut, cream, milk, almond extract, and salt until well blended; stir in the remaining cup of untoasted coconut; chill thoroughly for several hours or overnight. Freeze in an ice cream maker according to manufacturer's directions. When the ice cream is nearly frozen, but still slightly soft, stir in the toasted coconut.

FROZEN CREOLE CREAM CHEESE

Frozen cream cheese is an old Louisiana delicacy that is luxurious on its own, even better topped with fresh strawberries or sliced peaches. This low-tech recipe is still the standard in many kitchens. It originally appeared in a pamphlet from the local utility company, New Orleans Public Service, circa 1940. If you use an ice cream machine, the results should be even smoother.

2	Creole cream cheeses with their cream (see Note)
1 cup	evaporated milk
1 cup	granulated sugar
½ teaspoon	vanilla extract
1	egg white (or an equivalent amount of reconstituted meringue powder), beaten to stiff peaks

Mash the cream cheese into the milk until smooth. Add the sugar and vanilla, then fold in the stiffly beaten egg white. Freeze in an ice cream machine according to the manufacturer's directions. (Or proceed the old-fashioned way: Pour into a 9-by-5-inch loaf pan or 2-quart metal pan and freeze with refrigerator temperature control set on coldest position. When frozen, reset control to normal operation.)

Note: Commercially packaged Creole cream cheese is seldom available outside of Louisiana. You may make it yourself by following the recipe on page 268, which will produce the equivalent of the two cheeses you need. Just add enough heavy cream to bring the total measure (curds and cream) to 1 quart and proceed as directed above.

hot finales!

They may seem like the latest outrage from the wild culinary frontier, but peppery desserts are nothing to sneeze at. In fact, they're well grounded in culinary history. Ancient Aztecs were the first to blend chocolate with ancho chiles. And even sturdy old European bakers approve of *Pfeffernüsse*, the traditional German "pepper nuts" seasoned with white and black peppercorns.

For a hot finale of a different sort, flaming Bananas Foster is a flashy ending for a Third Coast dinner. Made famous by Brennan's Restaurant in New Orleans, the spiced tropical fruit, sizzled in butter and rum, has roots in Mexico and Cuba.

HOT-CHA CHOCOLATE
and chipotle brownies

MAKES 16 BROWNIES

At first, all you taste is dark chocolate and cinnamon, maybe a touch of coffee liqueur. The chipotle spark comes after, along with an extra dimension of flavor and texture from sweet-hot roasted pecans. As one of the tasters said, "These brownies are kickin'!"

⅓ cup	unsalted butter
6 ounces	best-quality bittersweet chocolate, coarsely chopped
2	eggs
1 cup	firmly packed dark brown sugar
1 tablespoon	Kahlúa or another coffee liqueur (or 1 teaspoon instant coffee powder dissolved in 1 tablespoon water)
½ teaspoon	vanilla extract
½ cup	all-purpose flour
1 teaspoon	ground chipotle chiles
½ teaspoon	ground cinnamon
½ teaspoon	baking powder
1 cup	Honey-Chipotle Pecans (page 37), coarsely chopped

1. Heat the oven to 350° F. Line a 9-inch square pan with aluminum foil; butter and flour the foil.

2. Melt the butter and chocolate in a small saucepan over low heat; cool to lukewarm. Beat the eggs in a mixing bowl until thick; add the sugar and continue beating until the mixture is smooth; beat in the coffee liqueur and vanilla. Add the cooled chocolate mixture, beating just until blended. Sift the flour with the ground chipotle chiles, cinnamon, and baking powder; add to the batter, stirring by hand just until blended. Fold in the chopped Honey-Chipotle Pecans.

3. Turn the batter into the pan; smooth the top with a rubber scraper. Bake for 30 to 35 minutes, or until the center springs back from a light touch. Cool completely, then use the foil to lift the brownies out of the pan before cutting them.

* * * food of the gods * * *

The scientific name for the cacao tree is *Theobroma cacao*, which officially designates the product of its fruit, chocolate, as "food of the gods," but we already knew that. The irresistible little bean was worshiped as an idol over 2,000 years ago by the Mayan people of Mexico, who reserved it for the exclusive use of their priests and royalty. The last Aztec emperor, Montezuma II, introduced it to explorer Hernando Cortés, who returned to Spain with the secret formula for *cacahuatl*, ancient ancestor of our hot chocolate. By the 1700s it was all the rage in Europe, and England's chocolate houses outnumbered its coffee shops.

Anything that tastes that good has got to be bad for you, right? Not so, say experts, after centuries of false reports that blamed the innocent little cacao bean for everything from diabetes to nymphomania. Recent research has also relieved it of the responsibility for acne, hyperactivity, and dental cavities.

It seems those cravings are all in our heads. Chocolate is not addictive and it is not high in caffeine. A typical 1.4-ounce bar or an 8-ounce glass of chocolate milk is roughly equivalent to a cup of decaffeinated coffee.

Major studies have confirmed that stearic acid, the main saturated fatty acid in chocolate, marginally increases levels of HDL cholesterol (the "good" cholesterol). More important, it does not raise levels of LDL cholesterol (the "bad" cholesterol).

Also, cocoa powder and chocolate contain antioxidants similar to those found in red wine, which could reduce the risk of heart disease and cancer. In fact, dark chocolate is packed with about eight times the antioxidant power of strawberries, which rank high among fruits.

Okay, so it's not exactly a health food, but you can add reasonable doses to your diet without guilt. And don't forget to give thanks to the gods.

* * * * * *

NUT BRITTLE THAT BITES BACK

MAKES 1½ POUNDS

A novel holiday gift for all of the chileheads on your list, nut brittle gets a surprising bite from chopped jalapeños (mildly hot), serranos (seriously hot), or habaneros (yow!). Mix and match according to your friends' tastes—or your level of veiled hostility. A base recipe follows, fine for the traditional peanuts, even better with the Tex-Mex flavor of piñons (pine nuts) or pumpkin seeds. The secret to success is low humidity, so save this project for a dry day.

2 cups	sugar
1 cup	light corn syrup
2 tablespoons	unsalted butter
¼ teaspoon	salt
¼ cup	water
1½ cups	(6 ounces) roasted pumpkin seeds, pine nuts, or salted peanuts
½ teaspoon	baking soda
3	or more fresh chiles, seeded and finely chopped (see headnote)

1. In a large nonreactive pot, stir together the sugar, corn syrup, butter, salt, and water. Bring to a boil, whisking to dissolve the sugar; reduce the heat and cook gently for about 20 minutes to the soft-ball stage (235–240° F on a candy thermometer). Stir in the nuts and simmer for about 15 minutes longer to the hard-crack stage (290–300° F). Add the baking soda and chopped chiles, whisking briefly until the bubbling stops and the mixture settles.

2. Meanwhile, butter a 16-inch length of heavy-duty aluminum foil (the thin stuff tears). Pour the nut mixture onto the foil and, using a wooden spoon, spread to a fairly uniform thickness of ¼ inch. Allow to set for at least 20 minutes, until cool and brittle, then break into pieces, which can be stored in airtight containers for several weeks.

TABASCO FIRE and ICE CREAM

SERVES 6

Now here's a fun finale for a cookout or seafood boil. It's also a sparky topping for apple pie or peach cobbler. The recipe is from the McIlhenny Company, which produces its famous Tabasco sauce on Avery Island, just off the Louisiana Gulf Coast.

½ cup	milk
1	medium cinnamon stick, plus 6 more for garnish
1	strip orange peel, plus 6 more for garnish
4	whole cloves
2 teaspoons	vanilla extract
1	(14-ounce) can sweetened condensed milk
1½ teaspoons	Tabasco sauce
2 cups	heavy cream, whipped

1. Heat the milk, 1 cinnamon stick, 1 strip of orange peel, and the cloves to boiling in a small pan over medium-high heat. Reduce the heat to low; cover the pot and simmer for 5 minutes to blend the flavors. Cool to room temperature; strain out and discard the solids.

2. Combine the spiced milk, vanilla extract, sweetened condensed milk, and Tabasco sauce in a large bowl. Gently fold in the whipped cream. Cover and freeze until firm, stirring once. To serve, scoop the ice cream into glasses or dessert dishes. Garnish each serving with a cinnamon stick and a twist of orange peel.

BANANAS FOSTER

SERVES 4

During the 1950s, when New Orleans was a major port of entry for Central
and South American bananas, Owen Brennan challenged Chef Paul Blangé to showcase
the tropical fruit in a new dessert. It was named for Richard Foster, then chairman
of the New Orleans Crime Commission, which was organized to stamp out vice
in the French Quarter. Definitely more successful than that hopeless enterprise,
Bananas Foster has since become an international classic. It is still the most
requested item on the menu at Brennan's Restaurant, where more
than 35,000 pounds of bananas are flamed each year.

Mexicans make a nearly identical dessert with ripe plantains, which are
sautéed in butter and seasoned with sugar, cinnamon, and rum (without the banana
liqueur). Instead of being ladled over ice cream, they're topped with a dollop of Crema
(page 267). Cubans serve the same plátanos dulces en mantequilla y ron (sweet plantains
with butter and rum) as a side dish for suckling pig or roast pork on special occasions.

¼ cup	unsalted butter
1 cup	packed brown sugar
½ teaspoon	ground cinnamon
¼ cup	banana liqueur
4	bananas, cut in half lengthwise, then halved crosswise
¼ cup	dark rum
4	scoops vanilla ice cream

Combine the butter, brown sugar, and cinnamon in a flambé pan or skillet. Place the pan over
low heat, either on an alcohol burner or on top of the stove, and cook, stirring, until the sugar
dissolves. Stir in the banana liqueur, then place the bananas in the pan. When the banana sections soften and begin to brown, carefully add the rum. Continue to cook the sauce until the
rum is hot, then tip the pan slightly to ignite the rum. When the flames subside, lift the
bananas out of the pan and place four pieces over each portion of ice cream. Generously spoon
the warm sauce over the top of the ice cream and serve immediately.

a little something sweet

From almond-scented Nun's Fingers to spiced fig *cuccidati*, Third Coast cookie jars are filled with little treats that are sophisticated enough for adults, but also fun for kids. And everyone will love the intriguing names. Crisp or cushy, soft or snappy, each has the strength to support a tingling mouthful of flavors and textures. Got milk?

NUN'S FINGERS
dedos de monja

MAKES 3 DOZEN

Maybe it was the long hours, or the hot ovens, but colonial bakers sure had their irreverent moments. From "virgins' belly buttons" to "priest's farts," many of the old French or Spanish names for Cajun and Mexican confections sound a lot more appetizing without their English translations.

These tender cookies are just like the ones I bought at a little bakery in the Mexican border town of Matamoros—ethereal crescents with a heavenly vanilla-almond flavor and soft dusting of confectioners' sugar. For Cuban-style galletas de almendras (almond cookies), shape the dough into 24 balls instead of crescents and roll the warm baked cookies in confectioners' sugar.

1 cup	sliced almonds, very lightly toasted to pale gold
1 cup	unsalted butter, softened
¾ cup	granulated sugar
2 teaspoons	vanilla extract
2 cups	all-purpose flour
	Confectioners' sugar (optional)

1. Heat the oven to 325°F. Place the almonds in the bowl of a food processor; pulse several times until the nuts are chopped, but not ground to a powder.

2. Cream together the butter, sugar, and vanilla in a mixing bowl until smooth. Stir in the flour and chopped almonds, kneading lightly in the bowl until the dough comes together.

3. Use your hands to form the dough into 36 thin crescents, about the size of a woman's little finger. (They'll expand and spread as they bake.) Bake on ungreased cookie sheets for 30 minutes, or until the edges are just barely browned. Cool for 5 minutes on the cookie sheets before removing to racks to cool completely. If desired, sprinkle with confectioners' sugar.

Plan ahead: These cookies actually taste better the second day. Store airtight at room temperature for up to 1 week. Freeze for up to 2 months.

MEXICAN ANISE and CINNAMON
sugar cookies
bizcochitos

MAKES 4–5 DOZEN, DEPENDING UPON SIZE

Crisp and spicy bizcochitos are a Christmas tradition throughout Mexico. Some cooks crisscross the rolled dough with a sharp knife to cut it into diamonds. Others use cookie cutters to make festive shapes. Either way, proceed with patience and a light hand, as the extra moisture from the sherry makes a delicate dough (and tasty cookies).

1 cup	unsalted butter, softened (for strict authenticity, use lard)
1 cup	sugar
1	egg
2 tablespoons	sweet sherry
2 teaspoons	aniseed
3 cups	all-purpose flour
1½ teaspoons	baking powder
1 teaspoon	ground cinnamon
½ teaspoon	salt
2	egg whites, lightly beaten
½ cup	sugar mixed with ½ teaspoon ground cinnamon

1. Heat the oven to 350° F. Cream the butter with the sugar in a mixing bowl until very fluffy. Beat in the egg, sherry, and aniseed. Sift the flour with the baking powder, cinnamon, and salt. Stir into the butter mixture.

2. Roll the dough on a floured surface to a thickness of ¼ inch. Use a sharp knife to cut into diamonds, or use cookie cutters to make different shapes. Brush the tops lightly with beaten egg white, then sprinkle generously with cinnamon sugar. Transfer to ungreased cookie sheets and bake until golden brown, 15 to 20 minutes. Cool for 5 minutes, then transfer to wire racks to cool completely.

Plan ahead: Store airtight at room temperature for up to 1 week. Freeze for up to 2 months.

SICILIAN ANISE DROPS

MAKES 6 DOZEN

*Sicilians also love the sweet licorice taste of anise, a flavor that appears in many
of their pastries, as well as in pasta sauces and other savory dishes. Meringue-like anise
drops, sprinkled with multicolored nonpareils, are a Christmas favorite, also an essential
decoration for St. Joseph's Day food altars (see page 259). Marilyn Macaluso Ortalano of
Marrero, Louisiana, agreed to share this family recipe.*

*"My cousin Agnes Plaisance, who has since passed away, came up with the idea
of letting the dough sit eight hours to rise. That really makes a difference, and it needs the
full eight hours," Ortalano told me. "Just spoon out the cookies last thing at night and bake
them first thing in the morning. You can buy the anise oil at some drug stores, but I get it
at Central Grocery in New Orleans."*

3	eggs
1 cup plus 2 tablespoons	sugar
1¾ cups	all-purpose flour
½ teaspoon	baking powder
½ teaspoon	salt
5 drops	anise oil
	Multicolored nonpareils

1. Beat the eggs with an electric mixer on high speed for 10 minutes, until light and frothy.
   Reduce to low speed and add sugar gradually. Beat at high speed for an additional 17 minutes,
   until very thick and light in color. Add the flour, baking powder, salt, and anise oil. Beat on
   high speed for 3 minutes longer.

2. Line the cookie sheets with waxed paper. Drop the dough onto the waxed paper by teaspoons.
   Sprinkle with the multicolored nonpareils immediately, before the dough dries out. Set aside
   at room temperature for 8 hours.

3. Heat the oven to 325°F. Bake the cookies for 8 to 10 minutes, then
   cool on the pans. The cool cookies should just pop off the waxed
   paper when lifted up.

*Plan ahead: Store the cookies
airtight for up to 1 week.*

SICILIAN DATE and FIG COOKIES
* cuccidati *

MAKES ABOUT 6 DOZEN

Sicilian cuccidati are spicy ancestors of Fig Newtons. Sweet dough is filled with a moist and toothsome paste of ground fruit and nuts, then it's topped with a pastel-tinted glaze and a sprinkle of multicolored nonpareils. Like the preceding anise drops, cuccidati are standard for both Christmas and St. Joseph's Day (see page 259). Unlike the anise drops, these cookies are a big project that could use a few extra helping hands. This version is adapted from an old family recipe contributed by Ann Kay Logarbo, M.D., who coordinates the St. Joseph's Day altar at her parish church in Covington, Louisiana.

FILLING

3½ pounds	dried figs, stems removed
2	small thin-skinned oranges, unpeeled and sliced, all seeds removed
1 pound	raisins
1 pound	crystallized fruit (as for fruit cake)
½ pound	chopped dates
½ pound	pecans
½ pound	dried cherries
1½ cups	sugar
2 teaspoons	ground cinnamon
2 teaspoons	ground allspice
2 teaspoons	grated nutmeg

DOUGH

1 pound	unsalted butter, melted
3 cups	sugar
4	eggs, beaten
1 cup	milk
1 tablespoon	vanilla extract
1 teaspoon	almond extract
8–10 cups	self-rising flour

4 cups confectioners' sugar
1 tablespoon fresh lemon juice
1 teaspoon vanilla extract
3–4 tablespoons light cream or milk, plus more if needed
Food coloring (optional)
Multicolored nonpareils

1. For the filling: Place the figs, oranges, raisins, crystallized fruit, dates, pecans, and cherries in the work bowl of a food processor. Grind to a rough paste. Scrape into a mixing bowl and stir in the sugar, cinnamon, allspice, and nutmeg. Add warm water, as necessary, to keep mixture moist.

2. For the dough: Mix all of the ingredients, adding enough flour to make a pliable dough. Working in batches, roll the dough on a floured surface into 12-inch squares, about ¼ inch thick. Cut each square into three 4-inch-wide strips. Spoon the filling evenly down the center of each strip. Fold one side of the dough lengthwise over the top of the filling, then continue to roll the dough over until the filling is enclosed in a long tube, ending with overlapping edges on the bottom. Trim the excess dough off each end, then slice into 2-inch cookies. (They'll look similar in shape and size to Fig Newtons.) Place on lightly greased cookie sheets, pressing lightly to flatten the bottoms of the cookies.

3. Heat the oven to 350° F. Bake the cookies for 25 to 30 minutes, or until lightly browned. Cool on racks.

4. For the glaze: Mix the confectioners' sugar with the lemon juice, vanilla, and enough cream or milk to make a medium-thin glaze. If desired, divide the glaze among three or four small bowls and use food coloring to tint it different pastel colors. Brush the glaze over the tops of the cooled *cuccidati* and immediately sprinkle with nonpareils before it dries.

Plan ahead: Store cookies airtight for up to 1 week or freeze for up to 3 months.

essential pralines

These sweet confections traveled with French colonials to the Third Coast, where the traditional hazelnuts and almonds were soon replaced by creamier native American pecans. The Creole candy also has a more buttery and yielding texture than the brittle caramelized sugar of classic European *pralin*. Though usually associated with New Orleans, pecan pralines are common throughout Mississippi, Alabama, Texas, and Mexico.

Please use only the freshest pecans, lightly toasted for extra depth of flavor. And note that an inexpensive candy thermometer (available in most supermarkets) yields the most reliable results.

PRALINE COOKIES

Like their namesake, praline cookies are thin and sugary, loaded with toasted
pecans to balance their sweetness. Bake them on parchment or buttered foil, otherwise
they might shatter when you try to remove them to a cooling rack. Much easier
than the traditional Creole candy, they don't require a bubbling kettle
or precise timing to succeed, but it's harder to eat just one.

½ cup	unsalted butter, softened
1 cup	packed brown sugar
1	large egg, beaten
1 teaspoon	vanilla extract
1 cup	all-purpose flour
¼ teaspoon	baking soda
¼ teaspoon	salt
1½ cups	coarsely chopped toasted pecans

1. Heat the oven to 325°F. Line baking sheets with parchment (preferred) or greased aluminum foil. Cream the butter and brown sugar in a mixing bowl until fluffy, then beat in the egg and vanilla until smooth. In a separate bowl, whisk together the flour, soda, and salt; blend into the batter. Fold in the pecans.

2. Drop by rounded teaspoons onto the prepared baking sheet, allowing about 3 inches in between for the cookies to spread. Bake for 15 to 20 minutes, until browned. Cool on the sheets for 5 minutes, then carefully remove to racks with a large spatula.

Plan ahead: Store airtight at room temperature for up to 1 week.

* * * hot nuts * * *

Toast pecans before using them in a recipe to intensify the flavor and add a crisp edge to their buttery texture. Just spread the nuts in a single layer on an ungreased pan and bake at 325°F until they're fragrant and lightly browned, about 10 minutes. For small amounts, a toaster oven is convenient.

* * * * * *

CREOLE PECAN PRALINES

*Serve one or two of these rich little patties with afternoon coffee, or as a
simple dessert. They're also good crumbled over vanilla ice cream, and a must
on holiday cookie trays in the Gulf South.*

1 cup	granulated sugar
1 cup	packed light brown sugar
½ cup	light cream
2 tablespoons	unsalted butter
1 tablespoon	vanilla extract (or 1 teaspoon vanilla plus 1 tablespoon rum or brandy)
1½ cups	very coarsely chopped, lightly toasted pecans

1. Stir together the granulated sugar, brown sugar, and cream in a heavy saucepan until smooth. Bring to a boil over medium heat and continue boiling, stirring occasionally, until the mixture registers between 234 and 240° F on a candy thermometer (soft-ball stage).

2. Remove from the heat. Stir in the butter, vanilla extract, and pecans. Cool slightly, beating with a wooden spoon until the mixture begins to thicken, but is still glossy. Drop by rounded teaspoons onto a greased marble slab or a pan lined with a double thickness of waxed paper.

Plan ahead: Store airtight at room temperature for up to 1 week.

* * * carrying on * * *
a sweet tradition

Anyone who thinks the wheels of government turn slowly has never been in New Orleans City Hall when "Tee Eva" Perry makes her rounds. That's when you can observe smartly attired young professionals galloping down stairwells, and hear interoffice phone lines buzz with progress reports.

"Tee Eva's here!"

"Where is she?"

"I think she's on the fifth floor."

"Oh no! Go find her and ask her to come back to four."

The cause of all the fuss is a tiny, fast-moving grandmother swinging a basket full of homemade pies and pralines. It's not unusual to hear her name paged as she scoots through the courthouse or to see downtown office workers chasing her on the sidewalk like kids after an ice cream truck.

"One time I even had the sherriffs come at me with their lights on and the sirens going," Perry said. "I thought, 'Oh Lord, what have I done?' But they had recognized my car and just wanted to buy pies."

She snagged the first of many film appearances by working the crowd that had gathered outside of a local high school to audition for Oliver Stone's *JFK*.

"I just went there to make my quota for the day," she claimed, although she did admit to wearing a nineteenth-century costume. "I sold my way through the door. Then I sold straight on up the line. Right to the casting table."

Perry has worked as a cook/manager in private homes and operated her own cafe, and has even done a few star turns as visiting chef at trendy West Coast restaurants. Snapshots of "Tee Eva" with assorted glitterati are tacked to a bulletin board in her office. Meanwhile, she continues on her rounds.

"I'm very proud to walk the streets with my basket. I strut when I walk the streets with my basket," Perry said, "because I'm part of a long tradition of black women who made a living and kept their independence selling pralines this way."

Want to sample her wares? Tee Eva has joined the Internet generation. (See Sources, page 385.)

* * * * * *

TEXAS BUTTERMILK PRALINES

Buttermilk adds a slight tang and helps cut the sweetness of these Texas-style pralines.
Tie some up in a bandanna and bring them along next time you're invited to a barbecue.

2 cups	sugar
1 teaspoon	baking soda
1 cup	buttermilk
1 tablespoon	light corn syrup
¼ cup	unsalted butter
1 tablespoon	vanilla extract
1½ cups	very coarsely chopped, lightly toasted pecans

1. Stir together the sugar, baking soda, buttermilk, and corn syrup in a heavy saucepan until smooth. Bring to a boil over medium heat and continue boiling, stirring occasionally, until the mixture registers between 234 and 240° F on a candy thermometer (soft-ball stage).

2. Remove from the heat. Stir in the butter, vanilla extract, and chopped pecans. Cool slightly, beating with a wooden spoon until the mixture begins to thicken, but is still glossy. Drop by rounded teaspoons onto a greased marble slab or a pan lined with a double thickness of waxed paper.

Plan ahead: Store airtight at room temperature for up to 1 week.

CHEWY MEXICAN PRALINES

MAKES 5–6 DOZEN

*Closer to a buttery toffee than the crisp Creole version, these toothsome candies
are a real mouthful. Watch your dental work!*

1 cup	granulated sugar
1 cup	packed light brown sugar
1 cup	light corn syrup
1 can	sweetened condensed milk
½ pound	unsalted butter
1 tablespoon	vanilla extract
½ teaspoon	almond extract
3 cups	very coarsely chopped, lightly toasted pecans

1. Combine the sugars, corn syrup, condensed milk, and butter in a heavy saucepan over medium heat. Bring to a boil and continue boiling, stirring constantly, until the mixture measures between 234 and 240° F on a candy thermometer (soft-ball stage).

2. Remove from the heat. Stir in the vanilla and almond extracts and pecans. Cool, beating with a wooden spoon until the mixture thickens. Drop by rounded teaspoons onto a greased marble slab or a pan lined with a double thickness of waxed paper.

Plan ahead: Store airtight, individually wrapped in waxed paper, at room temperature for up to 1 week.

* * * instant gratification * * *
southern style

If you're willing to abandon tradition and endure the scorn of serious cooks, you can make pralines in a microwave. Just mix together a pound of light brown sugar and a cup of heavy cream, then microwave at full power for 13 minutes. (I learned this from one of those photocopied recipes that makes the rounds of offices and teachers' lounges.) Be sure to use an extra-deep, 2-quart bowl. (I learned this from bitter experience.) Stir in 2 cups of lightly toasted chopped pecans and a tablespoon of vanilla extract, then drop the mixture by rounded teaspoonfuls onto a pan lined with a double thickness of waxed paper. These heathen "instant pralines" are slightly grainy, but surprisingly good.

* * * * * *

part 6

BACKYARD BACCHANALS and BEACH PARTIES

Fire, food, music, storytellers: the elements of a great bash have changed very little over the past few thousand years. And here on the Third Coast you never have to dress up to have a good time, unless it's a masquerade. From Mardi Gras to Mexico's Day of the Dead, there's always something to celebrate and people willing to take off work to do it. Grab a plate and join the party.

food for a crowd

LIGHT THE FIRE

* ✳ *

BIG SANDWICHES

light the fire

One of the most enduring American food fads got off to a fiery start in 1941, when James Beard published the landmark *Cooking Outdoors* and the suburban backyard barbecue was born. It was inspired by the old Texas barbecues, utilitarian affairs organized to feed hungry cowboys, who got the name from the even older Mexican tradition of *barbacoa*.

And then there's the ancient feast of a roast suckling pig—that's *cochon de lait* to Cajuns, *lechón asado* in Mexico and Cuba, or an invitation to a "pig pickin'" in Mississippi. Louisiana's seafood boils are Florida's land's-end stews. And everybody loves a good fish fry. Of course, people have been cooking outdoors since the dawn of time, but the more sophisticated our kitchens become, the more settings of china and silver we collect, the more fun it is to rattle our pots over an open fire and eat with our hands.

TIPSY CHICKENS

SERVES 4–6

Rude, but not tasteless, the whole fowl is impaled astride an open can of beer, which steams the inside as the outside roasts. Also known as drunken chicken, or beer-in-the-rear chicken, it's trendy party fare in Texas and Louisiana, mainly because of the boffo presentation, but also because the upright posture makes it possible to fit several birds onto a barbecue grill or oven rack. Use the garlicky rosemary seasoning in this recipe or any rub you like.

More show biz: some Louisiana cooks like to spritz their chickens with the pepper spray that is sold elsewhere as a mugger repellent. Use the water-based version, as oil-based propellants are inedible.

2	(3-pound) fryers, cleaned and patted dry
1	lemon, cut in half
	Freshly ground black pepper
4	garlic cloves
	Kosher salt or any coarse-grain salt
6	large sprigs fresh rosemary
4 tablespoons	olive oil, plus more for basting
2 cans	beer
2 cups	mesquite or hickory chips, soaked in water for 1 hour

1. Rub each chicken inside and out with a lemon half and black pepper. Mash the garlic to a paste with salt; rub the chickens inside and out with the paste, using your fingers to carefully work it under the skin of the breasts. Insert one rosemary sprig under the skin on either side of each chicken's breastbone; place one sprig inside each chicken's cavity. Rub the chickens inside and out with olive oil.

2. Remove the pull-tab from the beers and empty out half of the contents. (Cheers!) Make two or three other holes around each top with a can opener. Insert one can upright into the cavity of each chicken and arrange its legs so it sits upright.

3. Place the chickens in the center of a heated grill over a drip pan, away from the heat source. (If using charcoal, mound the hot coals in two piles at the edges of the grill. If using gas, light only half of the burners and place the chickens on the opposite side of the grill.) Scatter the soaked wood chips over the hot coals or place them in the smoker box of a gas grill. Cover the grill, adjusting the vents as needed to maintain the temperature at a steady 350°F until the chickens are browned and cooked through (165°F at the thickest point of the thigh), about 1½ hours.

PETE GERICA'S SHRIMP BOIL

MAKES 10 POUNDS (WITH DIRECTIONS FOR BIGGER BATCHES)

Pete Gerica was coming in with a good catch as I walked around the back of his house, which faces his boat dock and a million-dollar view across the wetlands of Bayou Sauvage in Louisiana. He had been out since 4 A.M. on one of the first days of brown shrimp season, chugging home along this tranquil waterway just a few miles from the rush-hour traffic on Interstate 10. The son of a Croatian fisherman, he has worked on the water all of his life, hefting 200-pound sacks of oysters as a teenager. His family recipe and tips for a successful shrimp boil follow.

Like many fishermen's wives, Clara Gerica helps to prepare and distribute the catch her husband hauls in. Whatever doesn't go straight from the water onto his truck (bound for area retailers) she processes herself, stocking a large freezer with half-pound vacuum bags of peeled and deveined meat. "But he's the one who knows more about cooking," she insists. "The day after we got married my mother-in-law knocked on the door with a stack of recipe cards, a dozen eggs, a frying pan, and a stick of butter. I really love my mother-in-law, but I still don't like to cook."

She does know her seafood, though. "You shouldn't buy shrimp that have a fishy odor," Clara Gerica advises. "They should be white or brown, with no pink showing. We say 'not red in the head.' When you get home, put them in the refrigerator in a bowl of ice and water, because the refrigerator is never cold enough for fresh seafood. If you're not going straight home, ask your dealer to put some ice in your bag."

	Water (twice the volume of the shrimp)
2–3 pounds	small red-skinned potatoes
4 bags	crab boil (Sources, page 384)
¼ cup	liquid crab boil (Sources, page 384)
¼ cup	fresh lemon juice
⅓ cup	oil
3–4	whole onions
1–2	heads garlic or 3 tablespoons garlic powder
¼ cup	Tony Chachere's Creole Seasoning (Sources, page 384)
10 pounds	shrimp
	Salt to taste, about ¼ pound
	Smoked sausage (optional)
	Frozen corn on the cob (see Note)

1. Bring a large pot of water to a boil and cook the potatoes until they're barely soft; remove and set aside. (Gerica cooks the potatoes in a net laundry bag so they're easier to fish out of the boiling water. He parboils them before adding the other ingredients to the pot, so they don't soak up too much seasoning or pick up a lot of debris from the shrimp.)

2. Add the bags of crab boil, liquid crab boil (Gerica uses both to intensify the flavor), lemon juice, oil, onions, garlic, and Creole seasoning to the pot. Cover and boil for 5 minutes, then add shrimp. Continue cooking just until shrimp float up to the surface of the water. Immediately take the cover off the pot and turn off the fire. Add salt, parboiled potatoes, sausage (if using), and frozen corn on the cob.

3. When the shrimp sink back to the bottom of the pot, taste one. The longer they soak, the spicier they will become. (Gerica recommends soaking for 15 to 20 minutes after the cover comes off.)

For larger or smaller groups: You may cut the recipe in half for smaller groups. For larger groups, you may use the same water to boil up to three batches. Just add an extra half-measure of each seasoning for the second batch, and again for the third.

Note: Gerica uses frozen corn on the cob because it is less likely to overcook when added with the rest of the ingredients in step 2. If you prefer fresh corn on the cob, add it during the final 10 minutes of soaking in step 3.

✳ ✳ ✳ now you're cooking with gas ✳ ✳ ✳

Large outdoor cooking rigs are common household equipment on the Third Coast, where they seldom have time to collect dust in the garage between crab boils and fish fries. The usual setup is a sturdy four-legged stand with a powerful gas burner, which is attached by a fuel line to a portable propane tank. Deep 25- or 50-gallon aluminum stockpots are used for boiling seafood or frying turkeys. Huge skillets turn out catfish and hushpuppies for a crowd. You'll find everything you need at hardware stores or discount marts in the Gulf South. Otherwise, contact one of the mail-order sources on page 384.

✳ ✳ ✳ ✳ ✳ ✳

CAJUN FRIED TURKEY

SERVES 10–12

Deep-fried whole turkey is a Louisiana indelicacy that is gaining popularity
across the country. One of the first journalists to chronicle the weird phenomenon was
New Orleans food editor Dale Curry. Unfortunately, shortly after her story ran,
she tuned into the TV news on Thanksgiving night just in time to see a man
standing in front of the smoking ashes of his former house, announcing that
he would never make another one of her recipes.

Since then, Curry has redoubled her emphasis of these vital safety precautions:
Never deep-fry a turkey indoors or under a carport. Set the rig on grass or sand, rather than
smooth concrete (where an oil spill could flare up). Be very careful not to slosh oil onto
the flame while cooking, or as you lower or raise the turkey in the pot. (Key to this
process is the frame you use to lower and raise the turkey; see Sources on page 384.
The fireplace-poker approach just don't cut it.)

Curry even gave me a tested and approved recipe from an actual fireman,
Richard "Ricky" Heyd. He fried turkey on Thanksgiving for his colleagues at the Aycock
Fire Station in St. Bernard Parish, Louisiana.

If you decide to tackle this enterprise, you'll need a proper outdoor cooking rig (see
page 353 and opposite). Southern supermarkets now sell the injection syringes, which are
used to shoot marinade deep into the flesh of the bird. If you can't find one,
see Sources on page 384. You start this the day before.

10 tablespoons	Tabasco sauce, plus more for final rub
10 tablespoons	Worcestershire sauce
4½ tablespoons	onion juice (stocked with spices at supermarket)
3 tablespoons	garlic juice (stocked with spices at supermarket)
4 tablespoons	liquid crab boil (optional) if you like it spicy (Sources, page 384)
3¼ cups	water
5 tablespoons	Louisiana spice seasoning, plus more for final rub (Sources, page 384)
1	(10- to 12-pound) turkey
3–5 gallons	peanut oil (see Note)

1. Before you even start, be sure to read all of the safety precautions in the introduction to this recipe. Place all ingredients, except turkey and oil, in a saucepan over medium heat; bring to a boil, stirring often. Cool; then pour the marinade into an injection syringe (Sources, page 384) and inject the turkey all over.

2. "Stick the needle all the way into the meat," Heyd instructs. "As you inject the turkey, draw back on the needle so that the mixture is distributed through all of the meat areas. Be careful not to draw out too far, as this mixture burns if it gets into your eyes. Trust me on this one." Refrigerate the turkey to marinate overnight.

3. When ready to cook, heat oil to 350° F. Before lowering turkey into oil, coat outside with an additional small amount of Tabasco sauce and Louisiana spice seasoning.

Note: The size of your pot will determine the amount of oil, but it should come at least 4 to 5 inches above the submerged turkey. If in doubt, place the raw bird in the pot and cover it with water, then drain and measure the water to gauge how much oil you'll need. Dry the pot completely before adding the oil.

4. Use a proper frame to slowly lower the turkey into the hot oil (see headnote). "Be extremely careful, especially when the oil goes into the cavity," Heyd cautions. Cook for 4 minutes per pound. Watch and adjust the temperature if needed. Carefully remove the turkey and place it into a pan lined with paper towels to drain.

* * * mississippi fish fry * * *

An old-fashioned fish fry makes a fine backyard party, especially if you don't have an electric deep fryer with a filtered lid to control odors indoors. All you really need is a heat source, a heavy skillet (purists swear by cast-iron), and a good clip-on thermometer to maintain ideal cooking temperatures. Big crowds can use an outdoor gas ring with an extra large skillet or kettle, plus a fry basket (Sources, page 384).

For a simple and dependable crust that adheres well, dredge salted and peppered fillets in flour, then liquid (two eggs per cup of milk), then cornmeal seasoned to taste. You might also try equal parts of cornmeal and corn flour for the third step. Less common but very good alternatives are flour/milk/bread crumbs and flour/beaten egg/chopped nuts (almonds or pecans). You'll need vegetable oil deep enough to float the fish, heated to 375° F. Don't overcrowd the pan. A single layer of fillets, uniformly cut, should be well browned in 3 to 4 minutes.

* * * * * *

✳ ✳ ✳ serious fun ✳ ✳ ✳
the ins and outs of beer tasting

Brillat-Savarin classified *Homo sapiens* as "that animal that fears the future and has a desire for fermented beverages." Since there's no better climate for a little of both than the Third Coast, convene a meeting of your favorite bipeds to review the latest in hot topics and cold brew.

A beer-tasting party is a great way to learn more about the ever-growing craft movement that's crowding Bud off the shelves with labels like Old Peculiar, Arrogant Bastard Ale, and Purple Haze. There are several ways to set it up. You could serve a half-dozen different styles (pilsner, ale, stout, etc.) or the same style from several different breweries. You could sample the beers of Louisiana, Texas, or Mexico, or a variety of regional brands. At any rate, six seems to be the magic number for a serious tasting.

Keep food simple during the official judging: just pretzels, breadsticks, crackers, or unbuttered French bread—something to clear the palate so there's no memory in your mouth when you go on to the next sample. Begin with the lightest varieties, progressing from pilsners through ales, to darker brews, like porters or stouts. If you want to try something exotic (with nontraditional ingredients like fruit or smoked malt), save that for last because it will definitely destroy your ability to taste anything else.

Be sure to buy the beers in a store where they move quickly because beer goes downhill the minute it gets into the bottle. And make sure to chill each style to the appropriate temperature. Check the label or ask the dealer.

Wineglasses are ideal for tastings because the stems prevent fingers from smudging the bowls, which should be clear for judging color and clarity. Use perfectly clean glasses. Wash them in mild detergent, as heavy detergents can leave a film that will cause bubbles to adhere to the sides, which will "kill the head." And you do want to form a head when you're pouring beer, so the carbonation comes out for a better aroma.

get out your scorecards

Beers are typically judged according to the following criteria:

Appearance
(clarity, color, beading, etc.)

Aroma

Flavor

Balance

Finish

Overall impression

Grade each on a score of 1 to 3 points. Blind tastings are usually for profes-sional purposes, but if you want to go all out, pour the beers in a room away from your guests, about 3 to 4 ounces per glass, and code the base of each glass with an adhesive label.

keep it lite

Above all, remember that it's a party, not a competition. Friendly arguments are part of the fun.

Finally, if you really want to profit from the experience, my niece Chris Hill, a rugby player and beer enthusiast, passed along this campus scam: "You call it an import party and everybody brings a different case to try. It ruins your house, but there are always tons of leftovers that you get to keep."

*　　*　　*　　*　　*　　*

⁕big sandwiches⁕

We're talking two-fisted, roll-up-your-sleeves, ooze-down-your-shirtfront sandwiches. The kind you get at finer establishments, where you can watch TV while you eat, drink right out of the bottle, and argue about politics with your mouth full. Come to think of it, why would you want to stay home?

CUBAN SANDWICH

SERVES I

Some time ago in Tampa's older neighborhoods, Cuban bakers used to deliver their crusty French-style bread. They'd just stick a yard-long loaf onto the outside of each house, where a nail was left protruding for that very purpose. Such service belongs to another era (as does the relaxed attitude about commercial food packaging), but Cuban sandwiches are more popular than ever.

Cut off a 9-inch length of Cuban bread (or po-boy or French bread); split it in half horizontally. Spread one side with butter and the other with mustard. Layer it with slices of Cuban-Style Pork Roast (page 175), baked ham, Swiss cheese, and dill pickle chips. Put the whole thing in a hot sandwich press or waffle iron; grill until the bread is flattened and brown and the cheese is melted.

PO-BOYS

Po-boys were born during a 1920s streetcar strike, when former conductors Bennie and Clovis Martin gave away free lunches to all "poor boys" (fellow union members) at their New Orleans sandwich shop. Today the foot-long extravaganzas, piled on toasted French bread, are commonly sighted from Alabama to Texas.

Po-boys might be stuffed with anything from meatballs to French fries, but the enduring favorites are roast beef and gravy, fried oysters, fried shrimp, or ham and Swiss cheese. Just add finely shredded lettuce or cabbage, sliced tomatoes, dill pickle chips, spicy brown mustard, and mayonnaise.

VIETNAMESE PO-BOYS

Though they've adopted the Louisiana name, the "po-boys" sold at Gulf Coast Vietnamese restaurants and delis are actually based on a popular street food of Vietnam. French settlers imported their distinctive crusty bread to both colonies, where natives still love to stuff it with spicy meats and crisp vegetables, and sometimes mayonnaise (a condiment common to all three cultures).

The authentic Vietnamese sandwiches incorporate a wide variety of pâtés and exotic cold cuts, but the shredded pork po-boy is the simplest for home cooks to reproduce. Just split open a baguette as you would a hot dog bun (don't cut all the way through) and brush the inside generously with vegetable oil seasoned by plenty of chopped scallions and roasted garlic. Stuff the sandwich with roasted pork loin cut into matchstick-size pieces, then top it with coarsely shredded carrot and daikon (Chinese radish). The unique flavor comes from a final drizzle of the ubiquitous seasoning sauce known as Nuoc Cham (page 49), plus a few hearty squirts of imported Tuong Ot Toi Sriracha Hot Chili Sauce. Sort of like a thick garlic Tabasco—and great on other foods—it's available in big plastic squeeze bottles at Asian markets (see also Sources, page 385). Look for the rooster on the label.

MUFFULETTA

SERVES 2–4

Ever since Sicilian immigrants imported their crusty muffuletta bread around the turn of the century, New Orleans delis have used the 8-inch rounds to build huge messy sandwiches that will feed four (tourists), two (locals), or one (with a death wish).

These impressive constructions are generally stacked with layers of ham, Genoa salami, provolone and/or Swiss cheese, sometimes mortadella or other imported cold cuts. They're always topped by plenty of oily chopped olive salad (Sources, page 384), which provides the gratifyingly sloppy finish. The bread is then cut into four even wedges.

The round seeded loaves are becoming more common elsewhere, now that muffulettas are nationally known, but you may use any sturdy Italian bread. Though the original version is unheated, many cooks prefer to broil the layered bottom half (to warm the meats and melt the cheese) while the oil-brushed top half toasts. This is a source of great controversy in Louisiana, where people take their food very seriously.

GRILLED VEGETABLE MUFFULETTA

SERVES 2–4

*Even carnivores will be satisfied by this fat and hearty vegetarian sandwich, big enough
to feed four or a feast for two. Stuff it with any grilled vegetables you like, including
portobello mushrooms, thinly sliced fennel bulbs, tomatoes, zucchini, sweet banana
peppers, poblano chiles, and roasted garlic.*

1	large red bell pepper
2	large yellow onions, unpeeled and halved from root to stem
1 cup	good-quality chopped olive salad (Sources, page 384)
	Freshly ground black pepper
2	small eggplants, trimmed and cut lengthwise into ¼-inch slices
2	small yellow crookneck squash, trimmed and cut lengthwise into ¼-inch slices
1	large muffuletta loaf (or a seeded loaf of crusty Italian bread)
	Sliced Provolone cheese (optional)
	Fresh basil leaves

1. Place the bell pepper on a hot grill, turning occasionally, until the entire surface is charred and blistered. Enclose it in a paper bag (trapped steam will loosen skin) for 2 or 3 minutes. When it's cool enough to handle, peel the skin away and discard it, along with the seeds and stem; slice the pepper lengthwise into wide strips.

2. Meanwhile, brush the cut side of the onions with oil from the olive salad; sprinkle them with pepper and arrange, cut side down, on an oiled grill; cook for 15 to 20 minutes, turning and basting as needed, until browned and tender. Brush the eggplant and squash slices with oil from the olive salad; sprinkle with pepper and add to the oiled grill for 5 to 10 minutes, turning and basting with oil as needed, until browned and just tender. (Don't overcook the eggplant and squash, or they'll disintegrate into mush.)

3. Split the muffuletta loaf in half; brush the cut sides of the top and bottom halves with oil from the olive salad; grill until toasted. Layer the sandwich with the peeled roasted peppers, peeled grilled onions, squash and eggplant slices, Provolone cheese (if using), fresh basil leaves, and olive salad. Cut into quarters.

icy glasses

DEMON RUM
Mojito * 365

Daiquiri * 365

Planter's Punch * 366

Fresh Fruit Daiquiris * 367

* ❊ *

TEQUILA!
Blue Margaritas * 369

Big Bruce's Ultimate Prickly Pear Grande Margaritas * 370

Rio Ritas * 371

Citrus Tequila * 371

* ❊ *

SANGRIA AND SANGRITA
Red Wine Sangria * 373

White Wine Sangria * 373

Sangrita * 375

* ❊ *

NONALCOHOLIC COOLERS
Cuban Fruit Milkshake (*Batido*) * 377

Mexican Hibiscus Tea (*Agua de Jamaica*) * 377

Yucatecan Rice and Almond Cooler (*Horchata*) * 378

Watermelon Cooler * 379

Southern Strawberry Lemonade * 380

Mango Iced Tea * 381

demon rum

It was first known as "kill devil," then "rumbullion," and finally (by 1667) as rum. Now bottled by most of the world's sugar-growing countries, it was born in the Caribbean. In fact, British sailors once sang the praises of grog, their acronym for the "grand rum of Grenada."

There are hundreds of varieties, depending upon the quality of ingredients and methods of fermentation, distillation, and maturation. Beginning with either pure sugarcane juice or (more commonly) molasses, the initial fermentation process can take anywhere from 48 hours to 12 days. After distillation the liquor is clear, but it may be colored by the casks in which it is stored or by the addition of caramel flavoring or burnt sugar.

Early planters made fortunes on their intoxicating harvest, one of the reasons King Sugar still reigns in the tropics. And on a hellishly hot day, it's still hard to resist Demon Rum.

MOJITO

SERVES 1

The bourbon-based mint julep is an Old South cliché, but you'll get the same kick from a chic and exotic Mojito. Like other retro cocktails, this old Cuban classic is back in fashion.

	Juice of ½ lime
1 teaspoon	superfine sugar
	Crushed ice
2 ounces	dark rum
	Club soda
2–3	fresh mint leaves, plus 1 small mint sprig for garnish

Stir lime juice and sugar in a highball glass until the sugar dissolves. Fill the glass with crushed ice. Add rum and club soda, then two or three mint leaves. Stir to crush the leaves. Garnish with a small sprig of mint.

DAIQUIRI

SERVES 1

Another fine old cocktail that has been mass marketed to ill effect (now extruded from machines in chain restaurants), the daiquiri also has a Cuban connection. Ernest Hemingway helped popularize the drink in Key West, though he liked his without sugar.

3 ounces	light rum
1 tablespoon	fresh lime juice
2 teaspoons	superfine sugar
2–3	ice cubes

Shake all ingredients vigorously in a cocktail shaker. Strain into a chilled cocktail glass.

PLANTER'S PUNCH

SERVES I

The cloying pink knockoff peddled in tourist bars is closer to Hawaiian Punch. Here is the original cooler from sugarcane country. There is no standard recipe, but according to tradition, it should be one part sour, two parts sweet, three parts strong, and four parts weak. That's interpreted here with lime juice, simple syrup, rum, and club soda. You could use the same formula with other mixers, but the rum is essential. Similar to the Mojito, but sweeter and more citrusy, it's scented by a fresh orange slice and a sprinkle of nutmeg.

	Crushed or finely cracked ice
3 ounces	dark rum
1 ounce	fresh lime juice
2 ounces	simple syrup (see Note)
1 dash	Angostura bitters
4 ounces	sparkling water or club soda
	Orange slices for garnish
	Freshly grated nutmeg

Half-fill a tall glass with crushed or cracked ice. Add rum, lime juice, simple syrup, and bitters; stir to mix well. Fill the glass with sparkling water; garnish with the orange slice and a sprinkle of grated nutmeg.

Note: Simple syrup is made by combining equal parts water and sugar, bringing it to a boil, and simmering for a minute or two. It lasts in the refrigerator for weeks.

✳ ✳ ✳ and we're touchy ✳ ✳ ✳
about it

Bourbon Street in New Orleans was named for the French kings, not the Tennessee whiskey.

✳   ✳   ✳   ✳   ✳   ✳

FRESH FRUIT DAIQUIRIS

*Hemingway would not approve, but these fruity frothy ices can be made
with or without alcohol. If you've only tried the synthetic versions, don't give up
on daiquiris until you've tasted the right stuff.*

2 cups	fresh fruit (see Note)
2 tablespoons	fresh lime juice
2 tablespoons	superfine sugar, or to taste
3 cups	ice
½ cup	white rum (optional)
	Additional fresh fruit for garnish

Combine all ingredients except fruit garnish in a blender container or food processor; purée
until thick and smooth. Pour into wine goblets and garnish with fresh fruit.

*Note: Use mango, papaya,
fresh pineapple, melon,
bananas, peaches, nectarines,
strawberries, raspberries,
blackberries, or blueberries (or
a combination). Depending
upon the sweetness of the fruit,
you may need to adjust the
amount of sugar. Reserve a few
berries or fruit slices to garnish
each glass.*

tequila!

In fashionable watering holes across the United States, bar shelves already crowded with a staggering array of single-malt scotches, artisan vodkas, and small-batch bourbons have been rearranged to accommodate yet another wave of connoisseurs. Thanks to revved-up imports of premium brands, fans who reside north of the border are finally practicing what the greatest Mexican distillers preach: "*Tequila es para saborear, no para emborrachar.*" (Tequila is for savoring, not for inebriating.)

BLUE MARGARITAS

SERVES 4

Blue Margaritas are an intoxicating reflection of azure Mexican skies.
The kitschy color comes from blue Curaçao, a citrus-based Caribbean liqueur that's
similar in taste to the more traditional Triple Sec.

	Coarse salt
	Lime wedges
	Ice cubes
1¼ cups	fresh lime juice
1 cup	premium white or gold tequila
⅓ cup	blue Curaçao
⅓ cup	sugar, or to taste

Place salt in a saucer. Rub the rims of four Margarita glasses or large goblets with lime wedges, then dip in salt to coat the rims. Fill a blender three-quarters full of ice cubes. Add lime juice, tequila, blue Curaçao, and sugar, then blend until frothy. Taste and adjust sugar. Serve in salt-rimmed glasses.

✴ ✴ ✴ belly up and order one ✴ ✴ ✴

Along the Texas coast, a margarita without salt is known as a "naked lady."

✴ ✴ ✴ ✴ ✴ ✴

BIG BRUCE'S ULTIMATE
prickly pear grande margaritas

Sweet-tart prickly pears, known in Mexico as tunas, contribute their electric fuchsia color and a sense of adventure to these trendy margaritas. Dealing with the fresh article can be rather—well, prickly—as you must hold the fruit with tongs over an open flame to scorch away its hairy little thorns. However, thanks to the fashionistas of food, there is a booming market for these unlovely desert blooms, now packaged for your protection as prickly pear cactus syrup. This recipe is from an Arizona-based supplier, Gunpowder Foods.

	Lime wedge
	Coarse salt
	Ice cubes
1½ cups	premium tequila
1¼ cups	prickly pear cactus syrup (Sources, page 385)
1 cup	water
½ cup	Grand Marnier
½ cup	fresh lime juice

1. Rub the lime wedge around the rims of six 6-ounce glasses; roll the rims in salt; set aside for a few minutes to allow the lime juice to dry, so salt will really stick.

2. Put ice into a shaker; add all remaining ingredients. Shake vigorously, then pour into the prepared margarita glasses.

RIO RITAS

If you want to be authentic, serve a real cowboy breakfast of fatback and tough sourdough biscuits, cooked over an open fire and washed down with sock coffee. (Spoon coffee into a clean white sock, tie, and immerse in boiling water. . . .) Then again, an opening round of Rio Ritas helps blur the distinction between old West and new. The zesty morning margaritas are made with Texas red grapefruit grown in the Rio Grande Valley near Brownsville, in season from October through May. The recipe is from TexaSweet Citrus Marketing.

½	Texas red grapefruit, peeled, seeded, and quartered
¼	orange, peeled and seeded
2 ounces	Citrus Tequila (recipe follows)
¾ ounce	Triple Sec
½ ounce	fresh lime juice
1½ cups	ice cubes
	Citrus rings for garnish

Blend everything together except the ice cubes and citrus garnish. Strain through a large-hole sieve and return to the blender with the ice cubes. Pour into 2 tall glasses and garnish with the citrus rings.

CITRUS TEQUILA

INFUSES 2 BOTTLES OF TEQUILA

6	Texas red grapefruits, peeled and quartered
3	oranges, peeled and quartered
2	(750-ml) bottles tequila
2	thumb-size pieces of fresh ginger, peeled and thinly sliced
1 cup	brown sugar
2	vanilla beans, split lengthwise

Combine all ingredients, cover tightly, and allow to infuse for 8 hours. Strain out and discard the solids.

sangria and sangrita

Though the name has lately been associated with soda-pop concoctions targeted for the youngest members of the drinking public, homemade wine coolers can add a pleasantly mild buzz to big gatherings and hot summer afternoons. Margaritas and microbrewed beers may have become more fashionable, but a big pitcher of sangria is still fun for Tex-Mex meals or backyard barbecues. In fact, the fruity Spanish cooler that was everywhere during the '60s and '70s seems almost exotic again.

A real Mexican bar would be more likely to serve the stronger sangrita, a sweet-sour-salty-spicy blend of orange and tomato juices, fortified by tequila and hot pepper sauce. Mix it all for an offbeat party punch, or serve it in traditional style, sans booze, as a chaser for tequila shots.

RED WINE SANGRIA

SERVES 6–8

1	bottle dry red wine
¼ cup	Grand Marnier or brandy
¼ cup	fresh lime juice
2 tablespoons	superfine sugar, or to taste
1	lemon, sliced
1	orange, halved and sliced
1	lime, sliced
1	(24-ounce) bottle club soda, chilled

Pour the wine, brandy, lime juice, and sugar into a large glass pitcher, stirring until sugar dissolves. Add the fruit slices and chill the sangria well. Just before serving, add chilled club soda and stir lightly to blend.

WHITE WINE SANGRIA

SERVES 4–6

1	bottle dry white wine
¼ cup	Cointreau (preferred) or Triple Sec
2 tablespoons	fresh lemon juice
2 tablespoons	superfine sugar, or to taste
1	lemon, sliced
2	oranges, halved and sliced
1	green apple, unpeeled and thinly sliced

Pour the wine, Cointreau or Triple Sec, lemon juice, and sugar into a large glass pitcher, stirring until sugar dissolves. Add fruit slices and chill the sangria well. Serve over ice.

✦ ✦ ✳ the right stuff ✳ ✦ ✦

Anyone with foggy memories of twentysomething drinking bouts, slamming shots of an oily moonshine between salt licks and lime, is in for a big surprise. Premium tequilas are downright palatable, suitable for sipping, and the last thing you want to do is kill the aftertaste. Choices range from a freshly distilled "silver," with the bite of spicy vodka, to oak-barrel-aged *añejos* with the rich natural colors and complex flavors of brandy—some costing upwards of $75 per bottle.

Authentic tequilas are very expensive to produce. The blue agave plant takes eight to twelve years to reach maturity, and then it will only yield about eight bottles. Not a cactus, as commonly believed, the gargantuan barbed plant is actually related to the lily. When harvested, the pineapple-like heart is baked to transform the starches into sugar, then it is ground, shredded, and rinsed. The fermented juice is later distilled to produce tequila, which must be at least 51 percent agave in order to carry the name. Premiums and super-premiums, made from 100 percent blue agave, are identified as such on the label.

In fact, a few other clues that appear on each label can lead you to the best buys in your liquor store. Freshly distilled tequilas are clear, designated as "white" or "silver." Golden varieties aged in oak barrels for two months to a year are labeled as *reposado* (rested). The best, aged for a year or more, are called *añejo* (aged). Some of the so-called gold tequilas, on the other hand, are actually fresh from the still and tinted with caramel color, identifiable by the term *joven abocado* (bottled when young) on the label.

NORMA *Official Mexicana* was created in 1978 to regulate quality in tequila, just as the French *Apellation Controllée* sets standards for cognac. The letters NOM or DGN, followed by four numbers and the letter I, are printed on every bottle that complies with the established norms.

✳ ✳ ✳ ✳ ✳ ✳

SANGRITA

1 cup	fresh orange juice
1 cup	tomato juice
1 cup	tequila
¼ cup	fresh lemon juice
2 tablespoons	Grenadine syrup
1 teaspoon	Worcestershire sauce
	Tabasco sauce to taste
	Salt and pepper to taste

Two options: Either stir together all ingredients and serve over ice for a party punch; or serve shots of tequila separately, with glasses of the nonalcoholic punch as a chaser. Either way, the juice mixture should be well chilled.

✳ ✳ ✳ white with jackrabbit, ✳ ✳ ✳
red with chicken-fried steak

Winemaking in Texas dates back to the mid-seventeenth century, when Jesuits brought cuttings from Spain to produce grapes for sacramental wine. Though the Val Verde Winery of Del Rio is more than 100 years old, the modern industry didn't really begin until the 1970s. However, many regional vintners can already answer cracks about "Chateau Bubba" with fistfuls of gold medals and rave reviews.

✳   ✳   ✳   ✳   ✳   ✳

✳nonalcoholic coolers✳

If ever there was a need for a long cool drink, it's on the Gulf Coast, where some of the best concoctions date back for centuries. Residents have made a virtue of necessity, producing some of the world's greatest cocktails, but also these nonalcoholic refreshers zinged by tropical fruit, citrus, and herbs.

CUBAN FRUIT MILKSHAKE
✳ batido ✳
SERVES 1

To Cubans, they're batidos. In Mexico, they're licuados. Tropical fruit milkshakes in beautiful pastel shades might be sweetened by papayas, guavas, mangoes, bananas, peaches, strawberries, melon, or any combination you like.

1 cup	cold milk
½ cup	diced ripe mango
½	ripe banana
1 teaspoon	sugar, or to taste (optional)
3	ice cubes

Combine the milk, fruit, and sugar, if using, in a blender; process until smooth. With the machine running, add ice cubes one at a time; process until frothy. Serve in a tall glass.

MEXICAN HIBISCUS TEA
✳ agua de jamaica ✳
MAKES 2 QUARTS

Hibiscus puts the red in Red Zinger tea, and Mexico's tangy agua de Jamaica is made with the fleshy calyx of the flower, also known as roselle, rosella, or Jamaican sorrel. It is sold in dried form at natural foods stores (often packaged as hibiscus tea) and Latin groceries (usually labeled as flor de Jamaica*). A standard on the carts of Mexican street vendors, this invigorating tisane is a colorful alternative to iced tea or lemonade.*

1 ounce	flor de Jamaica (see headnote)
1	cinnamon stick
2	wide strips of orange zest, each about 3 inches long
1 cup	sugar, or to taste
2 quarts	boiling water

Combine all ingredients in a nonmetallic heatproof pitcher, stirring until the sugar is dissolved. Cover and set aside at room temperature for 2 to 24 hours. Strain into a glass pitcher or large glass jar and refrigerate until well chilled. Serve over ice.

YUCATECAN RICE
and almond cooler
* horchata *

SERVES 4–6

The refreshing almond-scented drink from the Yucatán is also popular in Florida's Cuban neighborhoods. It's one of those surprisingly good recipes that is best served without reciting the ingredients, as the taste is considerably better than the sum of its parts. Rice juice—who knew?

½ cup	uncooked long-grain white rice (not converted rice)
⅓ cup	slivered blanched almonds
	Zest of 1 lime
6 cups	boiling water
½ cup	sugar, plus more if needed
½ teaspoon	vanilla extract
¼ teaspoon	ground cinnamon
Dash	of almond extract

1. Combine the rice, almonds, and lime zest in the work bowl of a food processor or blender; process to a fine powder. Scrape into a heatproof pitcher; add all of the remaining ingredients, stirring to dissolve the sugar. Cool to room temperature, cover, and refrigerate overnight.

2. Strain through cheesecloth, wringing the cloth to extract as much liquid as possible. Discard the solids. Taste and add more sugar, if necessary. Serve over ice.

WATERMELON COOLER

SERVES 6

*My tourist guidebook for Mexico had warned me not to consume tap water,
fresh produce, or food from market stands. So the sight of those huge glass barrels
brimming with watery melon juices on the vendors' carts—a triple threat—
was especially irresistible. Maybe it was the lure of forbidden fruit, or the brutal
summer heat, but soon I was wondering exactly what sort of bug I might catch.
I mean, would it kill me, or just make me feel kinda queasy? When I finally succumbed
to temptation, the tepid pink drink was a big disappointment, closer to oversweetened
Kool-Aid than the sun-drenched tropical cooler I had expected.
This is how I thought it would taste. Serve this unauthentic licuado de agua in
a big glass jar (with a ladle) or tall glasses, along with plenty of ice, fresh mint leaves,
and little wedges of watermelon.*

6 cups	diced seedless watermelon
1 cup	water
½ cup	fresh lemon juice
⅓ cup	superfine sugar, or to taste
	Small thin wedges of watermelon for garnish
	Fresh mint sprigs for garnish

Purée the watermelon and water in a food processor or blender until completely smooth.
Transfer to a large jar or pitcher; add lemon juice and sugar to taste (adjusted according to the
sweetness of the watermelon), stirring until the sugar is completely dissolved. Serve over ice,
garnished with little wedges of watermelon and fresh mint sprigs.

SOUTHERN STRAWBERRY
lemonade

MAKES ABOUT 2 QUARTS

Fill your tallest glasses with cracked ice and raid the cookie jar. Pink-hued strawberry lemonade is great for children's parties, backyard picnics, or lazy afternoons on the front porch.

⅔ cup	sugar
5 cups	cold water
	Zest from 2 lemons
1 cup	fresh lemon juice, plus more if needed
1 cup	fresh strawberry purée
1	lemon, thinly sliced and seeded
	Whole strawberries for garnish
	Fresh mint sprigs for garnish

Stir the sugar with 1 cup of the water in a small saucepan over medium heat until sugar dissolves. Cool. Pour into a 2-quart glass pitcher with lemon juice, strawberry purée, and remaining water; stir well to blend. Adjust tartness to taste, adding up to ¼ cup of additional lemon juice. Add lemon slices and fill the pitcher with ice cubes. Garnish each glass with a fresh strawberry and mint sprig.

MANGO ICED TEA

*Iced tea has been called the house wine of the South, and a big pitcherful is a good
alternative to beer at barbecues and seafood boils. Lemon and mint are classic garnishes,
but icy glasses could also be adorned with berries or thin slices of orange, lime, nectarine,
or green apple. Or you might season chilled tea with a few drops of almond extract,
vanilla, or fruit syrup. Here's another idea with a Third Coast flavor.*

1½ quarts	water
1	thumb-size piece of fresh ginger, peeled and sliced
2	cinnamon sticks
5–6	whole cloves
3	mangoes, peeled and sliced (8 thin slices reserved for garnish)
6	tea bags or 3 family-size tea bags
	Superfine sugar (optional)
	Lime wedges for garnish

Bring the water to a boil in a nonreactive saucepan over high heat with the ginger, cinnamon
sticks, cloves, and mangoes. Remove the pot from the heat and add the tea bags; steep the tea
with the seasonings for 5 minutes, then remove the tea bags. Stir in sugar to taste, if desired,
then set aside the spiced tea until it cools to room temperature. Strain the tea into a glass
pitcher filled with ice; discard the solids. Add a fresh mango slice and lime wedge to each glass.

bibliography

* Bayless, Rick. *Rick Bayless's Mexican Kitchen*. New York: Scribner, 1996.

* Bayless, Rick, and Deann Groen Bayless. *Authentic Mexican*. New York: William Morrow & Company, 1987.

* Beranbaum, Rose Levy. *The Cake Bible*. New York: William Morrow & Company, 1988.

* Brittin, Phil, and Joseph Daniel. *Texas on the Halfshell*. New York: Dolphin Books, 1982.

* Chalmers, Irena. *The Great Food Almanac*. San Francisco: Collins Publishers, 1994.

* Cormier-Boudreau, Marielle, and Melvin Gallant. *A Taste of Acadie*. Fredericton, New Brunswick, Canada: Goose Lane Editions, 1991.

* Creen, Linette. *A Taste of Cuba*. New York: Plume, 1994.

* DeWitt, Dave. *The Chile Pepper Encyclopedia*. New York: William Morrow & Company, 1999.

* Emmons, Bob. *The Book of Tequila*. Chicago: Open Court Publishing Company, 1997.

* Feibleman, Peter S. *The Cooking of Spain and Portugal*. New York: Time-Life Books, 1969.

* *Fiesta: Favorite Recipes of South Texas*. Corpus Christi, Tex.: The Junior League of Corpus Christi, 1976.

* *From Woodstoves to Microwaves: Cooking with Entergy*. New Orleans: Entergy Corporation, 1997.

* Gassenheimer, Linda. *Keys Cuisine*. New York: The Atlantic Monthly Press, 1991.

* Geddes, Bruce. *World Food: Mexico*. Hawthorn, Victoria, Australia: Lonely Planet Publications, 2000.

* Hafner, Dorinda. *A Taste of Africa*. Berkeley, Calif.: Ten Speed Press, 1993.

* Herbst, Sharon Tyler. *Food Lover's Companion*. Hauppauge, N.Y.: Barron's Educational Series, 2001.

* ———. *Never Eat More Than You Can Lift*. New York: Broadway Books, 1997.

* Hutson, Lucinda. *¡Tequila!* Berkeley, Calif.: Ten Speed Press, 1995.

* Kennedy, Diana. *My Mexico*. New York: Clarkson Potter, 1998.

* Kerr, W. Park. *The El Paso Chile Company: Beans.* New York: William Morrow & Company, 1996.

* ———. *The El Paso Chile Company: Chiles.* New York: William Morrow & Company, 1996.

* ———. *The El Paso Chile Company: Tortillas.* New York: William Morrow & Company, 1996.

* LaFray, Joyce. *¡Cuba Cocina!* New York: Hearst Books, 1994.

* Nelson, Mary Sue Koontz. *Stolen Recipes.* San Antonio, Tex.: The HK Ranch, 2000.

* Philcox, Phil, and Beverly Boe. *The Sunshine State Almanac.* Sarasota, Fla.: Pineapple Press, 1999.

* Quintana, Patricia. *The Best of Quintana.* New York: Stewart, Tabori & Chang, 1995.

* ———. *Cuisine of the Water Gods.* New York: Simon & Schuster, 1994.

* *Rare Collection.* Galveston, Tex.: The Junior League of Galveston County, 1992.

* *Recipe Jubilee!* Mobile, Ala.: The Junior League of Mobile, 1993.

* Routhier, Nicole. *The Best of Nicole Routhier.* New York: Stewart, Tabori & Chang, 1996.

* Voltz, Jeanne, and Caroline Stuart. *Florida Cookbook.* New York: Alfred A. Knopf, 1996.

sources

* ✻ *

Melissa's/World Variety Produce, Inc.
Post Office Box 21127
Los Angeles, CA 90021
(800) 588-0151
www.melissas.com

You've probably seen their label on exotics in the produce section of your supermarket, but the company maintains a mail-order website, as well. It's the largest distributor of specialty produce in the United States, a great source for hard-to-find Latin and tropical fruits and vegetables, including plantains, prickly pears, blood oranges, guava, figs, passion fruit, key limes, jicama, yuca, and habanero chiles. The online catalog also offers a good variety of dried chiles (ancho, chipotle, guajillo, japone, and many others), as well as pickled chiles, epazote, flor de Jamaica (hibiscus tea), banana leaves, corn husks, basmati and other aromatic rices, pepitas (raw pumpkin seeds), pine nuts, canela (Mexican cinnamon), lemongrass, and crystallized ginger. The sugarcane swizzle sticks are just right for the shrimp cakes on sugarcane skewers (page 48), and they're also a fun garnish for the rum drinks on pages 364–367.

Adriana's Caravan
(800) 316-0820
www.adrianascaravan.com

An international inventory includes every spice imaginable, whole and ground chiles, chipotles en adobo, *panko* (Japanese bread crumbs), rice noodles, rice papers, pickled ginger, wasabi, orange flower water, a world of coffees and teas, crab boil, Creole mustard, remoulade sauce, Italian olive salad, and some 1,500 other ingredients.

The Louisiana General Store
524 St. Louis Street
New Orleans, LA 70130
(800) 237-4841
www.nosoc.com

Creole Delicacies
#1 Poydras Street
Riverwalk Mall, Store 1116
New Orleans, LA 70130
(800) 786-0941
www.cookincajun.com

Both of these New Orleans–based food shops incorporate cooking schools and mail-order companies. Check out their websites for a full range of Creole/Cajun goods, such as Steen's cane syrup and cane syrup vinegar, seasoning mixes, crab boil, Italian olive salad, Tabasco products, hot sauces, bottled remoulade sauce, fish fry (seasoned corn flour), Creole mustard, filé, French-roast and chicory coffees, and turkey injection syringes.

Zachary Dupre's Cajun Market of New Orleans
(888) 43-CAJUN
www.cajunmarket.com

This mail-order company offers many of the regional foods listed above, as well as smoked andouille and other Louisiana sausages, cast-iron cookware, fry pots and deep fryers, turkey fryers with outdoor cooking rigs, Zapp's potato chips (yum), regional music, even voodoo supplies. Fun website.

Hoppin' John's
(800) 828-4412
www.hoppinjohns.com

You can also order heavy-duty turkey frying equipment from author John Martin Taylor, who named his online shop after his Low Country cookbook. Taylor sells his own line of stone-ground grits, cornmeal, and corn flour; shrimp and crab boil; and small-batch pickles and preserves.

Latingredients

(305) 463-6680

www.latingredients.com

Online orders only for this virtual Latin grocery, where you'll find everything from papaya nectar to Cuban cosmetics. A good variety of fresh fruits and vegetables includes chayotes, yuca, and plantains. Also look for frozen tropical fruit purées, corn husks, dry-cured chorizo, Latin cheeses, Badia Jamaican curry powder, and a wide variety of dried beans and other legumes.

Asia Foods

(877) 902-0841

www.asiafoods.com

Check this mail-order company for Tuong Ot Toi Sriracha Hot Chili Sauce, Squid-brand fish sauce, rice papers, rice noodles, pickled ginger, wasabi, *panko* (Japanese bread crumbs), lemongrass, and dried chiles.

Perrone's Progress Grocery

4512 Zenith Street

Metairie, LA 70001

(504) 455-FOOD

www.progressgrocery.com

One of the original New Orleans delis that popularized the massive Sicilian sandwiches known as muffulettas, Progress will send you the round muffuletta loaves and Italian olive salad to make your own. They'll even FedEx the complete sandwiches, a colorful (if sloppy) alternative to flowers or candy. You can also get Cajun andouille sausage here.

L. L. Lanier & Sons Tupelo Honey

Post Office Box 706

Wewahitchka, FL 32465

(850) 639-2371

lltupelo@digitalexp.com

Contact these third-generation producers for authentic tupelo honey from the Florida swamps.

Tee Eva's World Famous Pies and Pralines

4430 Magazine Street

New Orleans, LA 70115

(504) 899-8350

www.tee-eva.net

Not fancy, just good. Tee Eva's simple homemade pies and pralines have been a welcome—if elusive—indulgence. Now one of New Orleans' most popular street vendors has opened her own shop, and out-of-towners can taste her wares via the Internet.

D'Hanus Pottery

HCR 8 Box 697

Beeville, TX 78102

(361) 358-0391

dhanus@dbstech.com

Debra Hanus makes custom dishes she calls "ranchware," emblazoned with the owners' brands or other insignia of choice, at her studio in the cattle country near the Texas Gulf Coast.

Premier Baking Company

1124 West Garden Street

Pensacola, FL 32501

(850) 438-1263

This Florida panhandle bakery makes and ships the hard-tack biscuits essential for Pensacola gaspachee salad.

Gunpowder Foods, Inc.

4514 East Desert Trumpet Road

Phoenix, AZ 85044

(480) 753-5556

www.gunpowderfoods.com

The prickly pear syrup makes quick work of prickly pear margaritas.

New England Cheesemaking Supply Company

Post Office Box 85

Ashfield, MA 01330

(413) 628-3808

www.cheesemaking.com

Check here for cheesecloth, thermometers, molds, how-to-books, and other essentials.

contributing restaurants

* ✳ *

Thanks to the many chefs and restaurateurs who provided recipes, cooking advice, local lore, and encouragement. You'll find their contributions throughout this book. And be sure to seek them out on your own travels around the Gulf Coast.

Anne's Other Place
360 Dock Street
Cedar Key, FL 32625
(352) 543-5494

Apache Mexican Food
511 20th Street
Galveston Island, TX 77550
(409) 765-5646

Bayley's Restaurant
10805 Dauphin Island Parkway
Mobile, AL 36582
(251) 973-1572

Bayona
430 Dauphine Street
New Orleans, LA 70112
(504) 525-4455

Bern's Steak House
208 South Howard Avenue
Tampa, FL 33602
(813) 251-2421

Brennan's Restaurant
417 Royal Street
New Orleans, LA 70130
(504) 525-9771

Cafe Annie
1728 Post Oak Boulevard
Houston, TX 77056
(713) 840-1111

Cafe Giovanni
115 Decatur Street
New Orleans, LA 70130
(504) 529-2154

Cha-Cha Coconuts
800 2nd Avenue Northeast
St. Petersburg, FL 33701
(727) 822-6655

Chef Eddie's Magnolia Grill
99 11th Street
Apalachicola, FL 32320
(850) 653-8000

Coco Palms Jamaican Restaurant
300 Front Street
Key West, FL 33040
(305) 296-0046

Columbia Restaurant
2117 East 7th Avenue
Tampa, FL 33605
(813) 248-4961

Commander's Palace
1403 Washington Avenue
New Orleans, LA 70130
(504) 899-8221

Dolores' Sweet Shop
29 Avenue E
Apalachicola, FL 32320
(850) 653-9081

Grand Casino
3215 West Beach Boulevard
Gulfport, MS 39501
(800) 946-7777

Gulf Bay Seafood Grill
Canal and Gulf Bay Roads
Orange Beach, AL 36561
(334) 974-5090

Hotel Galvez
2024 Seawall Boulevard
Galveston Island, TX 77550
(409) 765-7721

The Island Hotel
373 2nd Street
Cedar Key, FL 32625
(352) 543-5111

Justine's
80 St. Michael Street
Mobile, AL 36602
(334) 438-4535

King Neptune's Seafood Restaurant
1137 Gulf Shores Parkway
Gulf Shores, AL 36542
(334) 968-5464

Louis Pappas' Riverside Restaurant
10 West Dodecanese Boulevard
Tarpon Springs, FL 34689
(727) 937-5101

Lulu's Sunset Grill
11525 U.S. Highway 98
Point Clear, AL 36532
(251) 990-9907

Mayan Dude Ranch
6th and Pecan Streets
Bandera, TX 78003
(830) 796-3312

Palace Cafe
605 Canal Street
New Orleans, LA 70130
(504) 523-1661

Pho Tau Bay Restaurant
3116 North Arnoult Road
Metairie, LA 70002
(504) 780-1063

Prejean's Restaurant
3480 Highway 167 North
Lafayette, LA 70507
(337) 896-3247

Ralph & Kacoo's Corporate Headquarters
314 Highway 98 East
Destin, FL 32541
(850) 837-3139

Sea Ranch Restaurant
1 Padre Boulevard
South Padre Island, TX 78597
(956) 761-1314

Taj Mahal Restaurant
923 Metairie Road
Metairie, LA 70005
(504) 836-6859

The Upperline Restaurant
1413 Upperline Street
New Orleans, LA 70115
(504) 891-9822
(504) 891-9919

Vaquero's Restaurant
4938 Prytania Street
New Orleans, LA 70115
(504) 891-6441

index

* * *

conversion chart *Equivalent Imperial and Metric Measurements*

American cooks use standard containers, the 8-ounce cup and a tablespoon that takes exactly 16 level fillings to fill that cup level. Measuring by cup makes it very difficult to give weight equivalents, as a cup of densely packed butter will weigh considerably more than a cup of flour. The easiest way therefore to deal with cup measurements in recipes is to take the amount by volume rather than by weight. Thus the equation reads: 1 cup = 240 ml = 8 fl. oz., ½ cup = 120 ml = 4 fl. oz. It is possible to buy a set of American cup measures in major stores around the world.

In the States, butter is often measured in sticks. One stick is the equivalent of 8 tablespoons. One tablespoon of butter is therefore the equivalent to ½ ounce/15 grams.

liquid measures

Fluid Ounces	U.S.	Imperial	Milliliters
	1 teaspoon	1 teaspoon	5
¼	2 teaspoons	1 dessertspoon	10
½	1 tablespoon	1 tablespoon	14
1	2 tablespoons	2 tablespoons	28
2	¼ cup	4 tablespoons	56
4	½ cup		120
5		¼ pint or 1 gill	140
6	¾ cup		170
8	1 cup		240
9			250, ¼ liter
10	1¼ cups	½ pint	280
12	1½ cups		340
15		¾ pint	420
16	2 cups		450
18	2¼ cups		500, ½ liter
20	2½ cups	1 pint	560
24	3 cups		675
25		1¼ pints	700
27	3½ cups		750
30	3¾ cups	1½ pints	840
32	4 cups or 1 quart		900
35		1¾ pints	980
36	4½ cups		1000, 1 liter
40	5 cups	2 pints or 1 quart	1120

equivalents for ingredients

all-purpose flour—plain flour
coarse salt—kitchen salt
cornstarch—cornflour
eggplant—aubergine
half-and-half—12% fat milk
heavy cream—double cream
light cream—single cream
'lima beans—broad beans
scallion—spring onion
unbleached flour—strong, white flour
zest—rind
zucchini—courgettes or marrow

solid measures

U.S. AND IMPERIAL MEASURES		METRIC MEASURES	
Ounces	Pounds	Grams	Kilos
1		28	
2		56	
3½		100	
4	¼	112	
5		140	
6		168	
8	½	225	
9		250	¼
12	¾	340	
16	1	450	
18		500	½
20	1¼	560	
24	1½	675	
27		750	¾
28	1¾	780	
32	2	900	
36	2¼	1000	1
40	2½	1100	
48	3	1350	
54		1500	1½

oven temperature equivalents

Fahrenheit	Celsius	Gas Mark	Description
225	110	¼	Cool
250	130	½	
275	140	1	Very Slow
300	150	2	
325	170	3	Slow
350	180	4	Moderate
375	190	5	
400	200	6	Moderately Hot
425	220	7	Fairly Hot
450	230	8	Hot
475	240	9	Very Hot
500	250	10	Extremely Hot

Any broiling recipes can be used with the grill of the oven, but beware of high-temperature grills.